By Miguel Covarrubias

INDIAN ART OF MEXICO AND CENTRAL AMERICA
(*1957*)

THE EAGLE, THE JAGUAR, AND THE SERPENT
INDIAN ART OF THE AMERICAS
North America: Alaska, Canada, the United States
(*1954*)

MEXICO SOUTH
THE ISTHMUS OF TEHUANTEPEC
(*1946*)

ISLAND OF BALI
(*1937*)

THESE ARE BORZOI BOOKS
PUBLISHED BY ALFRED A. KNOPF IN NEW YORK

The Eagle, the Jaguar, and the Serpent

INDIAN ART OF THE AMERICAS

North America: Alaska, Canada, the United States

MIGUEL COVARRUBIAS

The Eagle, the Jaguar, and the Serpent

INDIAN ART OF THE AMERICAS

North America: Alaska, Canada, the United States

New York   Alfred A. Knopf   1967

DRAWING ON TITLE PAGE: *Beaver crest painted on a skin shirt.*
From Haida, Queen Charlotte Islands, Canada (MfVB).

L. C. catalog card number: 52–6415

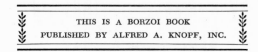

THIS IS A BORZOI BOOK
PUBLISHED BY ALFRED A. KNOPF, INC.

Published November 1954
Second Printing, September 1967

Contents

CONTENTS

Color Plates

vii

Illustrations in the Text

ix

ILLUSTRATIONS IN THE TEXT

ILLUSTRATIONS IN THE TEXT

xi

An Album of Photographs

(FOLLOWING PAGE 294)

AN ALBUM OF PHOTOGRAPHS

Abbreviations

AMNH: *American Museum of Natural History, New York*

ASM: *Arizona State Museum*

BM: *Brooklyn Museum*

BMAS: *Buffalo Museum of Arts and Sciences*

BrM: *British Museum*

ChIA: *Chicago Institute of Art*

ChMNH: *Chicago Museum of Natural History*

CiMA: *Cincinnati Museum of Art*

CMA: *Cleveland Museum of Art*

DAM: *Denver Art Museum*

EMS: *Ethnographic Museum, Stockholm*

FAM: *Fogg Art Museum, Boston*

FGAW: *Freer Gallery of Art, Washington*

GP: *Gila Pueblo, Globe, Arizona*

IACB: *Indian Arts and Crafts Board, Department of Interior, Washington*

LACM: *Los Angeles County Museum*

LASF: *Laboratory of Anthropology, Santa Fe*

MAIHF: *Museum of the American Indian, Heye Foundation, New York*

MAM:	*Museo Arquelógico de Madrid*
MfVB:	*Museum für Völkerkunde, Berlin*
MfVH:	*Museum für Völkerkunde, Hamburg*
MfVW:	*Museum für Völkerkunde, Wien*
MIA:	*Minneapolis Institute of Art*
Ml'H:	*Musée de l'Homme, Paris*
MMA:	*Metropolitan Museum of Art*
MMANY:	*Museum of Modern Art, New York*
MMFA:	*Montreal Museum of Fine Arts*
MNAG:	*Museo Nacional de Antropología, Guatemala*
MNAM:	*Museo Nacional de Antropología, Mexico*
MNRJ:	*Museu Nacional, Rio de Janeiro*
NGA:	*W. R. Nelson Gallery of Art, Kansas City*
NGS:	*National Geographic Society, Washington*
OSM:	*Ohio State Museum, Columbus*
PMC:	*Peabody Museum of Cambridge, Harvard University*
PMV:	*Provincial Museum, Victoria, British Columbia*
SarM:	*Sarawak Museum, Borneo*
SFM:	*Santa Fe Museum*
SNMP:	*Shilo National Military Park, Tennessee*
TMCS:	*Taylor Museum, Colorado Springs*
UCM:	*University of California Museum, Berkeley*
UMP:	*University Museum of Pennsylvania, Philadelphia*
UO:	*University of Oklahoma*
USIS:	*United States Indian Service, Rapid City, Iowa*
USNM:	*United States National Museum, Washington*
WA:	*Wadsworth Atheneum, Hartford*
WSM:	*Washington State Museum, Seattle*
YUM:	*Yale University Museum, New Haven*

The Eagle, the Jaguar, and the Serpent

INDIAN ART OF THE AMERICAS

Introduction

THE coming of the white man was a major disaster to the American aborigines. In the north they were dispossessed and exterminated or, at best, reduced to "reservations" and cut off from progress and from participation in the growth of a new America. While the unsubmissive redskin of the north was shot down by a well-placed bullet or cheated out of his lands by one-sided treaties, great Indian civilizations in Middle and South America were brought under the feet of the Spanish conquerors by a ruthless and patient labor of attrition. The immediate objective of the Spaniards was the Indians' gold, but they were also concerned with the future spoils of conquest, and they set out in earnest to break down the culture and pride of the Indians and make them into impotent vassals. Everywhere the Indians were betrayed and robbed, despised and treated with contempt; their works of art were generally regarded as heathen abominations to be destroyed, or as bizarre curios, products of an unfathomable, barbaric people.

Nowadays everybody knows that the Indians contributed many of the material assets that have since become basic to our modern civilization: corn, beans, tobacco, chili peppers, sweet and "Irish" potatoes,

3

tomatoes, squashes, and pineapples. They discovered chocolate, qui-
nine, cocaine, and cascara; they were the first to use rubber, chicle, and
petroleum, and they domesticated turkeys, llamas, and alpacas. In various places in Middle and South America the Indians had built great
civilizations with cultures and arts comparable to those of their civilized Asiatic contemporaries. These Indians lived in great cities that
awed the Spaniards. They practiced intensive agriculture and had effective systems of law and government, elaborate literatures, hieroglyphic writing, and powerful and lively arts. As craftsmen many of
them were unexcelled. They painted frescoes, carved magnificent monuments of stone, and worked jade, crystal, obsidian, turquoise, gold,
platinum, silver, and copper into jewelry and implements. They wore
splendid clothes of cotton and wool, and decorated their persons with
luxurious ornaments of glittering feathers and delicate mosaics of turquoise. A well-known sample of their scientific achievement is the
knowledge of astronomy and mathematics, by which the Maya had
devised a calendar considerably older, more exact, and more efficient
than the Julian calendar, the most advanced in Europe at the time of
the Conquest. The concept of the zero and the significance of numeri-
cal position, basic for higher mathematics, were Maya inventions, used
by them for at least one thousand years before they were known in Europe.

Practically the whole of the American continent is a vast archæological site. From Point Hope, Alaska, to the southernmost tip of Tierra
del Fuego there is an amazing variety of buried evidences of human
culture. Throughout the centuries layer after layer of remains left by
successive peoples—ruined temples, funerary mounds, tombs, refuse
dumps—covered one another; many old Catholic churches rise over
the ruins of Indian temples or were built with their stones; everywhere
the peasants' plows unearth broken pottery, clay figurines, and some-

4

times even great works of art, fine jades, or caches of gold objects; and everywhere professional pothunters are in search of ancient treasures like those which have gone to make great private and museum collections all over the world. When these ancient remains are dug up systematically and the objects found are studied, they reveal the cultural affiliations and the evolution of the various settlers of a given zone. Slowly the painstaking and methodical excavations of the archæologists bring to light cities, sumptuous tombs, fine stone monuments, and jewels and ornaments of the Indians, so that one day we may have a complete picture of ancient American civilization. But American archæology is still a young science; the work is slow and far from complete. Every new discovery tears down an old concept: the rubber stamps with which the Indian cultures formerly were designated have become largely obsolete, and modern scientists are trying to readjust and order the pieces of the gigantic and chaotic puzzle that is our knowledge of the cultural history of native civilized man in America.

The speculative and often fancy-free archæology of the nineteenth century has now given way to the painstaking, systematic archæology of today. Many of the oversimplified and comfortable beliefs about the age, origins, and identity of the Indians are being discarded and are undergoing a most devastating revision. Cultures are no longer called by doubtful linguistic and legendary names, which have often proved wrong and misleading, but preferably by the names of their most important sites. Often as many as five or six cultures, different in time and character, occupied one site, leaving superimposed layers of broken pottery and utensils; when studied by a careful system of stratigraphical sequence taking into account the changing nature of the clays employed, shapes, style of decoration, and so forth, these remains permit us to establish the scope and chronological position of each phase, as well as the evidences of contact with other peoples. For these studies, fittingly called "dirt archæology," the earth of an undisturbed refuse dump is peeled off by layers, and each shovelful of dirt is examined for potsherds and other remains. The results are classified and studied to establish the various phases of successive cultures. Digging trenches as deep as twenty-five or thirty feet before finding rock or soil sterile of potsherds is not uncommon—a hint of the long duration of human occupation.

Dirt archæology is also concerned with the exploration and reconstruction of architectural remains and the study of tombs and their contents when the archæologist is lucky enough to find them untouched. Tomb-rifling is an old and profitable profession. It began early with the Indians themselves, and had a great boom after the Conquest, when the Spaniards discovered that the Indians buried gold with their dead. Today treasure-hunting continues unabated, and often the success of an archæologist in his explorations depends on whether or not he can beat grave-robbers to the place. But even in rifled tombs important discoveries have been made, revealing objects overlooked by the treasure-hunters in their haste or inexperience.

Dirt archæology is complemented by such specialized studies as the correct interpretation of the finds; the reading of pictorial manuscripts and of mural and vessel decorations; the identification of the personages, deities, and symbols represented; the uses and purposes of the utensils; the reconstruction of buildings; the dress, customs, and modes of the ancient peoples; analysis of their art styles, techniques, and inventions; interpretation of their physical characteristics, their economic life, their institutions, their recorded histories, traditions, and legends (not always reliable), both in the chronicles of the rare early historians and missionaries who were interested in the Indians beyond their use as slave laborers and in the writings of those Indians who learned Spanish or wrote Indian languages in Latin characters. A most

6

intricate and difficult science is the reading of the pre-Spanish hiero-
glyphics written by the Indians of Middle America on stone monuments or in books of paper or deerskin. In this field the reading of Maya
dates is thus far the most significant achievement.

However insufficient for an over-all knowledge of American Indian culture the reliable archæological data may be, enough artistic
material is available to permit us to look into aboriginal American art
and theorize about its significance, its probable evolution, and even its
origins and to judge it from stylistic points of view. A true primitive
man, such as the Java or the Peking man, has not been found on the
American continent; consequently it is taken for granted that man as
we know him today came to America from elsewhere. But when and
whence did the Indians come? From what sources and by which process did their cultures develop? What contacts, inside and outside the
Americas, influenced their arts? These are still largely unanswered
questions, and new discoveries are constantly revising the accepted
dogmas of the cultural history of the American Indian; the horizon of
his life on this continent is steadily being pushed back, as is the time of
his change from a wild hunter and gatherer into a civilized human being sensitive to art and capable of development. In Mexico and Peru
great and mysterious mother cultures have been identified recently,
though they are not yet fully understood; fascinating archæological
finds have been made that cast new light on the cultural status of the
Americans long before the coming of the white man.

The first aim of the following pages is to present the Indians' main
artistic achievements, to discuss the characteristics and idiosyncrasies
of their art, and to expound a hypothesis of the history of American Indian art from Alaska to Tierra del Fuego. This will perforce remain a
hypothesis, for there are still too many blind spots, too many unex-
plored areas and little-known cultures, to allow us to establish with

7

certainty the evolutionary processes, chronologies, contacts, interrelations, and changes in the prehistoric cultures. Consequently our primary concern is with Indian art, not necessarily because it is Indian, but because it is an important and little-known part of our continental artistic heritage. Indian art has not been studied sufficiently from the combined points of view of its æsthetic values and its historical implications in an effort to understand the mental process of its creators and the social factors that helped its formation.

FACING: *Fantastic Alaskan Eskimo carved and painted driftwood mask, 38 centimeters high (UCM).*

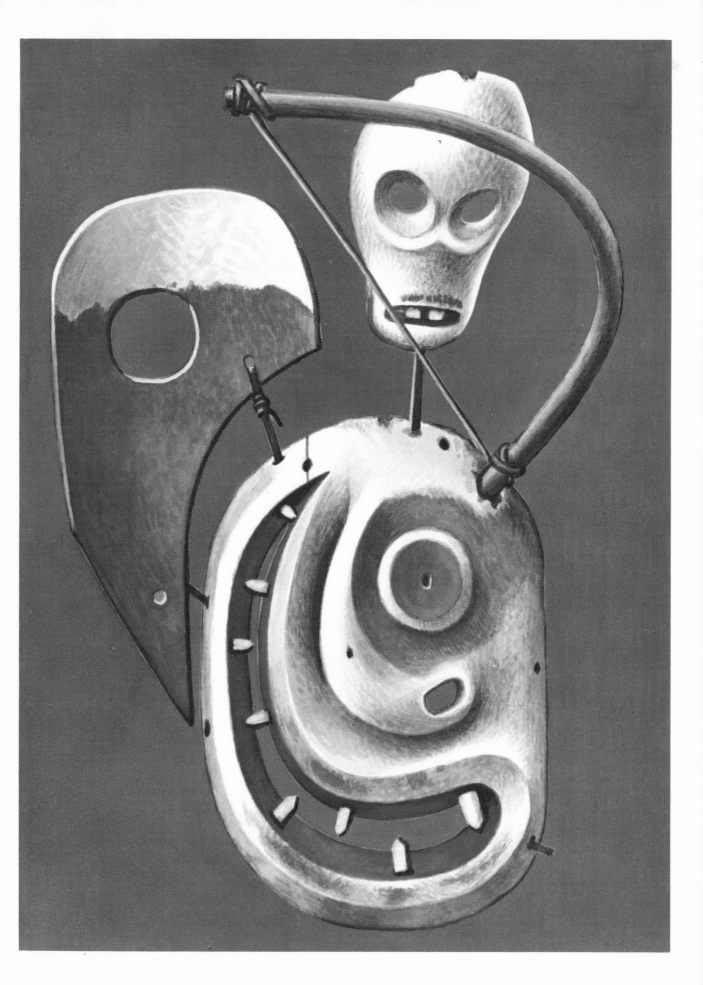

CHAPTER I

Origins of the American Indians

THE problem of the origins of the American Indians has occupied professional and amateur chroniclers, historians, and anthropologists since Indians and Europeans first met. There was always the question of the Indians' physical resemblance to Asiatics, and it was long a favorite pastime to trace the Indians of Mexico back to the Egyptians because they both built pyramids. Dilettante speculation as to where the amazing arts of Middle and South America originated has been considerable and constant: Egypt, China, the legendary Atlantis of Plato, and the absurd "Continent of Mu" of Churchward have all taken turns as explanations of the presence of high civilization in America. As early as the middle of the sixteenth century the Spanish friar Bartolomé de Las Casas rationalized his love and admiration for the civilized but oppressed Mexican Indians by calling them descendants of the ten lost tribes of Israel. Other friars saw them as the descendants of the Phœnicians and Carthaginians, and Lord Kingsborough spent a fortune and many years in the publication of his colossal work *Antiquities of Mexico*

(1831–48) to prove Las Casas's theory that the ancient Mexicans were descended from the Jews.

The great Toltec culture-hero Quetzalcoatl was identified by the early Spanish friars with Saint Thomas because he wore a Maltese cross among his insignia and because he was described by the Indians as white and bearded. In 1590 José de Acosta, desiring to reconcile the existence of human beings on the American continent with the Scriptures, expounded the belief that as Adam was born in the Old World, and as all mankind was descended from Adam, the Indians must have come from the Old World. In 1643 Hugo Grotius (Huig de Groot) asserted that they were Vikings or Norse, and in the same year Johannes de Laet first presented the theory of an Asiatic land bridge, maintaining that they were Scythians.

These speculations, however wild and baseless, continue to plague the serious students of ancient history, art, and anthropology; the scientific world is now sharply divided into "diffusionists" (those who believe in an early diffusion of Asiatic and Pacific cultural traits through America) and "isolationists" (those who claim that all Indian culture was a local development). There are of course extremists in both camps. G. Elliot Smith traced the origins of all culture to Egypt and saw elephants, complete with mahouts, in the Maya stelæ of Copán; Ameghino believed that man originated in the Argentine pampas, whence he spread to populate the world. On the other hand, the most intolerant of the "isolationists" reject all evidence and see in the "diffusionists" an effort to rob the Indian of the glory of reinventing culture all by himself.

Arguments for and against both theories are strong, but the "isolationist" camp has been losing ground in the last few years because though the endemic, and for the most part superficial, comparison between Old World and American cultures has subsided, more substantial

10

and striking similarities have been pointed out by more serious historians and archæologists. This tendency culminated in 1949, at the Congress of Americanists held in New York, where "diffusionism" spoke with renewed vigor in a disturbing exhibition entitled *Across the Pacific: Did the Ancient Civilizations of the Far East Contribute to American Indian Civilizations?* prepared for the occasion by the American Museum of Natural History and presenting an overwhelming mass of Asiatic-Pacific-American parallels (Ekholm, 1950). The distinguished anthropologists present heatedly argued the pros and cons of the subject and cautiously named a committee to give it further study. The findings of the committee of scholars not being available, a review of the case is presented here, beginning with what anthropologists believe.

MAN supposedly crossed from Asia into America at a relatively late date, some fifteen thousand years ago, over the natural land bridge of Bering Strait and the Aleutians, which became free of ice at the end of the Quaternary. These Asiatics were still in a Stone Age state: they lived in caves and shelters and hunted wild animals with the aid of dogs and crude darts tipped with splinters of stone and bone and propelled by spear-throwers. They had to move south constantly to find new happy hunting grounds and to escape the raw climates of the northern land, each successive wave pushing the other farther and farther south until they had spread all the way from Alaska to Tierra del Fuego. For some reason that the anthropologists did not explain, soon after the arrival of the new immigrants all communication with their home in Asia was cut off. Furthermore, these people must all have been of the same stock, for it was dogmatically asserted that they eventually developed into a homogeneous race, the American Indian, who then set about the task of reinventing all culture and duplicating in, say, two thousand years what man in the Old World took about six millennia to invent. Such is the essence of the rather oversimplified and comfortable theory generally accepted by anthropologists to explain the origins of the American Indians.

It has taken a long time and considerable controversy to establish the presence of fossil man in America. Every reported discovery of human remains or of artifacts found under apparent conditions of great antiquity was carefully scrutinized by the more conservative anthropologists and stubbornly rejected as insufficient evidence. But the discoveries have become more frequent and convincing: beautifully made spear points of pressure-flaked flint of two types ("Folsom" and "Yuma" [1]) were found in the Southwest and in many other places in North America, from Alaska to the Mississippi, sometimes associated with the bones of such animals of the Pleistocene as giant sloths, American camels, horses, saber-toothed tigers, extinct bison, and mastodons. More recently, in a cave in the Sandia Mountains near Albuquerque, New Mexico, the spear points of an even earlier man were found mixed with the bones of extinct animals beneath a typical Folsom stratum, the two separated by a sterile layer indicating that between them occurred a long uninhabited period during which the floor of the cave must have been under water (Hibben, 1942). The age of the Folsom remains has been estimated to be between 10,000 and 13,000 years; consequently those of Sandia could be assigned an approximate age of from 15,000 to 20,000 years (Bryan and Ray, 1940).

The men of Folsom and Sandia are ghosts; their bones have not been found. But well-authenticated remains of early man have been dis-

[1] The term "Yuma" has since been dropped because it included almost all the unfluted points with parallel flaking which have been grouped in new types: "Scotts-bluff," "Oblique," "Eden," "Browns Valley," "Nebo Hill," "San Jon," etc. I have retained the term "Yuma" so as not to clutter the reader's memory with names. There are other types of points of great antiquity besides those mentioned here: Clovis fluted, Gypsum Cave, Clear Fork, Abilene, Lake Mohave, Pinto Basin, and so forth.

covered in various places, from the Great Lakes to Brazil. Examples are the burial of the man (or rather the girl) of Browns Valley, Minnesota, in a tomb lined with red paint, with flint implements of the Yuma type, which may be some 12,000 years old (Jenks, 1937); the man of Tepexpan, the articulated skeleton of an adult male found in the Valley of Mexico by a geologist (de Terra, 1949) in an Upper Pleistocene level, near the skeletons of imperial mammoth, with an estimated age of about 10,000 years; the man of Lagoa Santa, discovered in 1835 in the east Brazilian highlands of Minas Gerais, but put in doubt by Boas and Hrdlička and forgotten until it was confirmed by recent finds of human remains, associated with the bones of horses and mastodon, in the Confins Cave of the same region; and the fossil Punín skull, from the Ecuadorian highlands, similar to that of Lagoa Santa, also with bones of extinct fauna (Sullivan and Hellmann, 1925). All these bones are like those of modern Indians, and the question of the existence of a truly primitive man in America remains unanswered. However scarce, the remains known have proved that the early Indians were far from homogeneous: some are longheaded, others have round heads, and there are some with Mongoloid, Australoid, and even Negroid traits (Rivet, 1943; Gladwin, 1947).

Artifacts of the early Indians keep cropping up over the entire continent, but they remain too scattered and yield too few data to reconstruct a full picture of the life and culture of early man in America. We know, however, that while the men of Folsom and Yuma were expert hunters of bison and mastodon, others, like the Cochise people of Arizona and those of the Lake Mohave and Pinto Basin cultures of California, seem to have preferred gathering, as shown by their millstones for grinding nuts and wild grains and their undeveloped hunting implements. Others lived off the sea, fishing and collecting mollusks; such were the ancient peoples who left great shell middens at Pisagua and Taltal on the north Chilean coast (Bird, 1943) and the accumulation of refuse mixed with artifacts in the caves of Palli Aike and Fell's found by Bird (1946) near the Straits of Magellan. In the lowest level of one of these caves there were cremated burials, with skulls rather like that of the man of Lagoa Santa, with bones of guanaco and extinct ground sloth, and fine-stemmed projectile points. Bird had calculated an age of 5,100 years for this level, based upon the rise of the land level in modern times, but a reading of radioactive carbon 14 gave an even greater age: 8,639 years. Some living examples of this elementary cultural level survive still; such are the more primitive tribes of California, some of the Athapascans of the Yukon, and the more backward peoples on the fringes of South America, in Patagonia and Tierra del Fuego.

Nowhere on the continent is there evidence of the art of these early people. There are no known representations of living beings or even decorative motifs, but only utilitarian implements, though it is likely that these men used body paint and tattooing and that in time they may have developed decorative basketry, painted bark cloth, and skin robes with geometric decoration. The beauty and technical perfection of the Folsom, Yuma, and Sandia points indicate a feeling for form and a highly advanced art of stone-chipping comparable to that of their Solutrean contemporaries in the Old World (Figure 1).

There is a great blank between the primitive early hunters, fishers, and gatherers and the sedentary agricultural peoples who developed ceramic, stone-carving, architecture, and so forth. Most of the great cultures appear in a state of full development, without clear-cut evolution, either because they were imported or because the intervening stages have not yet been found. There are exceptions to the rule, notably in the Southwest of the United States, the most thoroughly explored area of the continent, where there is a gradual development of the art of pottery-making from elementary stages to the classic styles.

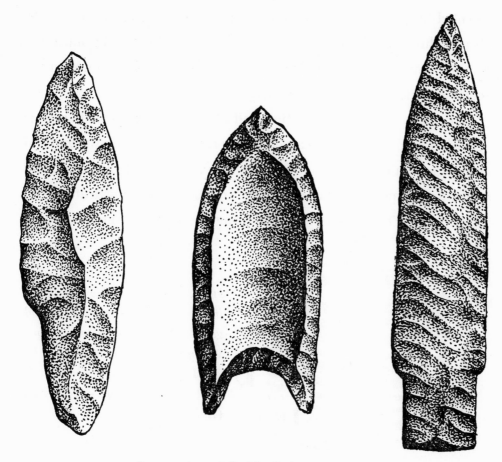

FIG. 1. *Spear points of the North American Stone Age:*
SANDIA; FOLSOM; *and* YUMA (*Scottsbluff*) *types.*

The Basketmakers of the Southwest clearly show an evolution from elementary agriculture and a geometric art based upon textiles to the eventual appearance of ceramic and the development into the classic Pueblo ceramic styles.

Interesting traces of early farmers without ceramic have been found in Peru, at Guañape and Cerro Prieto in the Viru Valley, Huaca Prieta in the Chicama Valley, Puemape near Pacasmayo, Aspero in Supe, and other places. The most elaborate of these, the Huaca Prieta culture, with an estimated date of from 3,000 to 1,000 B.C., belongs to a coastal people who depended mainly on shellfish and sea food, supple-

15

mented by such gathered or cultivated local plants as squash, gourds, beans, chilies, achira, and lúcuma. They made percussion-flaked scrapers and knives, but they had no hunting weapons and knew nothing of ceramics (Bennett and Bird, 1949).

Perhaps the most interesting find at Huaca Prieta was two little gourds whose covers were carved in low relief with highly stylized human figures, a mask of a sort of jaguar man and a double bird head in a style already pointing the way to the complex and sophisticated style of Chavín (Fig. 2). Another surprising development in the Huaca

FIG. 2. *The oldest known art object from South America: a small carved gourd from Huaca Prieta, Chicama Valley, Peru. It was excavated by Dr. Junius Bird in a pre-ceramic level dated at before 2000 B.C. (AMNH).*

Prieta culture is indicated by the finding of pieces of bark cloth and cotton textiles miraculously preserved in the bone-dry deserts of the Peruvian coast: string made without spindle-whorls, twined fabrics, looped and knotted pouches, fishing nets, and even true weavings. Junius Bird, the discoverer of Huaca Prieta, suggests northern Peru as the probable center of dispersion of the textile arts and suggests a partly Asiatic origin. It seems logical, if the coastal peoples first sowed the seeds of culture in the central Andes, that the textile arts in Peru had an antecedent in the early fishing peoples' art of making nets, carrying-bags, and gauzes.

The early hunter led a hard, uncertain life, having to move con-

16

stantly to find virgin hunting grounds, suffering cold and hunger whenever luck was not with him. His property was limited to what he could carry on his back; his society was reduced to the members of his tribe and his hungry dogs. To him every other human being was an enemy, an intruder and competitor in the wearisome search for food. Not much better was the lot of the gathering tribes, whose scanty and limited food supply did not permit the development of culture beyond the most elementary stages. But somewhere, somehow, an event took place that rapidly civilized the hunters and gatherers: this was the introduction of agriculture and the development of a tall wild grass into maize.

Years of experimentation and study have not solved the riddles of where, when, or from which wild grass maize originated. It was first believed that its ancestor was a wild plant called *teocentli,* "maize of the gods" (*euchlaena*), native to the Mexican plateau, where, consequently, maize would have originated (Spinden, 1922). Later another tall grass, *tripsacum,* from Mexico and Central America, was thought to have shared the ancestry of maize, but more recently it has been demonstrated from conclusive genetic evidence—the number of chromosomes—that neither *teocentli* nor *tripsacum* could have been its wild prototype. It was then suggested that the elusive ancestor of maize was a more primitive species, with the grains encased in a sheaf—podcorn (*Zea mays tunicata*)—or a vanished relative of it. The place of origin was then moved to somewhere in tropical South America, perhaps the upper Amazon basin or the Paraná-Paraguay valley (Mangelsdorf and Reeves, 1939). It now seems that when maize spread north and met with *tripsacum,* the two produced a hybrid, *teocentli,* which by repeated back-crossing gave birth to the endless varieties of maize typical of Mexico and North and Central America, but unknown in South America.

The most recent and significant discoveries on the subject of maize evolution were made in Bat Cave, New Mexico (Mangelsdorf and Smith, 1949). They revealed an accumulation of corncobs, and even kernels of corn, covering a period of about two thousand years, with the most primitive maize encountered in the lowest of the six levels found. The oldest ears, dated by carbon 14 at about 1500 B.C., were hardly the size of the little finger and were of two types: pod-corn and popcorn. The more primitive types of maize persisted relatively late, and there is a progressive increase in the size of the cobs and kernels throughout the sequence to the top level, dated by pottery from between A.D. 500 and 1000. The appearance of maize in the middle of the second millennium B.C. in a place so far removed from its probable southern place of origin (the evidence shows that it was not the Southwest) pushes back the probable date for the introduction of agriculture, and consequently the beginning of the development of American Indian culture, to at least 3000 B.C.

Maize was undoubtedly the greatest single factor in the development of American civilization, but all sorts of other native plants came to be domesticated, including beans, yams, and sweet potatoes; tomatoes; pumpkins and squashes; peppers; tobacco; cotton; cacao; peanuts; pineapples; sunflower; agave (for drink and fibers); cassava; quina (*chenopodium*); mate; coca; ipecacuanha; and copaiba. Beans were perhaps responsible for a great cultural impetus, for their rich content of proteins complemented the starch corn diet (Linton, 1940); the combination of maize and beans continues to be the basic diet of a great many Indian peoples. The discoveries of Bat Cave did not solve the main problem of the origin of maize as a wild plant, and it is a curious fact that while the wild prototypes of Eurasian cultivated plants are known, the ancestors of American domesticated plants have resisted identification. The increasing interest in interoceanic contacts has focused attention on certain transfers of food plants from Asia to

America and vice versa, of which at least three are proved to have traveled: the bottle gourd (*lagenaria*), found at Huaca Prieta, was used before maize and beans; the coconut, which is known to have been present on the west coast of Central America before 1539; and the sweet potato, which existed in Polynesia long before Spanish contact. Other cultivated plants whose American ancestry is beginning to be put in doubt are: cotton (*gossypium*), also present at Huaca Prieta, which probably originated in India; the sunflower (*amaranthus*); and, surprisingly enough, even maize and beans (Carter, 1953).

The next great unsolved problem concerning native American man is that of his age and the age of his culture. Great progress has been made in the knowledge of the early history of mankind in the Old World, mainly because of extensive discoveries of fossil man and because ancient civilizations left written historical records that go back to remote times. In America the oldest recorded Mexican histories go back to the end of the first millennium of our era, the older inscriptions on Maya monuments having defied interpretation except for the reading of dates, some of which fall in pre-Christian times. Estimates of the age of the earliest hunters of the Stone Age have fluctuated between 8,000 and 25,000 years, with a tendency to settle toward the latter date. Some rough-guess horizons have been established by archæologists, with initial dates steadily pushed back from the formerly accepted ones. For example, the cultures of Middle America are now supposed to have begun around the middle of the second millennium B.C. This pushing back has been done mainly to relieve what Dr. Alfred V. Kidder calls "chronological claustrophobia," for it is becoming harder to jam so much cultural achievement and the long cultural sequences of places like the Valley of Mexico into the impossibly short space of 1,500 years.

Ancient Mexican myth expounded that the earth had lived four epochs, called "suns," and had survived four catastrophes. Four times the sun and the world had been destroyed, once by each of the four elements: earth, wind, fire, and water. There are various versions of the myth, and in every one the exact number of years each epoch lasted is carefully specified as beginning with a certain date, which of course varies with each story, to mark the beginning of the world. An Aztec pictorial manuscript in the Vatican Library (Codex Vaticanus 3738) allots an average duration of from four to five thousand years to each epoch, with a grand total of 18,015 years since the creation. The Maya had also a mythical zero date from which time was counted, the beginning of the world on 4 *Ahau,* 8 *Cumhu,* which has been interpreted as October 15, 3373 B.C. (Spinden correlation) or as August 12, 3115 B.C. (Goodman-Martinez-Thompson correlation). However useless for scientific purposes these dates may be, they show that the Indians were conscious of their great age and that to establish historical chronologies was of great importance to them.

The archæologists have wrestled for over fifty years with the problem of dating the ancient Indian cultures. There have been fantastic estimates of great antiquity, but the predominant tendency has been toward cautious conservatism. None of the developed cultures was supposed to go back beyond the beginnings of the Christian era. Every imaginable device to date the ancient cultures has been tried, and some ingenious methods have been developed, until it can now be said that Indian chronology is beginning to tread more solid ground. The age of the remains of early man has been roughly dated by geological and paleontological clues: the geological strata in which they were found or their association with bones of extinct fauna. But geological dates are too general and uncertain, and there is also the question of whether the mammoth, horse, camel, ground sloth, and other beasts of the Pleistocene did not survive in America after they were extinct in the Old World.

Next are the clues provided by stratigraphic archæology, such as deep layers of remains in places occupied over a long period of time, which permit the identification of various phases of development of pottery styles, implements, and so forth, and the stratification of architectural ruins or tombs. If one or more phases in such sequences can be correlated to a known archæological style or period, a good guess can be made as to the relative chronological position of the earlier phases. This of course requires the finding of articles of trade or other objects identifiable with cultures of known antiquity.

There are, further, such written records as the pre-Columbian codexes; Indian genealogical pictorial manuscripts, many of which have been accurately interpreted. We know today the most minute details of the history of the dynasty of the aristocratic Mixtecs of Tilantongo in Oaxaca, Mexico, which lasted from A.D. 692 to 1642, 950 years of uninterrupted history for one dynasty (Caso, 1949); and the traditions and histories recorded by many of the missionaries and Indian aristocrats of the sixteenth century, such as the chronicles by the friars Sahagún, Torquemada, Burgoa, Bishop Landa, Prince Ixtlilxóchitl, Tezozomoc, and others in Mexico, or Garcilaso de la Vega and Guzmán Poma de Ayala in Peru. These have been invaluable for knowledge of the history of the Indians at the time of European contact. For dates of earlier periods the most important have been those inscribed on Maya monuments. The most brilliant of the Maya epigraphers—Thompson, Morley, Gates, Beyer—have spent lifetimes trying to read the Maya inscriptions. They have not had much success beyond the reading of the dates and of a handful of astronomical glyphs. The Maya dates have been correlated to our calendar, however, by the two systems of correlation mentioned above, which differ by 260 years. As the known Maya dates go back to the first centuries of our era and possibly even earlier, they provide a good anchor to which to tie the various styles of sculpture, painting, and architecture associated with these dates, as well as a way to establish the contemporaneity of other cultures that did not practice date-recording with the intensity of the Maya, but had trade and other contacts with them.

No extensive historical records like those from Middle America exist for either North or South American Indian cultures, and the age of these was guesswork until two new methods were discovered for dating ancient remains: one, *dendrochronology,* tree-ring dating, developed by Dr. A. E. Douglass, the science of establishing the age of a piece of wood by the varying thickness of the concentric rings trees develop every year, which vary according to the degree of dryness or humidity of that year. When a long-range pattern, extending over 2,000 years, of the climatic characteristics of the Southwest of the United States had been established, a master chart of the varying thickness of the tree-rings provided a means by which the date of a piece of wood from a ruin could be read with absolute accuracy. This technique has been applied to the ruins of the Southwest with great success because the dry climate has preserved the beams of ancient buildings, thus establishing a sure range of nearly two millennia of dates for the Southwest cultures. The earliest date thus recorded, A.D. 217, is that of a pole from a storage pit in a Utah cave.

The other and most sensational technique is the already famous carbon-14 method for dating archæological materials, invented by Dr. Willard F. Libby, of the Institute of Nuclear Studies at the University of Chicago. This method is based upon the principle of the transformation of nitrogen atoms in all living matter by bombarding with cosmic rays a radioactive, unstable isotope of carbon named carbon 14. This process ceases with the death of organic matter, after which the radio-activity of the isotope is lost in a constant, regular manner that can be measured by intricate laboratory processes and instruments of great precision. These measurements give the date of the death of such materials as charcoal, wood, textiles, teeth, and ivory with an average margin of error of only 250 years either way.

This almost incredible process is still in the experimental stage and was only recently made known to archæologists (Arnold and Libby, 1950; Johnson, 1951). It has already given positive results with remains of known antiquity, such as archæological Egyptian materials; the results of carbon-14 tests on American archæological materials have proved surprising and revolutionary, and have been for the most part extremely consistent. This means that Dr. Libby's process actually works, thus taking the guesswork out of future studies of early Indian history. When the margin of error has been eliminated, it will also solve such problems as the deadlock developed between the two correlations for reading Maya dates and the true age of Middle American and central Andean civilizations. Preliminary carbon-14 tests on charcoal and wood from early Mexican and Peruvian remains have given dates going back to the first and second millennia B.C., much earlier than any accepted before. I have adopted these dates here, in however preliminary a way, with enthusiasm and relief, because they provide the best antidote against Dr. Kidder's "chronological claustrophobia" when trying to establish a time-sequence for Indian art history. Carbon 14 will perhaps perform the miracle of pushing back the borderline between history and the dim prehistory of the early settlers of America.

ALONG with the "isolationist" theory of a single migration through Bering Strait to America are the theories of the "diffusionists," of whom there are two types: those who believe that the essentials of American civilization were brought from the Old World, and those who believe that there has been some contact between Asia and America since the Stone Age. Rivet is probably right in his belief that since prehistoric times the New World has been a center of affluence of peoples and races, the contrary of southern Asia, which has always been a center of human dispersion. This tendency has been greatly intensified since the discovery of America and continues unabated today.

According to Rivet (1943), other migratory currents besides the basic Mongoloid migrations crossed Bering Strait. For example, he thinks that the ancient inhabitants of the South Pacific islands, the Melanesians, always extraordinary seamen, also came in waves across the ocean and landed at various places on the Pacific shores of the Americas. Rivet's argument to support this is the traditional ability of the Melanesians and Polynesians in navigation: they discovered all the South Pacific islands, and even today, at the lowest ebb of their culture, they undertake voyages of 4,500 miles. Americans and Melanesians used similar boats, implements, dwellings, and weapons; made bark cloth, played on panpipes, and hunted with blowguns. Furthermore, the Hokan languages of California, Mexico, and Central America are closer to Melanesian than even Polynesian is, and Rivet claims that the skulls of the extinct Pericu Indians of Lower California are almost identical with those of the Melanesians. Rivet also believes in another, later, more limited (and less feasible) migration of Australoids across the ice wastes of Antarctica to Tierra del Fuego. Only by the admixture of the original Mongoloids from northern Asia with other peoples can he explain the striking lack of unity—physical, linguistic, and ethnological— among the American aborigines. These seemingly fantastic theories are well backed by persuasive arguments and the provoking similarities among the Indians, the Melanesians, and the Australians.

The fact that such voyages across the Pacific Ocean are quite feasible was demonstrated by the cruise of the *Kon-Tiki*, a wooden raft built strictly along Polynesian lines, with a cabin of plaited bamboo walls roofed with banana-leaf thatch, with only a radio as a modern convenience. It was manned by Thor Heyerdahl, a young Norwegian ethnologist, and five others, and sailed from Callao, Peru, on April 28, 1947. The voyage covered 4,300 miles, taking a direct westward course on the Humboldt Current before the trade winds, with a top speed of four knots and an average daily distance of 42.5 nautical miles. The trip ended three months later on a reef in the Tuamotu Archipelago, only about 450 miles from the objective, the island of Tahiti. Had the voyagers counted on a larger crew, the raft could have been paddled and thus saved from beaching on the reef (Heyerdahl, 1950).

THE endless similarities between the Old World and the New and the presence of the most varied physical traits in the Indians have been rationalized by Gladwin (1947) into the most elaborate existing theory on the question of American origins. He believes in no less than six successive migrations: (1) Australoid, (2) Negroid, (3) Algonquin, (4) Eskimo, (5) Mongoloid, and (6) Melanesian-Polynesian. This is roughly what Gladwin believes happened:

The first migration, between 25,000 and 15,000 B.C., of some sort of primitive east Asiatic Australoids, crossed Bering Strait, moved down the Pacific coast, spread east across the southern United States, and then moved southward again until it reached the Isthmus of Panama, where it split, one branch moving down to Ecuador, the other along the Brazilian Atlantic coast. This is suggested by the Australoid characteristics of certain skulls found from Lower California to the Texas Gulf coast, as well as of the Punín skulls of Ecuador and those of Lagoa Santa, Brazil. The early Cochise people of southern Arizona are among the suggested representatives of this migration, hunters and gatherers who brought the spear-thrower and who collected and ate wild oats, acorns, caterpillars, and oysters. They used millstones, and made coiled baskets.

The second migration consisted of Asiatic Negroids, and is supposed to have taken place sometime between 15,000 and 2500 B.C. They also came across Bering Strait, this time through the middle of North America, by way of the corridor opened at that time in the ice-sheet, along the edge of the Western Plateau. These Negroid immigrants, expert hunters, are identified by Gladwin with Folsom man, makers of fine flint spear points. They were stopped in the southern United States by the Australoid occupation (no Folsom points appear farther south), and there they mixed with the Australoids, as is shown by the skulls of the Basketmakers, which have characteristics of both races. The Negroid Folsom people moved eastward to the Mississippi basin, becoming the ancestors of the Archaic Woodland peoples, and eventually their Negroid strain vanished.

The third migration, entering by the same route, between 2500 and 500 B.C., brought people from northeast Asia, perhaps about 1000 B.C. These ancestors of the Algonquin Indians introduced a peculiar type of Asiatic pottery, its surface textured by a paddle wrapped in cords, made in northern China and Siberia since 2500 B.C. Cord-marked pottery of Asiatic shapes is restricted to a band that stretches from Idaho to Maine; hence the surmise that the Algonquins did not go south of this line because of the combined Australoid and Negroid barrier. The Algonquins brought with them, among other things besides Asiatic neolithic-style pottery, polished stone celts, twined basketry, and canoes and buckets made of bark. In support of Gladwin's belief must be mentioned the fact that at about this time metallurgy was introduced in eastern Asia, and that sometime later there appears in the

FIG. 3. *Hammered copper implements of the archaic Old Copper culture of Wisconsin and Minnesota. They show such Old World traits as stems, sockets, and holes for riveting (ChMNH).*

Great Lakes area a culture called "Old Copper," with typical early Asiatic tools and weapons made of hammered copper (Fig. 3).

The fourth migration, about 500 B.C., is supposed to have been that of the Eskimo, who also crossed from Siberia by the beaten path of Bering Strait, and spread along the Arctic fringe of North America as far as Greenland, prevented perhaps by the Algonquins from going south, and remaining isolated today.

The fifth migration was of Mongoloids, northern Chinese, according to Gladwin, who were running away from the Huns and from the chaotic situation that followed the breakup of the Chou dynasty of China, about 300 B.C. This migration, he believes, was numerous and prolonged, entering also by Bering Strait and reaching Mexico and Central America. It could have brought such of the essentials of Middle American culture as jade ornaments, figurines, human sacrifice, and the sinew-backed bow. Gladwin does not explain why it did not bring along the typical Chinese achievements of the time—unexcelled bronze-casting, glassmaking, hieroglyphic writing, and the wheel—or the fact that the bow and arrow were a late introduction into Middle America, probably not earlier than A.D. 900.

The sixth and last migration, between 300 B.C. and A.D. 500, coming directly by boats across the Pacific, consisted supposedly of "Melanesians who later turned out to be Caribs, and Polynesians who later turned out to be Arawaks." They landed on the Pacific coast from Mexico to Peru, crossed the Isthmus of Panama, and spread to the Antilles and Florida, as well as along the coasts of Venezuela and the Guianas. Gladwin's arguments in support of his theory are the numerous and complex Oceanic traits in this area; they also refer to Nordenskiöld (1931), who lists forty-nine such common traits, of which thirty-eight occur in Colombia and Panama. He also explores the possibility that such a native American delicacy as the sweet potato was imported into Polynesia from America before European contact; sweet potatoes are called *kumar* by the Quechua Indians of Peru, *kumara* by the Polynesians.

Gladwin's conclusions are, roughly, that it is highly improbable that all the traits of native American Indian civilizations were invented without any contact or influence from the Old World; that most, if not all, of the duplications of Old World traits found in the Americas were brought in from Asia, either through Alaska or across the Pacific; that the prototypes of North American culture have traits confined exclusively to China and northeast Asia, while those of the Mexican (Middle American) and Andean cultures are traceable to Polynesia, Melanesia,

28

India, and the Near East. Thus he explains the common Australoid traits found in far North and South America by the wedge driven between them, across the middle of the continent, by the migrations of the Caribs and Arawaks (Melanesians and Polynesians).

Gladwin's ingenious theory has not been received kindly, and has not been properly discussed, partly perhaps because of the defiant, wisecracking attitude with which it was presented in his book *Men Out of Asia,* partly because of the cautious horror with which "Dr. Phuddy Duddy" (his name for the old-guard archæologist) regards diffusionist ideas. The theory has many weak points, particularly in regard to the Near Eastern and Chou Chinese migrations; its outdated estimates of the age of Middle American cultures; and the fact that it leaves unexplained the sources of the most purely Asiatic culture, that of the Indians of the Northwest Coast of North America. On the other hand, the theory is stimulating and highly illuminating in regard to such confused factors as the presence of Australoid, Negroid, Mongoloid, and Oceanic traits in America. The identification of the Algonquins with the Siberians by their common and exclusive traits is brilliant.

It is thus clear that the problem of cross-Pacific contact cannot be disposed of by simply ignoring it or by doggedly supporting the highly improbable theory of absolutely independent duplication of inventions. It is becoming more and more evident that the possibility of various influences and contacts among America, eastern Asia, and the South Pacific is more real than the guessings of rash diffusionists. There is a tantalizing similarity between the art styles and spirit of some American Indian cultures and the arts of pre-Buddhist China, Malaysia, and the South Seas. These similarities have been pointed out by such serious art historians and archæologists as Fenollosa, Osvald Sirén, Leonhard Adam, Berthold Laufer, H. G. Creel, Carl Hentze, and, particularly, Gordon Ekholm, Carl Schuster, and Dr. Robert von Heine-

Geldern, a leading authority on the archæology of southeast Asia who has made the most serious studies on the subject.

The similarities between the arts of Asia and those of America have been generally attributed to coincidence or explained by a common psychological base. Heine-Geldern (1949) points out, however, that many of these analogies are so close and specific that they not only repeat a considerable number of characteristic decorative motifs and designs, but also extend into the basic character of certain art styles—for example, the styles of Ulua in Honduras and Tajín of Veracruz and the late Chou or Huai art of China (650–200 B.C.); the style of the Dongson culture of Indochina (of about 750 B.C.–A.D. 100) and that of western South America; or the art of the Chinese Shang dynasty (1700–1100 B.C.) and the arts of southern Alaska, British Columbia, and the island of Marajó in the mouth of the Amazon.

The great drawback in trying to correlate these similarities has always been the difference of time between the early Chinese cultures and those of the Americas, generally regarded as having developed much later, and the fact that no Asiatic objects have ever been found on the American continent. This thorny problem has been tackled by Heine-Geldern in a sound, scientific manner by analyzing the basic component elements of these Asiatic cultures and their obvious extensions into Malaysia and the South Pacific and establishing a chronological framework within which the spread of these influences could have taken place. First he postulated the existence of a basic, prehistoric culture, probably native to eastern Asia as early as the third millennium B.C. or even earlier, the "Old Pacific style." This he believes to underlie the great cultures of pre-Buddhist China (Shang and Chou) and to have spread through the islands of Malaysia and the Pacific until it reached the coasts of America. Its most characteristic trait is the making of

sculptures, mainly of wood, based upon the principle of combining human and animal figures with a genealogical, heraldic, or mythological
significance, usually in series, arranged in vertical columns towering
one above another. Another trait of the "Old Pacific style" is that of representing figures with the same meaning in low relief, painting, or
weaving as if they were split in two and the halves then spread over the
surface. This style survives in its purest forms among the coastal tribes
of southern Alaska and British Columbia, in New Ireland, parts of New
Guinea, and among the Philippine Igorots, the Dyaks of Borneo, and
the Bataks of Sumatra.

About 1800 B.C. the "Old Pacific style" combined in China with the
"Dniestro-Danubian" style of southwest Russia, Transylvania, Hun-
gary, Romania, and the north Balkans, characterized by spiral motifs
and the technique of bronze-casting, to produce the great art of the
Shang dynasty and the later Chou periods, as well as the Dongson style
of Indochina. The influence of these cultures spread far and wide into
Malaysia and across the Pacific, eventually reaching the coasts of
America, producing in turn many local styles that survive today on
South Pacific islands, and even in such places as the American Northwest Coast and the Amazon basin. Thus Heine-Geldern believes Chinese influences came into America at various times and from various
sources, mostly second-hand by way of the South Pacific islands; for
example, the style of the Amazon and Ucayali rivers is often almost
identical with that of the Marquesas Islands, which is in turn an off-
shoot of Chinese Shang art, suggesting that it came by way of the
Marquesas. Heine-Geldern (1937) has collected much evidence of
strong cultural influences spreading from southern or central China between the fifth and the third centuries B.C. This would account for the
extraordinary resemblance between the Tajín and Ulua styles of Mid-

31

dle America and that of late Chou art, which could have come, by indirect ways and in relays, on the wake of the collapse of the Chou dynasty in China.

The time difference is really no obstacle to the soundness of the
theory. On the one hand, the true age of American civilizations is still
undetermined. On the other, there is a great probability that the cultural waves that started from eastern Asia between 1200 and 200 B.C.
spread gradually across the Pacific by successive infiltration of styles
from one place to another from various sources and at various times, a
process that must have taken very long. What traveled, consequently,
was the styles acquired second-hand by different peoples, not the actual objects from Asia. The reluctance of some peoples to abandon
Archaic types of culture is typified by the survival of the styles of the
Neolithic and Bronze ages—for instances, among the Naga of Assam,
the hill tribes of Burma, and in Indochina, Malaysia, and Melanesia. It
is generally recognized that the Polynesians came from India at a time
when metallurgy was well advanced in Asia; yet they lost it on the way,
along with such even simpler techniques as pottery-making and textile-
weaving.

However controversial and "heretical" the theory of Heine-Geldern may be, it is thus far the most scientific and conscientiously built. I
have attempted to reduce it to the traditional nutshell in the chart
shown in Fig. 4 (facing).

I have always been struck by similarities in the concepts and styles
of the arts of America, eastern Asia, and the South Seas, and have become hopelessly guilty of subversive diffusionist convictions. The theories of Rivet, Gladwin, Heine-Geldern, and others have all helped to
clarify my own impressions on the matter of cross-Pacific contacts. To
present my case I shall begin with a selected list of art motifs and cultural concepts common to the Old World and the New:

32

DNIESTRO-DANUBIAN STYLE

The Bronze Age style from southwest Russia, Romania, Transylvania, and the north Balkans. Represented by spiral motifs and bronze-castings. Came to China probably about 1800 B.C.

"OLD PACIFIC STYLE"

The probable native style of east Asia (3rd millennium B.C. or before), represented by totemic posts, bilateral representation (and perhaps "hockers")

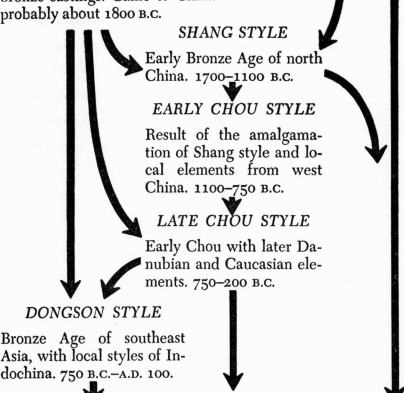

SHANG STYLE

Early Bronze Age of north China. 1700–1100 B.C.

EARLY CHOU STYLE

Result of the amalgamation of Shang style and local elements from west China. 1100–750 B.C.

LATE CHOU STYLE

Early Chou with later Danubian and Caucasian elements. 750–200 B.C.

DONGSON STYLE

Bronze Age of southeast Asia, with local styles of Indochina. 750 B.C.–A.D. 100.

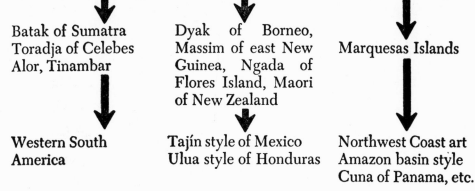

Widespread influences in Malaysia, Melanesia, and Polynesia, reaching the Americas through various channels and at various times. Examples:

Batak of Sumatra
Toradja of Celebes
Alor, Tinambar

Dyak of Borneo, Massim of east New Guinea, Ngada of Flores Island, Maori of New Zealand

Marquesas Islands

Western South America

Tajín style of Mexico
Ulua style of Honduras

Northwest Coast art
Amazon basin style
Cuna of Panama, etc.

FIG. 4. *Chart illustrating the Heine-Geldern theory.*

The *"Hocker" motif*, the most widespread common trait, a figure with arms and legs outstretched in frog fashion, is a circum-Pacific element, and is typical of early China, Malaysia, Melanesia, and Polynesia. It appears with dots or disks between knees and elbows; in series, often losing the head and becoming a decorative pattern; or as hockers with claws, horns, death's-head, and visible spinal columns, suggesting that it represents a spirit of the dead (Schuster, 1951). A peculiar as-

FIG. 5. *Two typical "hockers" carved on stone slabs, from Manabí, Ecuador. One has circles between knees and elbows; the other is a monster with claws and visible spinal column.*

34

pect is a Mexican and Peruvian hocker with the extremities ending in animal heads; this is repeated in Borneo and New Guinea. In some cases (Northwest Coast, Mexico, Peru, Borneo) hockers are flanked by two animals, which Spinden identifies with the guardians of the sun god in Mexico and Peru (Figs. 5, 6, 7, 8, 9).

Bilateral splitting of an animal, shown as two profiles joined by the head, is identified with a heraldic motif of the "Old Pacific style." It is found in early China, the Amur River area of Siberia, on the Northwest Coast, in Mexico, in Brazil, and elsewhere (Fig. 10).

Totemic posts, with figures arranged in vertical series as a heraldic or mythological motif of the "Old Pacific style," are typical of the Northwest Coast, Melanesia, Polynesia (New Zealand), and Malaysia (Batak and Igorot). The similarity between the totem poles of the Northwest Coast and those of New Zealand is underlined by the common use of ornamental inlays of haliotis shell. A variation of this concept, faces arranged in series, gives a striking similarity to the carved bones of Shang China and the decoration of the façades of Puuc style of Yucatán (Figs. 11, 12).

The *interlocking spiral motif,* a widespread motif originating in the Dniestro-Danubian Bronze Age, is found all over America, southeast Asia, and the Pacific. In both Java and America this motif seems to derive from stylized interlocking bird motifs.

Eyes and faces on the joints and hands are found on the Northwest Coast, in Aztec reliefs, in the Mississippi Basin, New Hebrides, New Guinea, and elsewhere (Schuster, 1951).

The *Makara motif,* a serpent head with upturned snout and with a human face in its mouth, from India, Java, Bali, and Sumatra, is comparable to the Mexican *Xiuhcoatl,* the fire serpent on the Aztec Sun Stone (Fig. 13).

Bird cults as basic art motivators are another circum-Pacific trait.

FIG. 6. *"Hockers" from early China and Brazil in similar styles:* ABOVE, *design on a bronze drum, Shang or Early Chou period (Collection of Baron Sumitomo, Osaka);* BELOW, *sherd of Shang-period kaolin ware (Sen-oku-Sei-sho, 1934);* FACING, *great funerary urn from Marajó Island, Brazil (MNRJ).*

For example: the albatross of the South Pacific, phœnix of China, tengu of Japan, rooster of Siberia, Garuda of India and Indonesia, thunderbird and eagle of North and Middle America, roseate spoonbill of the eastern United States, raven of the Northwest Coast, condor and pelican of South America. In both Oceania and America there are mythical birdmen like the *tangata-manu* of Easter Island and the endless humanized birds of the Woodlands, Mexico, and South America.

37

FIG. 7. *"Hockers" with extremities ending in animal heads:* UPPER LEFT, *on a Dyak woodcarving from Borneo (Tilhmann Collection, Amsterdam);* UPPER RIGHT, *on a clay stamp from Guerrero, Mexico (Collection M. C.);* CENTER, *painted on pottery from Nicoya, Costa Rica (after Lothrop);* BELOW, *woven on tapestry from the central Peruvian coast (YUM and John Wise Collection).*

FIG. 8. "Hockers" with joint-marks and faces on arms and legs: LEFT, bear on a house panel, Haida, Queen Charlotte Islands (DAM); BELOW LEFT, pictograph from Venezuela (Schuster, 1951); ABOVE, alligator-god repoussé on a gold disk from Coclé, Panama; BELOW, Aztec earth-god carved on a stone box (MfVH).

FIG. 9. *"Hockers" between two protecting animals:* ABOVE, *design on a spindle-whorl of wood from the Northwest Coast (PMV);* CENTER, *carved side of a Dyak wooden coffin, Borneo (courtesy of Carl Schuster);* BELOW, *stone lintel from Cajamarquilla, Huaraz, Peru (after Tello).*

40

FACING: *Pelvic bone of a large mammal carved into a fantastic mask, Tlingit, Alaska, about 60 centimeters high (Collection M. C.)*

FIG. 10. *Examples of bilateral splitting from China and America:* TOP, *design on an early bronze ax from China, Shang period (NGA);* SECOND ROW, LEFT, *on a Shang bronze vessel (Collection of C. T. Loo);* SECOND ROW, RIGHT, *on a pre-Columbian clay stamp from Guerrero, Mexico (Collection M. C.);* THIRD ROW, *bear design on a Haida silver bracelet (Collection of Alice Rahon Fitzgerald);* BOTTOM, *split jaguar, design in champlevé technique on a clay urn from Marajó, Brazil (MNRJ).*

FIG. 11. *Carvings with figures arranged in series, from Polynesia, Melanesia, and Indonesia:* LEFT TO RIGHT, *ivory fan-handle, Marquesas Islands (UMP); carved post from New Zealand (EMS); post of rank of tree-fern root, four meters high, from Malekula, New Hebrides (Nevermann, 1933); funerary post topped by a reconstructed human skull (ChMNH); Bontoc ceremonial fork, Philippine Islands (Collection M. C.); upper part of a Toba Batak shaman's staff, Sumatra (Collection M. C.).*

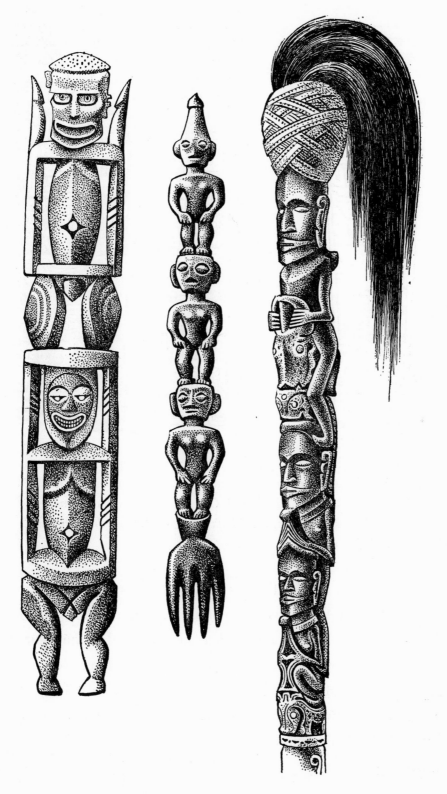

FIG. 12. *Faces arranged in series:* LEFT, *fragment of a bone spatula with masks of the jaguar T'ao-t'ieh, Shang period, from Honan, China* (Collection M. C.); RIGHT, *superimposed masks of the jaguar Chac, the Maya rain-god, from a building at Kabah, Yucatán.*

Feline cults, basic to the arts of early China, early Middle America, and the central Andes, have important variations: *Tiger and Jaguar Mask Panel,* the *T'ao T'ieh* of China, has a parallel in the jaguar rain-god masks of Mexico. Some late Chou jades resemble Mexican double representations of rain-god and tiger or jaguar faces. The *alter-ego motif,* a protective feline spirit that appears on the famous Shang bronze in the Sumitomo Collection, has counterparts in the sculptures of San Agustín and Popayán in Colombia, and of the Trombetas River

44

of Brazil, the monoliths of Zapatera Island in Nicaragua, Chimu bronzes, and the bone clubs of the Salish of the Columbia River (Figs. 14, 15). *Feline-head helmets,* in the shape of jaguars (as well as of birds and alligators), of Mexico and Peru are similar to the tiger helmets in Shang bronzes, and are a development of the protective animal spirit, as is shown clearly by the tiger caps of appliqué cloth worn even today by Chinese children for good luck (Fig. 16). The bear cult of the Northwest Coast and of the Ainu of Japan could be a variation of the jaguar cult.

Serpent and dragon cults of China, India, Indochina, and Indonesia (Naga), as well as the feathered serpent of Mexico, have an implication of "precious"; the Naga of India has a jewel in its tail, and Quetzalcoatl means "precious serpent" in Mexico. Priests were called "serpents" in Mexico, India, Java, and Bali. The sky-dragon was a rain-giving divinity in Mexico and southeast Asia, a variation of which is the *two-headed serpent* found in late Chou jades, on the Northwest Coast (*sisiutl*), the Maya ceremonial bar, the Tajín stone "yokes," Paracas textiles of Peru, Calchaqui bronze disks from Argentina, and elsewhere (Figs. 17, 18, 19). In Bali a two-headed serpent represents the rainbow that sucks water from the sea to produce rain. American two-headed serpents often assume the form of a double spiral, curvilinear or angular, a motif identical with the *lei-wen,* the lightning pattern basic to the design on all the early Chinese bronzes (Fig. 20). Furthermore, there is a striking similarity between the general style of the art of pre-Buddhist China—Shang and Chou—and the styles of Middle American art, specifically that of the Mexican Gulf coast (Tajín style) and, to a certain extent, that of the Maya. The same scroll patterns representing clouds and sky monsters turned into almost abstract decorative patterns can be found in Chou dynasty bronzes and jades and in Mexican stone-carvings. Figs. 21, 22, 23 show some such tantalizing parallels.

45

FIG. 13. *The fire serpent:* ABOVE, *Aztec, from the Sun Stone* (MNAM); BELOW, *Maya, from Altar O at Copán, Honduras;* FACING, *a* Makara *from the ruins of Borobodur, Java.*

All sorts of architectural elements are common to Mexico, Guatemala, India, Java, and Indochina, the most striking of which are the

pyramids with receding stages, faced with cut stone, and with stair-ways leading to a sanctuary on top, also of stone; in many there are surprising common traits such as *serpent columns and banisters, vaulted galleries and corbeled arches, attached columns, stone cut-out lattices,* and *Atlantean figures,* which are typical of the Puuc style of Yucatán. The most striking and highly specialized of these traits is the *lotus motif interspersed with seated human figures* common to Chichén-Itzá and Amaraviti, southern India (Fig. 24). Amaraviti is dated about the second century of our era, but it exercised a powerful influence over the Hindu-Buddhist art of Cambodia, Champa, and even modern Bali. It is significant that temple pyramids in Cambodia do not antedate the eighth century, and only became important in the ninth and tenth centuries, a time coinciding with the beginning of the Puuc period of Yucatán (Heine-Geldern and Ekholm, 1951).

Carved jade for ornaments and funerary offerings, typical of Mexico, Guatemala, Costa Rica, and Colombia, is also characteristic of early China and New Zealand. Identical jade celts are found in Amer-

FIG. 14. *The protective feline:* LEFT, *Chinese bronze from the Shang period* (*Collection of Baron Sumitomo, Osaka*); RIGHT, *Chimú bronze from north Peru* (*Collection M. C.*).

ica and in New Guinea, as well as in neolithic Europe; the Northwest Coast Indians carved labrets and adzes of jade, and so did the Eskimo. Furthermore, in both China and Mexico the funerary jades found in tombs were painted with red cinnabar.

Funerary mounds of earth of Mexico, Guatemala, the Mississippi Valley, and Brazil resemble those of early China. Those of Kaminaljuyú (Miraflores phase) in Guatemala are rather like the Shang tombs with stepped vaults and wooden planks where the corpses were laid, and

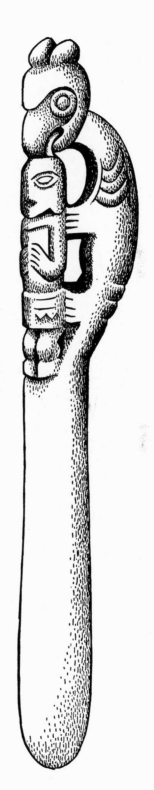

FIG. 15. *The alter-ego motif:* ABOVE, *Chinese jade ornament of the early western Chow* (*Collection of A. W. Bahr*); BELOW, *stone-carving from the Trombetas River, Brazil* (*Nordenskiöld, 1930*); RIGHT, *Salish bone club, Washington State* (*ChMNH*).

FIG. 16. *The feline helmet in Mexico and China:*
ABOVE LEFT, *the great Mixtec conqueror "Eight Deer" (Codex Nutall);*
RIGHT, *head from a clay urn of Monte Albán III period, Oaxaca, Mexico*
(MNAM); BELOW LEFT, *bronze pole-end from early China, Shang period*
(MIA); RIGHT, *tiger cap of cloth worn by modern Chinese children as an*
amulet.

FIG. 17. *Two-headed serpent and jaguar motifs:* ABOVE, *tattooing designs from wooden stamps, Kayan tribe, Borneo (SarM);* CENTER, *designs from clay stamps from Guerrero, Mexico (Enciso, 1947);* BELOW, *double jaguar motifs painted on Recuay pottery from Peru.*

there is a stone sarcophagus at La Venta, Mexico, like those from the Yamato tombs of Japan. A strange similarity exists in the use of *conical adobes* for construction in Sumerian Mesopotamia and in the Cupisnique ruins of Peru. A good deal has been said about the *megalithic stone constructions* of Easter Island, Peru, and Bolivia. The Tahitian *maraes*, stepped platforms or pyramids, placed across one end of an

FIG. 18. *The two-headed serpent with central mask, in China and America.* TOP TO BOTTOM: *Chinese jade ornament, Chou period (FGAW); on a Mexican clay urn from Oaxaca (MNAM); on a stela at El Mesón, Veracruz, Mexico; the* sisiutl, *the mythical two-headed serpent of the Northwest Coast: carved in wood, Kwakiutl (Boas, 1897), carved ivory "soul-catcher" from a shaman's paraphernalia (Inverarity, 1950).*

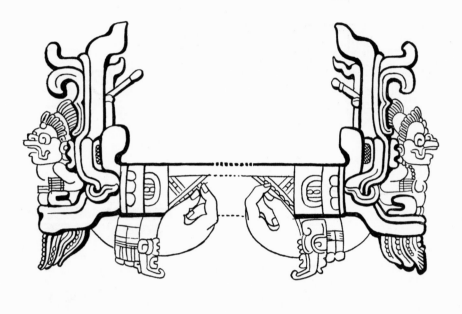

FIG. 19. *The Maya two-headed serpent:* ABOVE, *ceremonial bar on Stela N at Copán, Honduras;* BELOW, *east side of Altar O at Copán.*

enclosed rectangular court, are similar to the Maya platform structures to the extent that both have an upright stone slab in front of the pyramids, among the Maya generally an elaborately carved stela.

Masks for the dead are widespread, but there is a specialized type

53

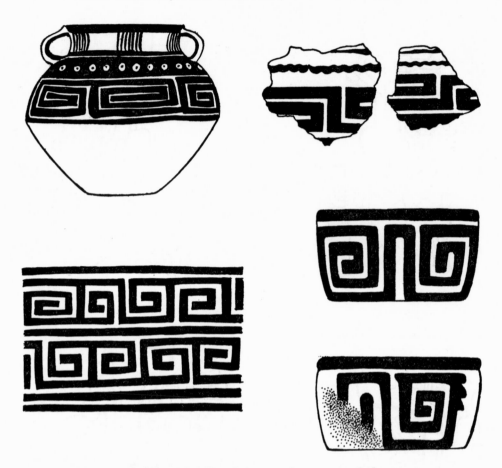

FIG. 20. *The neolithic Chinese thunder motif,* lei-wen, *and the Mexican* xone-
cuilli *(light-worm):* ABOVE LEFT, *clay pot from Kansu, Ma Chang period
(Andersson, 1943);* RIGHT, *two sherds from Hsien Tien (Andersson, 1943);*
BELOW LEFT, *design on a cylindrical clay stamp, Valley of Mexico (Enciso,
1947);* RIGHT, *purple-red on white pottery bowls, Las Charcas and Zacate-
pequez phases, pre-Classic Guatemalan period.*

made of sections: of shell and bronze in Shang and Chou tombs, of
ivory among the Ipiutak of Alaska, of jade in Monte Albán II and Miraflores, of gold in Chichén-Itzá, and of bronze in the Chimu and central
Peruvian mummy bundles.

Turquoise mosaics were made in ancient Mexico, the central
Andes, and the North American Southwest, as well as in Shang China,
India, Persia, and Tibet.

54

FIG. 21. *Similar decorative motifs from China and Mexico:*
ABOVE, *design on a Chinese bronze vase, Chou period*
(*FGAW*); CENTER, *design on a Chinese bronze brick, Chou
period* (*ChMNH*); BELOW, *decorative border carved in stone,
from El Tajín, Veracruz, Mexico;* RIGHT, *paddle-stone in Tajín
style* (*Collection of W. Paalen*).

Feather mosaic, a highly specialized technique, was common to
Mexico, California, the central Andes, the Amazonian forests, Chile,
Hawaii, New Zealand, and New Guinea. *Ornaments made of cut-out
feathers* were used by the Plains Indians, the Californian Hupa, and
the natives of the Admiralty Islands and New Guinea.

55

FIG. 22. *Tiger profile with prolonged snout:* ABOVE, *from China, bronze ornament, probably from the armor of a horse, Chou period* (ChIA); BELOW, *from Middle America, on a Maya stone-carving from Quiriguá, Guatemala* (*Proskuriakoff, 1951*).

Lacquer, a typical Asiatic technique, was used in Mexico, Guatemala, and Peru in pre-Columbian times.

Al-fresco mural painting, characteristic of the great civilizations of the Mediterranean, China, Korea, and India, was practiced with intensity in Mexico. Murals painted on adobe are known from Awatobi in Arizona and from the Huaca del Sol in Peru.

FACING: *Carved and painted Tlingit partition screen from the house of Chief Shakes, Wrangell, Alaska, about 5 meters high. The hole between the bear's legs served as a door.* (DAM.)

FIG. 23. *Mythical personages:*
ABOVE, *on a Chinese door-hinge
of bronze, Chou period* (FAM);
BELOW, *sea monster carved on
black slate, Haida, Queen Charlotte Islands, Canada* (Boas,
1927).

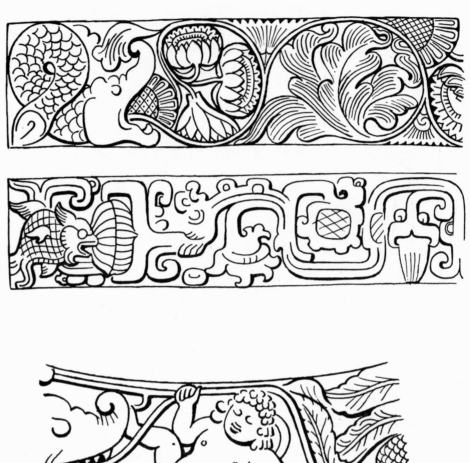

FIG. 24. *Decorative architectural motifs:* FIRST THREE, *from Amaraviti, southern India;* BELOW, *from Chichén-Itzá, Yucatán (Ekholm, 1950).*

Pottery techniques—that is, coiled or paddled pottery, polished and painted, cord-marked and stamped—are curiously separated by areas in both Asia and America. Gladwin (1947) lists twenty common traits: red polished ware with black interior; white or cream, and red or black slipped surfaces with painted designs; gray or brown wares with textured or cord-marked patterns; large jars shaped by the paddle-and-anvil method; coiled ribbon of clay to build pottery walls; slips of contrasting colors; patterns incised on sun-dried surfaces before baking, or engraved after baking; embossed ornaments and human features on vessel surfaces; paint rubbed on incised or engraved patterns; lead glaze in painted decorations; tripod or tetrapod bowls and trays (Figs. 25, 26); handles and rims for suspension; pottery spindle-whorls; clay figurines with "coffee-bean" eyes (and hollow effigy-vessels); baked clay tiles; stamp seals; cylindrical seals; wheeled clay toys; pot-stands.

Basketry techniques include lattice and split-cane baskets with identical shapes and designs among the Dyaks of Borneo and the Chitimacha of Louisiana; shallow-tray baskets of China and Indonesia like those of the Guiana Arawaks; imbricated baskets of the Northwest Coast, Sumatra, and Ceylon.

Bark cloth (or tapa) is widespread in Middle and South America as well as in Polynesia, Melanesia, and east Asia. Painted bark cloth exists with identical motifs and colors in the upper Ucayali in Peru and Bolivia, and in New Guinea (Fig. 27). Identical grooved stone beaters for making bark cloth are from Mexico and Celebes.

Head-hunting is a world-wide trait known from England, France, and Germany (as late as A.D. 879), Iran, West Africa, Assam, Indochina, Borneo, Celebes, the Philippines, Formosa, New Guinea, the Solomons, and other places. In America head-hunting was practiced intensively on the Northwest Coast, in California, Mexico, Colombia,

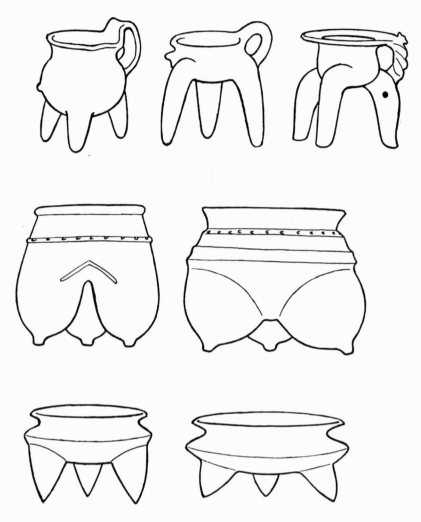

FIG. 25. *Ceramic parallels from early China and America:* ABOVE LEFT, *Ting tripod, prehistoric, from Shih Li P'u, Kansu;* CENTER & RIGHT, *pre-Classic Guatemalan (Miraflores period, Las Charcas phase, and from San Andrés Sajcabajá);* CENTER LEFT, *Li tripod, prehistoric, from Sha Ching, Kansu (700–500 B.C.);* RIGHT, *Mexican pre-Classic (about 500 B.C.) from Chupícuaro (Collection M. C.);* BELOW LEFT, *Li Ting tripod, Yang Shao, Honan (2200– 1700 B.C.);* RIGHT, *late pre-Classic from Chupícuaro, Mexico (MNAM). (All the Chinese examples after Andersson, 1943.)*

Ecuador, and Peru, and on the Amazon. Related to this is the *skull and head trophy* cults, equally widespread, with curious parallels such as

FIG. 26. *Clay bowls painted in black over a white slip:* ABOVE, *from Ma Chia Yao, Kansu, China (early prehistoric, Yang Shao period) (Andersson, 1943);* BELOW LEFT, *from Bennett's Peak, New Mexico, Anasazi culture, Pueblo II–III period;* RIGHT, *Whitewater, Pueblo II–III period (Roberts, 1940).*

the Aztec *tzompantli* racks for the skulls of the thousands of victims of sacrifice and the pyramid of ninety thousand skulls said to have been built by the Mongol Timur at Bagdad. A carved skull from Kaminaljuyú, Guatemala (Fig. 28), has counterparts in carved skulls from Borneo and decorated trophy heads from New Zealand, the Marquesas,

61

FIG. 27. *Bark cloth painted in yellow and black:* ABOVE, *from Collingwood Bay, New Guinea* (AMNH); BELOW, *from Cochabamba, Bolivia* (ChMNH).

and New Guinea. Other variations are the practices of ceremonial can-nibalism and the scalping of an enemy among the Scythians, Ostyaks, Samoyeds, Turks, and Mongols, and among the Indians of the North

American Plains, the Eastern Woodlands, Venezuela, Brazil, and the Paraná.

There are endless common traits in the general aspects of culture among America, Asia, and Oceania. Those which have been repeatedly

FIG. 28. *Carved trophy skulls:*
LEFT, *from tomb at Kaminaljuyú, Guatemala, Esperanza period* (*Kidder, Jennings, and Shook, 1946*); RIGHT, *from Borneo* (*MʹH*).

listed by the diffusionists include *implements of war:* the spear-thrower; specialized types of bows and arrows; stone, bone, and wood war-clubs; star- and pineapple-shaped stone mace-heads; stone-bladed swords; the blowgun and boomerang; shields of rawhide and basketry; armor of slats, quilt, or basketry; *identical musical instruments,* such as panpipes, bamboo flutes, nose flutes, conch-shell trumpets (end- and side-blown), clay ocarinas, long trumpets, slit wooden gongs, and, of course, rattles and skin drums. Among the *articles of dress*, ornaments, and paraphernalia of rank are: earplugs, nose plugs, shell gorgets, cheek plugs, and labrets, bracelets of shell, penis-cover, V-motif as chest decoration (Schuster, 1951); face- and body-painting, tattooing, and scarification; blackened, filed, and inlaid teeth; as well as the use of litters, fans, and parasols for dignitaries. There are, further, identi-

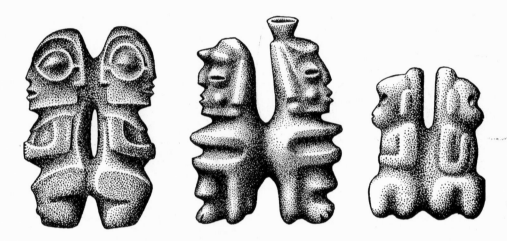

FIG. 29. LEFT, *Double tiki figurine of black basalt, Marquesas Islands (Collection of Georges Salles)*; CENTER & RIGHT, *twin figurines of metadiorite and green granite from Guerrero, Mexico (Collection M. C.)*.

cal double stone figures joined back to back in the Marquesas Islands and Guerrero, Mexico (Fig. 29); duplicate forms of stone mauls and pestles from the South Pacific islands, Kamchatka, and North and Middle America (Fig. 30); similar masks of painted bark cloth, house types, canoes and paddles, liana bridges, wooden pillows, four-footed trays and stools, net bags, folded books with wooden covers, games such as the parchisi of India and the Mexican *patolli,* the *volador* game, mirrors of pyrite, betel- and coca-chewing, with lime and tobacco, as well as gourd containers for the lime; shell money; birchbark shelters and canoes; and the identical containers of birchbark with curvilinear scraped design from Siberia and North America; string-crosses as prayers from Tibet, India, Assam, Mexico, and Peru; the custom of fishing with poison; shell fishhooks (Fig. 31); the use of agricultural terraces in southeast Asia, Peru, and Bolivia; and—last, but not least—the cultivation of cotton, practiced since early times in Asia and America (Hutchinson, 1947). It has been claimed that even maize, that most typical of American cultivated plants, was in use in Asia before Columbus came to this continent (Stoner and Anderson, 1949).

Looking again at the present state of the problem of American Indian origins, we can weed out the following conclusions from the quagmire of theories, impassioned arguments, and scanty evidence: the Indians are predominantly Mongoloid, but present among them are other racial traits, variously identified as Australoid and Negroid. In Asia there are also remnants of Negroids, from the Philippines to Malaya—the Negritos and Pygmies—and of Australoids, such as the Dravidians of India and Ceylon. It is generally accepted that the Asiatic immigrants began to arrive in America at a time guessed to have been some twenty to twenty-five thousand years ago, and all the evidence seems to indicate that no single mass movement of peoples or culture occurred from Asia to America. Consequently, the peopling of the Americas must have been accomplished over a very long period of time by successive, limited-scale waves of Asiatic immigrants, each of a different racial, linguistic, and cultural character.

The lack of linguistic unity is striking. There are over one hundred unrelated language groups without known Asiatic relatives in the American Babel, and the same can be said of the cultural characteristics of each area, which vary from the most elementary stages of human culture to great and complex civilizations. Taking into consideration the slow pace at which the early cultures of the world evolved and the

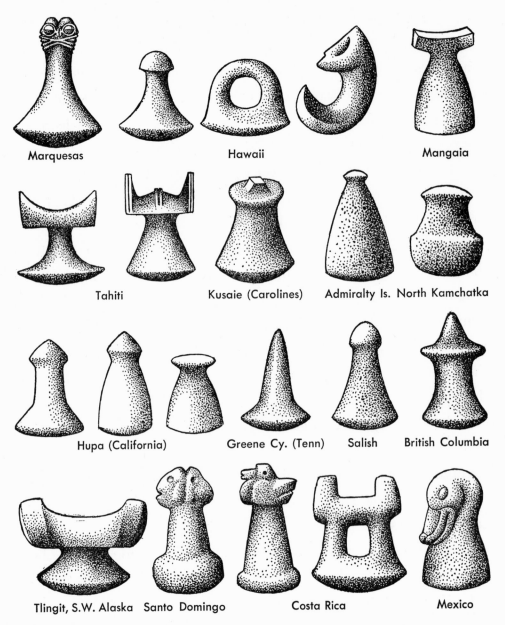

Marquesas

Hawaii

Mangaia

Tahiti

Kusaie (Carolines)

Admiralty Is. North Kamchatka

Hupa (California)

Greene Cy. (Tenn)

Salish

British Columbia

Tlingit, S.W. Alaska   Santo Domingo

Costa Rica

Mexico

FIG. 30. *Stone mauls and pestles from the South Seas, Asia, and America.*

long time it took for inventions to develop and travel, it is reasonable
to suppose that conditions in America were not necessarily different
from those in the Old World, and that the development and differentia-
tions of American Indian languages and cultures must have taken place

66

over several millennia, perhaps during the last ten thousand years (Lewis, 1947).

There is no reason to suppose that the influx of immigrants ceased completely while the autochthonous American civilizations were in the process of differentiation and development. Substantial signs exist of intensive contacts across the Pacific; the great numbers of more or less

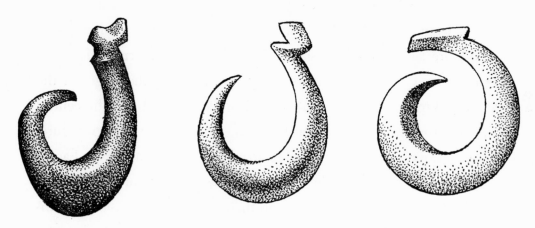

FIG. 31. *Fishhooks:* LEFT, *from Easter Island (Collection of Stephen Chauvet);* OTHERS, *from southern California, of bone and mother-of-pearl (AMNH).*

scattered Asiatic and Oceanic traits that have infiltrated various Indian cultures cannot be ignored, and it seems that the only possible explanation for their presence is importations and influences brought over by each new wave of immigrants. For instance, the early Chinese influences could have come, not only direct from northern Asia, but also, as Heine-Geldern believes, indirectly across the Pacific, already digested and mixed with the cultural traits of their carriers, the predecessors of the Melanesians and Polynesians. Recently a similar situation brought foreign elements of culture to Europe from Asia, Africa, and America, and flat denial of the possibility of carrying Asiatic and Oceanic traits into America would be as unfounded as if, some centuries from now, it were claimed that the habit of drinking chocolate, chewing gum, or smoking pipes or cigarettes was a European re-invention because there is no evidence of mass migrations of American Indians into medieval Europe.

Thus I feel justified in agreeing with Rivet (1943) that "the Indians created great autochthonous civilizations, and at the same time retained some of the heritage of the peoples that contributed to their making." Perhaps Gladwin is right in his belief that the earliest immigrants were predominantly Australoids in a low stage of culture, men who were succeeded by Asiatic Negroids and northern Mongoloids bringing new cultural elements. They may have set the stage for the sudden florescence of high culture in Middle America and the central Andes, brought about no doubt by the introduction of agriculture, while new immigrants continued to arrive by sea, settling on the Pacific shores and bringing with them elements of art and culture which were originally Asiatic. These peoples and their cultures were eventually absorbed into the established Indian populations. Some, more conservative than others, retained many of the archaic traits they brought with them. A striking example of such Asiatic settlement could be the Indians of the Northwest Coast, of Alaska and British Columbia, who had no high cultures near at hand to absorb them. Isolated geographically, and surrounded by tribes with simpler cultures, they developed and elaborated their art until it reached the highly individual personality and style characteristic of the coasts of southern Alaska and British Columbia, which, however, retain a strong Asiatic flavor.

Next looms the problem of the development and differentiation of the ancient Indian cultures, which took place on the American continent, and the question of whether or not and to what extent they had contacts among themselves. Looked at as a total picture, the art of Indian America is a striking mosaic of the most varied cultures in every possible stage of development, with the most abrupt contrasts of character and personality. Some are barren and elementary like that of the underprivileged inhabitants of Tierra del Fuego, who content themselves with making crude masks by cutting holes in a piece of bark, and painting lines and dots on the branches of their shelters; or the Athapascans of the Yukon and the Mackenzie, whose only artistic expression is the embroidery of fillets of dyed porcupine quills on their garments of caribou skin. But these are extremes. The great majority of the American peoples practiced the arts intensively, with the most diversified ideologies and techniques, from the inventive, gay Eskimo, who made a specialty of delicate ivory-carving, to the refinement of the Indians of the Mississippi basin, the irreproachable good taste and color sense of the Southwest Indians, the grandeur of the class-conscious aristocrats of the Northwest Coast, and the barbaric elegance of the warlike Indians of the Plains.

These are still, however, more or less independent and isolated cultural developments, clearly differentiated from the two great focuses of high civilization with which American Indian art reaches a grand climax: *Middle America,* with its center in southern Mexico, and the *central Andes,* centered in Peru, whose achievements in the arts and sciences compare favorably with those of the ancient civilizations of the Old World. In the map (Fig. 32) I attempt to show the relative position of the principal art-culture areas, with an emphasis on the two basic civilizations (black zones A and B) that constitute a sort of nexus from which a number of neighboring satellite cultures irradiate. The cultures within the sphere of influence of Middle America and the central Andes (shown in dark, stippled areas) generally have personalities of their own and seem to have developed from local elements, though their link with the senior cultures is often evident (C, the Southwest; D, the Eastern Woodlands; E, the Isthmus; F, the Antilles; G, the northern Andes; H, the tropical forests; and I, the southern Andes).

69

Farther removed from these centers are the more elementary cultures of marginal North and South America (shown in white), which seem to have had few if any contacts with the great civilizations. There are: L, the Northern Woodlands, represented by nomadic tribes of hunting Athapascans and Algonquians; M, the Indians of the Plains; N, the primitive Indians of the Far West; O, the little-known cultures of the Paraná basin, and P, the backward inhabitants of the pampas and Tierra del Fuego. Some of these cultures seem to represent the fossilized remains of earlier stages of human culture, perhaps representative of the first inhabitants. Others could be those of barbaric later arrivals who exerted constant pressure upon the centers of culture, sometimes learning enough from them to become civilized and give rise to new peripheral cultures. Such barbaric tribes would be responsible for the wedge driven deep into central Mexico and separating the cultures of the Gulf coast and of the North American Woodlands from those of the Southwest. On the other hand, the lack of cultural continuity between the Andes and the lower Amazon is explicable by such adverse geographic factors as the Andean barrier and the impassable jungles, with, however, two narrow threads of communication: one along the north coast across Venezuela, and the other through the upper reaches of the Amazon and Ucayali rivers.

A curious correspondence is evident among the characters of these three types or classes of cultures. For instance, the Middle American and central Andean areas have a parallel psychological personality and range of achievement. The same is true of the intervening region: the northern Andes and the Isthmus, as well as their peripheral areas—for instance, the similarities between the cultures of the Southwest and that of the Diaguita of the southern Andes, as well as among the Amazon area, the Antilles, and Florida, as if they were the result of concentric waves radiating from the Middle American and central Andean

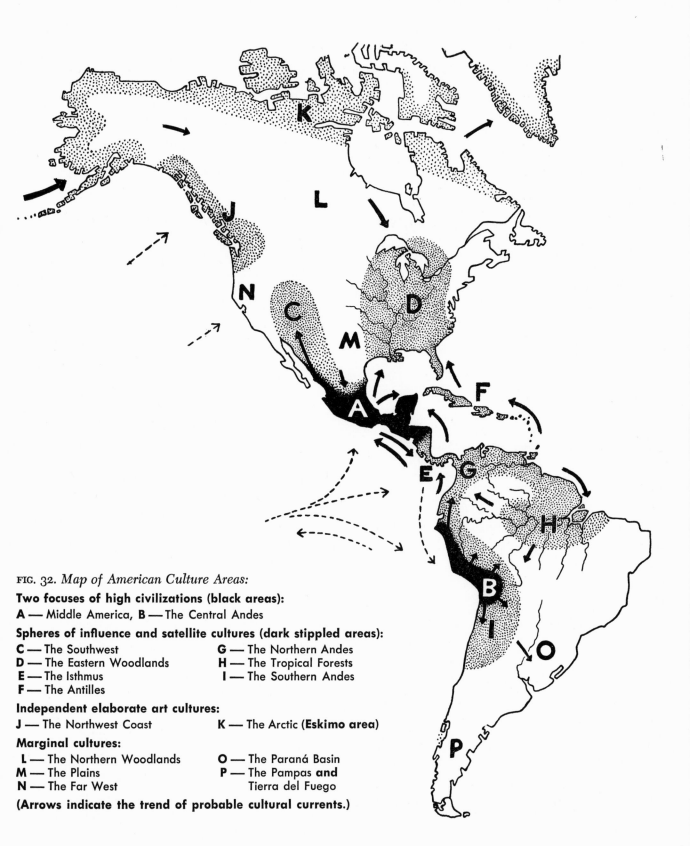

FIG. 32. *Map of American Culture Areas:*

Two focuses of high civilizations (black areas):

A — Middle America, **B** — The Central Andes

Spheres of influence and satellite cultures (dark stippled areas):

C — The Southwest	**G** — The Northern Andes
D — The Eastern Woodlands	**H** — The Tropical Forests
E — The Isthmus	**I** — The Southern Andes
F — The Antilles	

Independent elaborate art cultures:

J — The Northwest Coast   **K** — The Arctic (**Eskimo area**)

Marginal cultures:

L — The Northern Woodlands	**O** — The Paraná Basin
M — The Plains	**P** — The Pampas **and**
N — The Far West	Tierra del Fuego

(Arrows indicate the trend of probable cultural currents.)

focuses of civilization. Again, the same stage of cultural development can be found in the marginal areas of outer North and South America, but here there is a significant differentiation: the marginal areas of North America have a distinctive northeast Asiatic, quite Siberian, flavor, unlike those of marginal South America, which have a more Oceanic character.

There remain two more independent, totally different, and extremely important cultural developments: the Northwest Coast and the Arctic or Eskimo areas (stippled areas J and K), which, surely because of geographic isolation, seem to have had no obvious contacts with the other areas since these peoples came from Asia.

CHAPTER II

The Basic Horizons for the History of Indian Art

THE determination of basic time periods or horizons for the Indian arts of America has been a slow and painful process. Cultural stratigraphy began in Mexico about 1909 when Manuel Gamio first noted that the remains buried in the deposits of the Valley of Mexico changed in style with each layer, indicating the existence of superimposed cultures. Since that time, stratigraphical explorations have been carried out over the entire continent: refuse dumps have been dissected with a surgeon's care; architectural remains have been taken apart for clues to their development; chronicles and codexes have been scrutinized for historical references; and even geology, genetics, and nuclear science have been called in to help. Archæologists have met at international congresses and round-table conferences in attempts to correlate their chronological sequences, compare styles, and establish cultural horizons. The results, however tentative and incomplete, have been fruitful and even spectacular. Alaska has yielded long Eskimo cultural sequences; the Southwest cultures of the United States have been dated with the greatest accuracy; and the Eastern Woodlands, all of Middle

73

America, the central and southern Andes, and even Tierra del Fuego have produced such a wealth of data in the last decade that I feel it possible now to attempt a hypothetical correlation of the periods and horizons established by archæology. Here I venture to present a table (Fig. 33) with such a hypothesis of correlation; I hope that the goddess of archæologists may not strike me dead.

The bases for this table are the long, well-established cultural sequences of the Valley of Mexico (under the column "Central Plateau" of Middle America) and the Maya ceramic and architectural periods, supported by the equally sound sequences of the Guatemalan highlands, Monte Albán, and the Gulf coast (Huaxtec I–VI), leaving out the more dubious western Mexican sequences. The dates have been compiled from historical records in the case of the late periods; from the Maya dates and the guesses of archæologists for the middle period; and from the geological clues and the tests for radioactive-carbon content for the early periods. Ideological and stylistic clues have permitted the establishment of the following periods for Middle America:

1. PRE-CLASSIC, *with early formative, florescent, and decadent phases;*
2. CLASSIC, *the great period of the theocratic metropolis;*
3. HISTORICAL, *with the Toltec and Mixteca-Puebla renaissance and the imperialist Aztec periods.*

In the case of South America, the bases have been the newly established and illuminating horizons (Bennett and Bird, 1949), which define the essential character and psychology of the cultures of the central Andes. These are:

1. EARLY FARMERS, the formative period;
2. CULTISTS, represented by the great early Chavín culture;

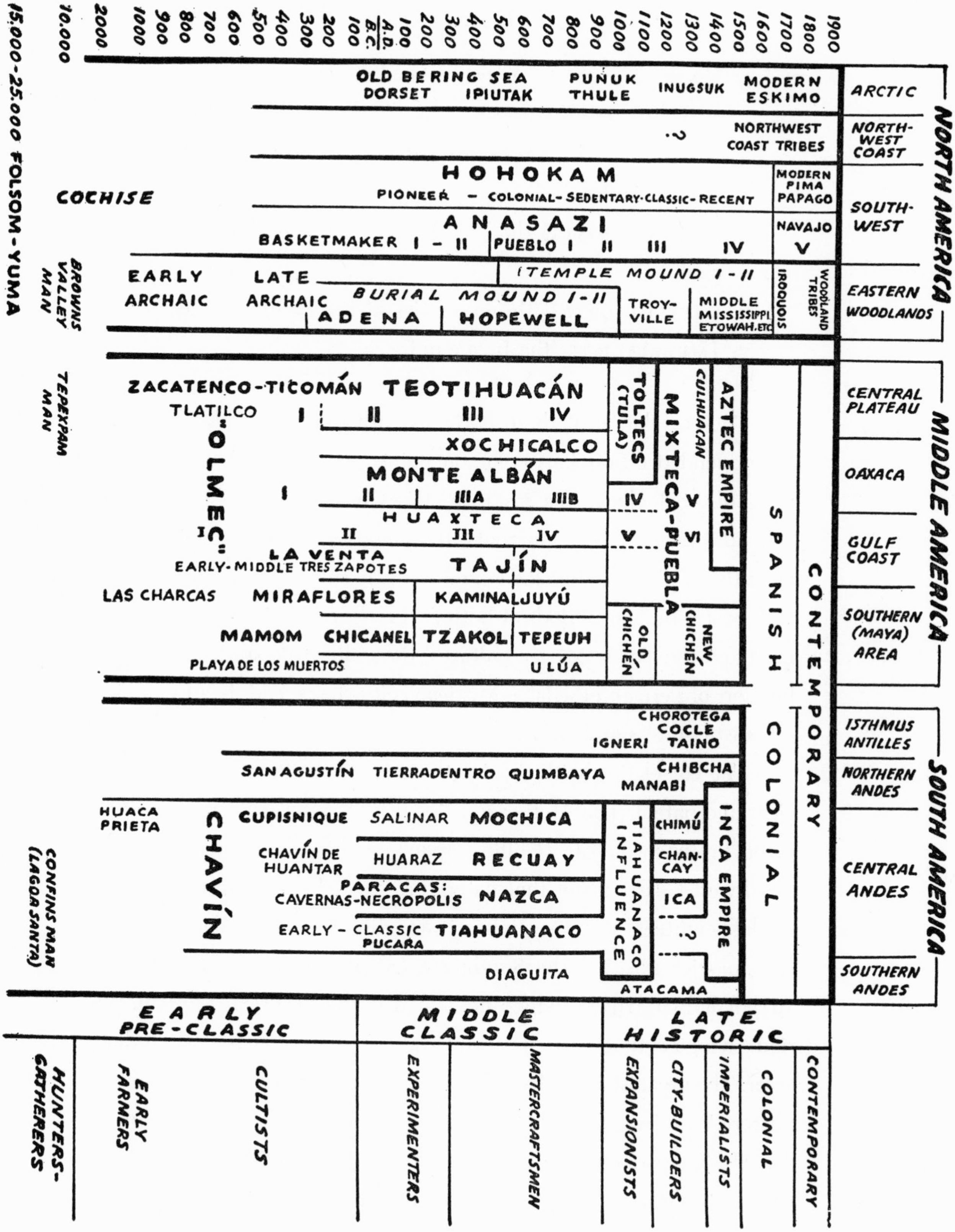

Time scale (left margin): 15,000–25,000 FOLSOM-YUMA · 10,000 · 2000 · 1000 · 900 · 800 · 700 · 600 · 500 · 400 · 300 · 200 · 100 B.C. / A.D. 100 · 200 · 300 · 400 · 500 · 600 · 700 · 800 · 900 · 1000 · 1100 · 1200 · 1300 · 1400 · 1500 · 1600 · 1700 · 1800 · 1900

COCHISE

BROWNS VALLEY MAN

TEPEXPAN MAN

CONFINS MAN (LAGOA SANTA)

NORTH AMERICA

		ARCTIC
OLD BERING SEA · DORSET · IPIUTAK · PUNUK / THULE · INUGSUK · MODERN ESKIMO		ARCTIC
NORTHWEST COAST TRIBES		NORTH-WEST COAST

HOHOKAM — PIONEER – COLONIAL – SEDENTARY – CLASSIC – RECENT — MODERN PIMA PAPAGO — SOUTH-WEST

ANASAZI — BASKETMAKER I – II · PUEBLO I · II · III · IV · V NAVAJO

EARLY ARCHAIC · LATE ARCHAIC · BURIAL MOUND I-II · TEMPLE MOUND I-II · TROYVILLE · MIDDLE MISSISSIPPI, ETOWAH, ETC · IROQUOIS · WOODLAND TRIBES — EASTERN WOODLANDS

ADENA · HOPEWELL

MIDDLE AMERICA

ZACATENCO-TICOMÁN · TEOTIHUACÁN (I · II · III · IV) · TOLTECS (TULA) · CULHUACAN · MIXTECA-PUEBLA (V · VI) · AZTEC EMPIRE — CENTRAL PLATEAU

TLATILCO

"OLMEC"

XOCHICALCO

MONTE ALBÁN (I · II · IIIA · IIIB · IV) — OAXACA

HUAXTECA (II · III · IV) · V — GULF COAST

LA VENTA · EARLY-MIDDLE TRES ZAPOTES · TAJÍN

LAS CHARCAS · MIRAFLORES · KAMINALJUYÚ

MAMOM · CHICANEL · TZAKOL · TEPEUH · OLD CHICHEN · NEW CHICHEN — SOUTHERN (MAYA) AREA

PLAYA DE LOS MUERTOS · ULÚA

SPANISH COLONIAL · CONTEMPORARY

SOUTH AMERICA

CHOROTEGA · COCLE · IGNERI · TAINO — ISTHMUS ANTILLES

SAN AGUSTÍN · TIERRADENTRO · QUIMBAYA · CHIBCHA · MANABI — NORTHERN ANDES

HUACA PRIETA · CHAVÍN · CUPISNIQUE · SALINAR · MOCHICA · CHIMÚ · INCA EMPIRE — CENTRAL ANDES

CHAVÍN DE HUANTAR · HUARAZ · RECUAY · CHAN-CAY

PARACAS: CAVERNAS-NECROPOLIS · NAZCA · ICA · TIAHUANACO INFLUENCE

EARLY – CLASSIC TIAHUANACO · PUCARA

DIAGUITA · ATACAMA — SOUTHERN ANDES

Bottom bands:
EARLY PRE-CLASSIC · MIDDLE CLASSIC · LATE HISTORIC · CONTEMPORARY

HUNTERS-GATHERERS · EARLY FARMERS · CULTISTS · EXPERIMENTERS · MASTERCRAFTSMEN · EXPANSIONISTS · CITY-BUILDERS · IMPERIALISTS · COLONIAL · CONTEMPORARY

FIG. 33. CHART: *hypothetical correlation of North American, Middle American, and South American cultures.*

3. EXPERIMENTERS, a transitional period represented by special types of pottery;

4. MASTER CRAFTSMEN, the great, classic period of the central Andes;

5. EXPANSIONISTS, the pan-Andean Tiahuanaco style period;

6. CITY-BUILDERS, the late cities of the Peruvian coast;

7. IMPERIALISTS, the Inca empire.

The correlation of these horizons with those of Middle America has depended on obvious common points, as well as on more subtle archæological clues—for instance, the Chavín and "Olmec" jaguar cults and megalithic monuments, the negative painted pottery of the transitional periods, the classic and realistic spirit of master-craftsman and master-builder periods of both areas, the expansion of the Tiahuanaco and the Toltec-Mixtec cultures, the militaristic spirit of the city-builders of Peru and the late "Mexican" city-states, and, finally, the imperialistic Aztecs and Incas.

The correlation with the North American cultures has been less clear and patent. The Arctic sequence is placed according to the dates given by its specialists (Collins, 1940); nothing is known about the Northwest Coast except that its culture existed in its present state in the late eighteenth century, when it was discovered; excellent and sure chronologies exist for the Southwest (Martin, Quimby, and Collier, 1947; Gladwin, 1937), which flourished in the historical Mexican period—a logical time given its peripheral position and conservative character. The greatest difficulty was encountered in the chronology for the Eastern Woodlands, where the long sequences, and the "Archaic," middle, and late periods, to judge from a stylistic point of view, seem to run parallel to the same periods in the cultures of Mexico. The dates given for the Woodland cultures have always seemed to me too conservative, and are mere guesswork, influenced perhaps by the important use of hammered copper in these cultures and the fact that metallurgy appears in Mexico about the tenth century of our era. But Mexican metallurgy is based upon the smelting and casting of gold and copper, while the hammered-copper tradition, typical of the Woodlands, is known to have begun in the Great Lakes area, at an early time, in the "Archaic" period. Furthermore, radioactive-carbon tests with Hopewell and Adena materials have given surprisingly ancient dates. So I feel justified in stretching back the age of the classic period of the Woodlands (Burial Mound I–II) considerably for this hypothetical correlation, trusting a new but sound scientific principle, that of the radioactive-carbon method, for determining the age of ancient remains, rather than leaving the chronology of the Woodlands to begin at the presently accepted, impossibly late date.

1. *THE EARLY (FORMATIVE) OR PRE-CLASSIC HORIZON*

ALSO known in Middle America as "Archaic" or "middle" cultures, these are the oldest known, being the cultures of simple communalistic peasants, agriculturists, and advanced ceramists, with an economy based upon maize and probably beans and squashes, supplemented by hunting and gathering. They raised and fattened edible dogs, cultivated cotton, and probably domesticated bees. Their religion was based upon a cult of the forces of nature and probably of the spirits of the dead, with burial offerings and mounds of earth as shrines. They did not represent deities except for a basic old fire-god, "Grandfather Fire," still venerated by the Huicholes of Mexico, and figurines of women with narrow waists and bulging legs.

Their art included the making of fine pottery of sober, original shapes, monochrome or bichrome, decorated with geometric and curvilinear designs, painted or incised—effigy vessels of animals, clay masks, stamps, and whistles. An innovation in the late phase of this horizon was the introduction of negative (batik) painting on pottery. They made realistic and expressive clay figurines, mostly of naked women modeled by hand and filleted and gouged with a stick, and large hollow figures of clay, painted red and highly polished. They also carved shell, stone, and probably wood, and somehow obtained polished jade ornaments and celts, probably by trade from other early but elaborate and not yet clearly determined cultures.

In the Valley of Mexico, where the horizon is best known, it has three phases: early, middle (Zacatenco I, II), and late (Ticomán). It is found all over Middle America, as far south as Honduras. Recent geological studies and experiments with radioactive carbon place this horizon in the first and second millennia B.C. No antecedents are known for the pre-Classic cultures, except for the rather nebulous stage established by the discovery of the late Stone Age man of Tepexpan and the subsequent "Chalco" cultures.

The mystery of the appearance of fully developed cultures is deepened by the presence in this early period of an intrusive, highly sophisticated culture with colossal statuary and beautifully carved figurines and masks and ornaments of jade. This apparently became a powerful factor in the shaping of the later civilization. This elusive and mysterious culture, known as "Olmec" or "La Venta," seems to establish a transitional period between the pre-Classic and Classic horizons and probably marks the ascendancy of an urban type of theocratic society preying upon the early peasant communities. Its creators were cultists, perhaps mystics or magicians, with an obsession about feline spirits,

78

jaguars with human traits and human beings with jaguar characteristics, as well as a cult of infants and dwarfs.

Besides the colossal monuments of stone, which probably appeared just before the collapse of this culture, "Olmec" art has significant traits suggesting an early stage in the development of the Classic cultures, particularly the Maya, Teotihuacán, Tajín, and Monte Albán: stelæ with dignitaries and altars of basalt; the jaguar-mask panel that develops into the various masks of the rain-god; the use of simple glyphs that seem related to the style of Maya writing; greenstone figurines; greenstone masks hollowed out in the back; earplug flares of jade; funerary red paint; cylindrical vessels. It also has some unique traits that seem to die with it: great anthropomorphic axes of stone; stone sarcophagi, fountains, and vessels; blue-green and blue-gray implements and ornaments of jade, such as spatulas, needles, chisels, hooks, replicas of jaguar teeth, shells, stingray tails, and such parts of the human body as toes, legs, and ears; concave mirrors of crystalline hematite, and so forth. The mystic spirit of "Olmec" art suggests the presence of highly intellectual sorcerers, who may have developed the astronomical knowledge basic for weather prediction and time-reckoning, culminating in the development of such liturgical traits as religious architecture, secret symbolic art, and glyphic writing.

The sophisticated jaguar cult, the cyclopean stone monuments, and the highly advanced techniques, appearing so early with simple peasant communalistic cultures, have a significant counterpart in the Andes, and were probably contemporary with the cultures of the "formative" and "cultist" horizons postulated for the central Andean zone: Chavín, early Paracas, early Tiahuanaco, and San Agustín. Thus it is possible to establish a common early horizon for Middle and South America, with elaborate mother cultures—"Olmec" and Chavín—

79

which must have been largely instrumental in the development and characterization of Middle American and Andean civilizations.

2. THE CLASSIC HORIZON

THIS was the apogee of Middle American civilization, the period of the great religious metropolises with high priests and rulers, an era of mystic master craftsmen and scholars, artists and astrologers. The communities of this epoch are great city-states dedicated to the cult of the rain-god and the sky-dragon, which gradually replaced the earlier jaguar deities, with accessory cults of the dead, Venus, the sun, the moon, maize, and so on, and the glorification and apotheosis of rulers. The art of its florescent phase is grandiose, aristocratic, and elegant, with great emphasis on ceremonial architecture of dressed and carved stone and stucco (temples on top of pyramids with great stairways, the Teotihuacán panel-and-slope architectural principle, the Maya corbeled arch, basreliefs, and decorative sculpture, ball courts, great plazas, etc.); al-fresco mural painting in temples and tombs; systems of hieroglyphic writing and the use of a calendar based on astronomical observation; rich funerary pottery with new forms and techniques of decoration, fine gorgets, beads, and earplug flares of emerald-green jade, and so forth.

The Classic horizon is divided into three phases:

1. An early, transitional period, marked by the consolidation of theocratic rule, and by an intensive cult of jaguar-like deities with strong "Olmec" traces, the gradual differentiation of local styles, and the appearance of many new elements, brought perhaps by new peoples from the south and east. This transitional art is still sober and realistic, but it has acquired an aristocratic spirit and an esoteric sym-

bolism, with a significant change in the human æsthetic ideal and a notable transformation of the ceramic arts from the fashions of the preceding early period. New pottery styles make their appearance (Teotihuacán II, Chicanel, Holmul I, and Monte Albán II), characterized by tetrapods, spouted handles, pot-stands, and elaborate large clay figures and urns.

2. A flourishing or "great" period, with the characteristic ceremonial architecture, frescoes, elaborate funerary pottery, mold-made figurines, green jades, and so on, described above (Teotihuacán III, Tzakol, Esperanza phase at Kaminaljuyú, Monte Albán III, etc.).

3. A decadent late period showing a marked stagnation of the creative capacity toward its end and a decided fossilization of the arts: more rigidity in the drawing of figures, with, in the lowlands, an increase of the baroque tendency in decoration, ending in a frankly rococo art. The personages in the Maya stelæ of the time are literally smothered under luxurious, extravagant dress and enormous fans of quetzal feathers; ornate, exclusively mold-made figurines (Teotihuacán IV, Monte Albán IV); new, and for the most part impoverished, pottery forms except in the Maya area, which has fine polychrome painted vases in this period (Tepeuh). In general, there is a total subordination of the arts to the machinery of the religious ceremonial and to the exaltation of the elite; abuse of ornamental meanders and intricate design replaces the classic beauty of form and line. The end of this horizon, sometime about A.D. 900, is characterized by a definite decline of artistic activity and often by a mysterious and sudden eradication of the cultures; all of the great cities in the highlands and in the lowlands of Middle America were either destroyed or abandoned.

Crop failure, famines, and epidemics caused by prolonged droughts are the reasons given most often for the collapse of the great cities of the Classic period: Teotihuacán, Cholula, Xochicalco,

Tajín, Monte Albán, and, to a lesser extent, the more isolated Maya cities, from Palenque to Copán. There is much to support the theory of drought, perhaps resulting from the destruction of the natural resources—for instance, the deforestation of the Mexican central plateau. It is obvious that great cities such as Teotihuacán and Cholula must have consumed enormous amounts of lumber for construction and fuel, not only to feed their large populations, but also for the sacrificial fires, and to burn the staggering amount of lime for stuccoing the thousands of pyramids, temples, and palaces. This is not to mention the destructive "slash-and-burn" technique of agriculture, which requires burning a part of the forest, cultivating the land thus cleared until exhausted (after five or six years), and then moving on to the next patch of virgin forest.

It has been dogmatically believed that the common people subjected by the city-states of the Classic period lived in a state of blissful peace and prosperity under the paternal rule of benevolent and cultured priests. The very exaltation of the aristocracy, the motivating factor of Maya art—for instance, noblemen shown standing on or in front of a vanquished enemy or a submissive slave—shows that a despotic autocracy must have prevailed. The peaceful spirit of the nobility is flatly denied by the ferocious battles shown in the Bonampak frescoes, of the Classic Maya period, against a naked population depicted as defeated, captured, and mutilated. Cities like Teotihuacán were deliberately and thoroughly destroyed, and it is therefore more likely that the prolonged droughts and famines set the stage for the discontented and oppressed serfs to rebel against their masters, who had lost prestige when their magic powers failed to control the weather and make rain. The great cities must have been islands of civilization in the sea of barbarians who constantly threatened the political stability of the city-states. This could have provoked a chain reaction of disturbances, perhaps peasant revolts and aggressions of the under-privileged tribes who must have haunted the fringes of the cities, rebellions similar to those which took place in the historical period, some five or six centuries later, and of which we fortunately have detailed accounts. At such times rival ruling houses and warlike barbarians would have taken advantage of the situation to fall upon the tottering theocratic states, bringing about the civil wars that killed the religious type of city and helped to create the more militaristic type of state characteristic of the historical period.

The Classic period of Middle America also has its counterpart in South America in the "master-craftsman" horizon of the central Andes, represented by such elaborate cultures as the Mochica and Nazca of Peru and the Classic Tiahuanaco of Bolivia. Perhaps the Classic horizon has a representative even in North America in the great Hopewell culture of Ohio and the Eastern Woodlands, though there is no absolute evidence, outside of their coincident sequences and their similar cultural spirit and personality, that these cultures were contemporary with the great civilizations of Middle America.

3. *THE HISTORICAL HORIZON*

Also known in Middle America as the "Late," "Renascentist," or "Mixteca-Puebla" period, this horizon was initiated at the beginning of the tenth century of our era by the waves of invasion of the civilized but decaying cities of the central Mexican plateau by hordes of northern barbarians, mostly of Nahua speech, called collectively Chichimecs ("of dog lineage"). The aggressive Chichimecs conquered the remnants of the ancient cultured inhabitants, gained uncontested political predominance, and rapidly became civilized, creating young and enterprising cultures endowed with a new vitality and a vigorous barbaric personality—with arts, however, mollified by the absorption of the arts of the preceding horizon.

The pattern of internal strife between warring houses for control of power, complicated by invasions of outlying barbarians, causing the collapse of long-established civilizations and the rise of new ones, seems to plague pre-Columbian Indian history. This is not unlike struggles for power among the old Asiatic feudal houses and with the barbarians of the northern and western steppes: the Hsiung-Nu, Mongol, and Tatar invaders of China. This is most evident in the historical period of Middle America, in the central Mexican plateau, which had its Genghis Khans and Kublai Khans in such famous warlords as the Toltec Mixcoatl (*circa* A.D. 900), the Chichimec Xolotl (A.D. 1172), the Mixtec conqueror "Eight Deer" (A.D. 972–92), and the military hero Itzcoatl (A.D. 1427–40), who consolidated the Aztec, or rather Mexica, empire.

The historical period thus begins about A.D. 900, with the arrival on the Mexican plateau of the hordes led by Mixcoatl, the founding of the city of Tollan or Tula, and the ascendancy of the Toltec empire. No historical records exist of events at this time in the heart of the Maya area on the south and central Gulf coast or in the important area of Puebla-Tlaxcala (probably Mixtec) around the ancient and venerable city of Cholula, but we know that powerful feudal dynasties were arising: the Huaxtec on the northern Gulf coast, the Mixtec of Tilantongo in Oaxaca, and the Itzá of Yucatán, establishing a series of new local cultures that show mutual contacts and influences. Three basic periods can be defined within the Historical horizon:

1. The Toltec empire, dated from historical records at about A.D. 900–1200, ended with the destruction of the city of Tula, the flight and apotheosis of the great culture-hero Topiltzin Ce Acatl (Quetzal-

coatl) (a sort of Mexican Huang Ti, the "Yellow Emperor" of China), and the mass exodus and dispersion of the Toltecs, all in the midst of catastrophic civil war. This period clearly establishes the struggle between the priest rulers of the old civil theocracies and the rise of an Oriental type of despotic and militaristic warlords. This is symbolized by the legend of the end of Tula, the defeat by black magic of the cultured and peace-loving Quetzalcoatl at the hands of the willful and contradictory Texcatlipoca, "Smoking Mirror," the war-god of the barbarians.

Typical of this phase are the introduction of metallurgy in Middle America (the casting of copper, gold, and silver), brought from Central America; a vigorous renaissance of monumental stone sculpture and architecture, with new traits (buildings with flat roofs, serpent columns, caryatids, Atlantean figures and standard-bearers of carved stone, circular temples dedicated to the wind-god, ball-courts with vertical walls and with stone rings as goals, elaborately carved colonnades, the reclining statues known as *chacmools,* and low reliefs with feathered serpents, collared tigers, eagles eating hearts, skulls, warrior friezes, and particularly a stepped meander called *xicalcoliuhqui,* which appears also in North and South America, variously interpreted as a serpent head or a bird (Fig. 34). The ceramics of the Classic period disappear completely, and new, more plebeian potteries take their place (Coyotlatelco, Mazapa, "Aztec I"), as do new trade wares, notably one made of a fine orange clay and one with a metallic glaze called "plumbate," imported from the east and south of Mexico. The art of making clay figurines persists, but the new types are carelessly molded into flat, rectangular little tablets.

The most important aspect of this period is the spread far and wide, from northern Mexico to Honduras, of such new techniques as gold- and copper-casting, and particularly of a new art style specifically

85

defined as the "Mixteca-Puebla" culture, which was largely instrumental in the formation of Toltec art. This widely diffused style has an interesting parallel in the central Andean "Expansionist" horizon, in which the style of Tiahuanaco spread all over Peru and parts of Bolivia and Chile.

2. The second phase, from about A.D. 1200 to 1350, is, on the Mexican plateau, a historical repetition of the preceding phase: the rise of new barbarians, notably the Chichimecs of the warlord Xolotl, who also became quickly civilized, and who rebuilt, on the ashes of the Toltec empire, the new, parvenu dynasty of Tenayuca (archæologically represented by the pottery called "Aztec II"), who coexisted and frequently fought wars with the older and more decadent city-states of the Valley of Mexico, such as Culhuacán, Azcapotzalco, Texcoco, and Chalco. In this phase Mixtec art flourished in Puebla and Oaxaca. The late Mixtecs did not distinguish themselves for their architectural and sculptural capacities, but on the other hand they were extraordinary craftsmen who produced objects of an unprecedented luxury and refinement: gold jewelry made by the lost-wax process of casting; fine carvings in wood, shell, and bone; translucent vases of alabaster; precious jewels of jade, rock crystal, amethyst, agate, opal, and polished obsidian; and the most delicate mosaics of turquoise, jet, shell, and the feathers of rare tropical birds. Formalized painting of an unmistakable style was practiced intensely in mural frescoes, in illustrated religious and genealogical books (of the Codex Borgia type), and particularly in the luxurious polychromed lacquer ware made mainly at Cholula. This phase is represented in Peru in the "City-Builder" horizon, the late Chimu, Chancay, Pachacamac, and Ica cultures, which seem to be contemporary with it, as characteristic Peruvian textile motifs appear in Cholula pottery, and the *xicalcoliuhqui* motif becomes basic to the Peruvian arts of this epoch.

FIG. 34. *Interlocked birds and derived spiral motifs from North America, Middle America, and South America: (A, B) painted on Anasazi pottery, southwestern United States (Mera); (C, D) painted on Mochica pottery, northern Peru (BrM); (E, F) woven on tapestries from the Peruvian central coast (AMNH); (G, H) on clay stamps from Guerrero, Mexico (Enciso, 1947); (I) painted on Mexican pottery from Cholula, Puebla; (J, K) stone mosaic wall-decoration from Mitla, Oaxaca.*

3. The last phase, the Imperialist period, lasted from about A.D. 1350 to 1521, the year of the Spanish Conquest. It began with the struggle for survival of the last autonomous nations of the Valley of Mexico: Culhuas, Tepanecs, Chalcas, Xochimilcas, and others, against the intrigues and aggressions of a ragged horde of ruthless and ambitious barbarians, coming this time from the northwest—the famous Aztecs, who later changed their name to Mexica (pronounced *méshi-ka*) and appointed themselves to the divine mission of ruling the world. The Mexica had the stormiest rise and downfall of any nation in America. Led by a long line of great military chiefs, merchants, and statesmen—Itzcoatl, Moctezuma the Elder, Ahuizotl, Moctezuma the Younger—in a relatively short time they conquered most of Middle America and from their vassals exacted not only goods for commerce and victims for sacrifices, but also artists and craftsmen to create the beauty and glory of their capital, Tenochtitlán, now Mexico City. The Mexica period saw a brilliant rise of the arts and a resurgence of monumental stone sculpture, producing the most emotive, original, and spectacular sculpture in the Americas. This was not necessarily because the Mexica were themselves great artists, but because they had the artists of all Middle America at their service and because they could imbue with a new vitality arts that had ceased to create. Thus a new and terrifying art based upon autocratic discipline and wholesale death flourished for a period of about one hundred years before the Spanish Conquest.

Mexican imperialism closes the cycle of Middle American civilization. It has a curious parallel in the rise, at the same time, of the Incas of Peru, the only other great empire in the Americas. It seems as if the evolution of the Indian civilizations of Middle and South America was ruled by a fixed pattern that can be correlated: from the early peasant

FACING: Amalaid, *the frontal ornament of a Tlingit chief's headdress, carved of cedar and inlaid with haliotis shell, Alaska, 16 centimeters high. It commemorates the whale and raven myth.* (Collection of W. Paalen.)

communities ruled by cultist elites, in time creating great theocracies of artists and craftsmen, to military despotism, city-builders, and finally a brilliant but ruthless imperialism that invited destruction, not only of the imperialists, but of all Indian art and culture.

CHAPTER III

The Technique and Æsthetics of American Indian Art

THE existing confusion in the appreciation of the artistic expressions of aboriginal peoples has been brilliantly analyzed by Linton (1941) as caused in good measure by the popular usage of the term "primitive art" with which they have been labeled, a term as vague and inappropriate as "heathen" or "pagan" if used in a comparative study of religions. The term "primitive art" has come to mean generally the art of peoples whose cultures fall outside the complex of Western civilization or the great cultures of the Orient; in the best cases it is understood to mean a simple and undeveloped form of a subsequently highly developed art. Our concept of art evolution originates from a dogmatic application of the novel evolutionary theories of the nineteenth century, which regarded the various human cultures as stages of a continuous line of evolution and classified the various cultures of the world according to the degree in which they differed from European civilization, then considered the climax, the perfect flower, of this evolutionary process.

There are in the world more or less complex ancient and contemporary cultures with phases more elementary than others, but few arts in the world can truly be called primitive. To think of arts as primitive is equivalent to regarding a mouse or a dog as a primitive stage of the elephant (Linton, 1941). It is equally unsound to compare these arts with the daubing of a child or with the pictures drawn by the insane, which are lyrical individual expressions, free of academic malice and technical knowledge. The so-called primitive artist repeats endlessly the forms and ideas he has learned, forms experimented upon by his ancestors, often for centuries, stylized and elaborated through a long selective process. Boas (1938) has ably stated that the "primitive artist" is concerned with giving emphasis to what interests him most and in minimizing and disregarding what he considers superfluous. His basic stimulus is the pleasure he derives from virtuosity and play with the technique. This leads to the creation of personality and style. As in all arts, there are good, mediocre, and inferior artists and craftsmen in every culture, and the measure of appreciation varies among groups having in common only the regard for good craftsmanship and technical virtuosity. Furthermore, a differentiation must be made between objects produced industrially to supply a popular market and those made by artists and specialized craftsmen for ceremonial purposes or for the use of the ruling elite. It often happens that a people will adopt arts or styles created by other cultures, which then lose their original significance. In time the artistic product acquires a new personality, and the motifs that once had a definite magic or religious meaning become purely decorative.

To the profane, a people's art is a language as unintelligible as a foreign tongue. It cannot be judged inferior because we cannot understand it. It is generally composed of elements and conventions with some sort of meaning; magic or religious, simple formulas to represent ideas, motivated, however, by an æsthetic urge. The more complex the culture, the more dominant the æsthetic elements become, until they overshadow their symbolical or useful purpose. This tendency culminates in the concept of art for art's sake, in which the art object has a function or meaning primarily æsthetic. Thus, the appreciation of a work of art may have an extremely wide range in the various cultural complexes: it may be valued for the purely sensuous pleasure it gives because of its texture, form, color, and design; or because of the technical skill lavished on its making; or it may combine all of these factors with symbolic expressiveness because of its subject-matter or ideological content, producing highly intellectual pleasure.

Two basic and totally opposite tendencies in art strongly influence our appreciation: one, which we can understand and accept readily, is the naturalistic representation of men, animals, and so forth, in which the artist delights in the deliberate and controlled re-creation of the forms of nature; the other, more difficult to grasp, is symbolical representation, in which he takes liberties with nature and often reduces the subjects of nature or parts of them for symbolical or decorative purposes, until all resemblance to the original model is lost. It is clear that this tendency is in many cases a deliberate intention to create a secret code expressing ideas that should be kept from the uninitiated.

These two tendencies are about evenly represented in American Indian art: the modern Eskimo, the Mochica of Peru, and the "Olmecs" and Aztecs of Mexico have arts of extraordinary realism. On the other hand, the arts of the prehistoric Eskimo, of the Southwest, the Plains, Teotihuacán, the Mixteca-Puebla, Chavín, Tiahuanaco, and the Amazon, are highly symbolic. Some, like the arts of the Northwest Coast, the Tajín style of the Mexican Gulf coast, and the Maya, combine the two tendencies—esoteric symbolism and naturalistic realism—with amazing success. Fixed forms and traditional subjects acquire through repetition certain idiosyncrasies and characteristic traits that constitute the basis for the development of styles in art. This may be perpetuated in a conservative, unchanging manner, or may in time branch out into other dependent styles, particularly in the more elaborate cultures with extensive outside contacts. Thus style alone can be a valid clue in the study of artistic development and can become an invaluable aid to the formulation of art history, especially when more tangible data are lacking.

In judging the arts of other peoples we are considerably handicapped by our established æsthetic traditions and by the prevailing dogma of racial superiority. It was only in the later part of the past century that the most restless intellectuals and artists revolted against the old academic dogmas and æsthetic prejudices and began to abandon the Greco-Roman ideal. Partly because of European interests in the Near and Far East and partly because of the decadence of Western art, which had drained dry its classic sources of inspiration, such artists of the time as Beardsley and Whistler and writers like Lafcadio Hearn experimented with the teachings of Oriental art as a means of liberation from academicism, creating in time a new artistic outlook. Later on, the cult of the exotic was given a new impetus by the European policy of colonial expansion. The romance of the savage colored people, the lure of the tropics, the charm and fascination of primitive life, became favorite subjects of such writers as Pierre Loti, Herman Melville, Rudyard Kipling, and Robert Louis Stevenson, and of painters like Paul Gauguin. Explorers, officers of military expeditions, and missionaries brought back from Africa, the South Seas, and Indian America great ethnographic collections that awed the civilized Westerner: the frightful sorcerers' masks, the blood-caked fetishes, the leering idols, the crude amulets, the knives, spears, and war-clubs. These were curios, trophies of war—ethnography, but not art.

Finally the revolutionary artists of the twentieth century—Picasso, Modigliani, Brancusi, Klee, Miró, Rivera, Henry Moore—and such art critics and poets as Apollinaire, Élie Faure, Marius de Zayas, Tristan Tzara, Stieglitz, Louis Aragon, Eluard, and Breton discovered and collected the "primitive arts" of Africa, Malaysia, Oceania, and Indian America. In this manner, our contemporary intellectuals drew from these arts a new æsthetic outlook and used it to feed and revitalize our contemporary art, thus creating our present æsthetic ideal.

To resume, the so-called "primitive arts" are by no means primitive, for they are generally the result of a long process of selection and stylization, and are generally conditioned by the development of technique. The component elements of these "primitive" arts often become purely decorative, even if they were originally symbolic, magic, or religious; whatever the meaning, the motivating force behind all art expressions seems to be primarily æsthetic and not religious.

Along with the symbolic or decorative arts, many cultures have realistic, or rather naturalistic, arts that represent living things and objects with careful observation of their true lines and forms, rearranged, however, and re-created to fit an æsthetic ideology and traditional style. Few if any of these arts aspire to the literal realism we inherited from the decadent aspects of Greco-Roman culture. Faced by an example of this sort of academic work of art, the aboriginal artist shows indifference or regards it as a useless fraud, an imitation of something impossible to imitate: life itself. Ralph Linton tells of a Polynesian sculptor of the Marquesas Islands who, upon seeing a picture of an academic marble nude, asked "what was the use of making a stone woman that did not feel or smell like a woman."

· · ·

94

Between the arts of Middle America and those of the central Andes there is a basic difference in spirit and ideology: Middle American art is more intellectual, more refined and mature, with a deeper and more emotional content and a more developed æsthetic sense in both the naturalistic and the symbolical fields. The Middle American artist often went beyond the limitations of tradition to create forms and compositions that bear the mark of true creative genius.

Central Andean art, on the other hand, relies more on technique and craftsmanship, remaining always within the limitations of traditional routine, mainly the production of luxury objects of the highest workmanship, but seldom creating a unique work of art. As Dr. A. L. Kroeber (1946) has remarked: "the Mexicans achieved best with their minds, the Peruvians with their hands." There are, of course, exceptions to the rule and many varieties of such technical achievements in both Middle and South America; for instance, the Mochica potters, the sculptors of Chavín, and the embroiderers of Paracas, all from Peru, often produced individual works of art of great æsthetic merit, while the Mexicans of the post-Classic "Mixteca-Puebla" culture produced delicate gold jewelry, ornaments of semiprecious stones, and mosaics of feathers and turquoise which were technical masterpieces, luxury articles more precious and decorative than the art objects of the earlier Classic epoch.

There is evidence of an interesting interaction between the baroque and ethereal art of the Gulf coast of Mexico, made of volutes, smiling faces, curvilinear, sensual, and realistic, and the solemn, dramatic, and stylized art of the highlands of the central plateau. This latter is essentially geometric, cubistic, austere, and forbidding; its lines are precise and barbaric, softened, however, by an innate sense of rhythm and feeling for the forms of nature. The coastal influence introduced ornamental curvilineal motifs and volutes, but as in the art

95

of Teotihuacán and Monte Albán, they become formalized and frozen. These two concepts—the Apollonian spirit of the art of the plateau as contrasted with the Dionysiac arts of the coast—have been interpreted by Jiménez Moreno (1948) as a clue to the basic psychology of the culture of pre-Columbian Mexico. These characteristics prevail even today among the Mexicans: the introverted serene and repressed personality of the Mexican highlands as opposed to the extrovert, gay, overflowing spirit of the coastal areas.

Curiously enough, this situation is repeated to a certain extent in the central Andean cultures. The austerity and colossal scale of the architecture and sculpture of the Bolivian and Peruvian highlands (Chavín, Callejón de Huaylas, Tiahuanaco, and Inca) are in sharp contrast with the realistic art of the Mochica, the flamboyancy of Paracas and Nazca, and the decorative preciousness of the arts and crafts of the central Peruvian coast. In both Middle America and the central Andes these two tendencies become interlocked, perhaps about the same time, around A.D. 900, and a general super-stylized and rather stiff style became universal: namely, the Mixteca-Puebla and Tiahuanaco or "Epigonal" expansions, which conditioned the arts of the later periods. These lost their Classic virtues and became inconsequential and mostly decorative, with one notable exception: the naturalistic sculpture of the Aztecs, which somehow retained, or rather revived, the magic creative spark.

The development of highly specialized techniques is one of the characteristics of American Indian art. Every culture has some sort of specialization, something unique, like the embroidery and weaving with dyed porcupine quills or the embroidery with moose hair on birch-bark of the Algonquians of the northern forests, which is not practiced anywhere else in the world. The more backward peoples with rather simple cultures sometimes developed techniques to unprecedented levels. For instance, the Pomo and other food-gathering tribes of California made the finest baskets in the world, from both the technical and the artistic point of view. The pastoral Navajo learned a simple technique from their neighbors, the Pueblo Indians: dry painting, the making of designs on the ground with colored sands, or on buckskin with the pollen of certain flowers. These were powerful magic prayers to restore the sick, and were developed to the level of a high art. This would also be a unique technique were it not for the fact that it is also reported from Tibet. No one else can carve ivory so well as the Eskimo, and no other people has the mastery of the Northwest Coast Indians in working wood. Many great works of art were produced by simple and even primitive techniques, such as the elementary but emotive and realistic paintings on skins by the Plains Indians, the abstract masks of painted rawhide of the Zuñi, or the super-stylized feminine figures of unbaked clay and wax of the Carajá Indians of the Brazilian jungles.

The high cultures have, of course, many elaborate techniques duplicated among the great civilizations of the Old World: monumental architecture of dressed and carved stone, decorative and luxurious funerary pottery, turquoise and feather mosaics, intricate textiles, lacquer, and metallurgy. We also find technical specialization in the high cultures of Middle America and the central Andes; the lapidary arts were typical of Mexico, and no other people in America carved and polished semiprecious stones such as jade, rock crystal, and obsidian as the ancient Mexicans did. Mural painting al fresco was also a Middle American specialty, and modeling with stucco was a purely Maya art. Elaborate techniques for soldering, gilding, and casting metals were practiced in Mexico, Central America, Peru, Bolivia, and Chile, but nowhere else did they reach the technical elaboration they had in Colombia and Ecuador. The most ambitious and intricate techniques in the world for dying and weaving wool and cotton can be found in Peru, particularly in Paracas on the south coast, where the finest embroideries were made some two thousand years ago. Here is a catalogue of the most important and typical achievements of native American technology, beginning with the simpler crafts and industries:

BASKETRY, one of the oldest crafts, has its best-known representatives in the Basketmakers of the Southwest, dating back to the beginning of our era, and in the contemporary tribes of the Far West, with the highest technical and artistic achievements among the Pomo, Washo, and Kern of California, and the Apache, Aleut, the Tlingit, Haida, and Salish of the Northwest Coast, the vanishing Chitimacha of the Mississippi Delta, and the Guiana Arawaks of South America. No extraordinary examples of basketry are known from ancient Middle America or the central Andes, though fine baskets are still made in Mexico and Ecuador, where the famous hats of Montecristo (known as "Panama hats") are made.

PAPERMAKING, also called bark-cloth- or tapa-making, was practiced in Mexico, where the product was used for making offerings, pictorial manuscripts, and maps, and in South America, surviving there for garments, often painted, on the upper Amazon and in Bolivia, as well as in Mexico among the Otomí of San Pablito, in the Sierra de Puebla, where it is made into magic effigies. Bark-cloth-making is a circum-Pacific trait that spreads from China (where it developed into paper manufacture) to the Marquesas, Hawaii, New Guinea, New Britain, the Solomons, etc.

TEXTILE-WEAVING, also an ancient technique, appears since pre-ceramic levels where conservation was possible: among the ancient Basketmakers of the Southwest and in Huaca Prieta in Peru, where it probably derived from net-making. Textiles were made of agave fibers and, principally, of cotton, though in places wool was used —of mountain goat and dog hair on the Northwest Coast. There is mention of rabbit-hair weaving among the ancient Mexicans, and of alpaca- and vicuña-wool weaving in Peru and Bolivia, where the highest development of the textile arts took place. There they reached an unprecedented technical quality, often as *tours de force,* made perhaps as curiosities of merit. Every imaginable technique for weaving was used, and even some for which no names exist. Here is a partial list of the textile techniques as practiced in Peru (Bennett and Bird, 1949):

Every variety of plain cloth in all degrees of fineness; striped in the warp or woof, checked or gingham, "repp" (ribbed cloth), twill, etc. Network, plain or figured, and gauze, determined by its technique of twisted warp structure and not by sheerness alone; double cloth, two-faced cloth done with two sets of warps and two sets of woofs; tubular weaving; woof loop pile weaves; velvet (pile knot fabric); shaped fabric (weaving to shape); simple and interlocked warp pattern cloth (patchwork); interlocked darning; bobbing or woof pattern (the insertion of colored threads over and under arbitrary groups of warps, done by manipulation of the bobbin); crocheting and needle-knitting, of which there is an extraordinary three-dimensional variety; and, of course, all sorts of brocades and tapestries: plain, sheer, interlocked (a variety of woven separate pieces), Kelim (with slits between adjacent color areas), and excentric (forcing the weave into curvilinear designs).

Other typical sorts of decorated cloth are: painted, stenciled, and stamped; intricate embroidery with copper or thorn needles; and two typically Oriental techniques of resist-dyeing: *plangi,* binding portions of the fabric with yarns or fibers before dyeing, to produce nucleated spots to form a pattern; and *ikat* or "tie-dye," tying small bunches of warp threads with waxed cord and dyeing the whole piece before weaving to form the design. This technique required an extremely careful and precise planning of the tying and dyeing, as well as of the final execution of the weave. Pre-Spanish *ikats* are known in Peru (Bird, 1947), and there are many contemporary examples from Mexico, Guatemala, and Ecuador.

No important pre-Spanish Mexican textiles are known to have survived, though representations in paintings and sculptures indicate that the art had reached a high level in Mexico. There are interesting new textile arts and modern survivals among the Navajo and in Mexico, Guatemala, Peru, Bolivia, and Chile.

FEATHER MOSAIC is a highly specialized and much appreciated technique with a rather restricted world distribution. The most notable examples come from pre-Columbian Mexico and Peru, but it was also practiced among such Californians as the Pomo, who made beautiful "gift" or "jewel" baskets covered with feather mosaic, and among the Paiute of Nevada and the Basketmakers of the Southwest, who made feather capes. There are also feather mosaics from Chile, and feathers as ornaments were widespread—among the Plains Indians, the Hupa of California, all over Middle America, and among the Amazon Indians. Outside of the Americas feather mosaic was a typical art of the Hawaiians, who used it for making fabulous royal robes and helmets; in New Zealand, in New Guinea (shields of feather mosaic from the Sepik River area), and in China (of kingfisher feathers to decorate jewelry made since the T'ang dynasty).

The finest mosaics known come from Mexico, where they were used for shields and headgear, as well as for capes and staffs like those of the Hawaiians (on the Maya Stela 7 of Piedras Negras and the

Bonampak frescoes). The Mexicans used the precious green feathers of the quetzal (*Pharomacrus mocinno*), turquoise and purple feathers of the *Cotinga amabilis*, red and yellow macaw feathers, pink ones from roseate spoonbills, and the minute opal-like feathers of hummingbirds. There was a special guild of feather-workers, the *amanteca*, who continued, after the conquest of Mexico, to practice their unique art for the Spaniards, making feather pictures of saints, church ornaments, and so on. The technique survives even today in the making of small souvenir feather pictures of birds, cockfights, and national coats of arms. The antiquity of the art was revealed by the discovery of a feather mosaic helmet from the early Cavernas de Paracas period in southern Peru (Carrión-Cachot, 1931), probably dating back to pre-Christian times.

PORCUPINE-QUILL EMBROIDERY AND BEADWORK. Embroidery on buckskin with dyed and flattened porcupine quills is a technique found only in North America, from the Yukon to the Atlantic coasts of the Labrador Peninsula and southward to the Delaware area and the Plains. Its highest exponents were the Ojibway (Chippewa) Indians of the Great Lakes region, who practiced a difficult and intricate variety of weaving with porcupine quills. After contact with the white men, this technique deteriorated, and was largely replaced by beadwork after the introduction of commercial beads in the early nineteenth century. There was an antecedent of beadwork, however, in the weaving of designs with wampum, beads of purple and white shell, typical of the old Iroquois, used to make the famous ceremonial wampum belts with which treaties were recorded. Elaborate weaving with colored shell beads was also practiced on the Peruvian central coast for funerary collars, aprons, and cushions. Beadwork reached its high point among the Plains and Woodlands Indians in the nineteenth century, and is practiced today among the Huicholes of Mexico and the Caribs and Arawaks of the Orinoco basin in South America.

SCULPTURE AND STONEWORK were a basic art in the Americas. There were excellent schools of sculpture at all times and in many regions. The oldest form of stonework is stone-chipping, and the oldest spear points, those of Folsom and Yuma, are among the most beautiful. An elaboration of the art of stone-chipping appears in middle American Classic times in the offerings of delicate, miniature flaked instruments of obsidian at Teotihuacán; the amazing excentric and elaborate flints of the Maya; the fine large spear points and swords of Hopewell and the middle Mississippi; and (in modern times) among the Californian Hupa, who made great ceremonial blades of chipped obsidian. Curiously enough, this art was not developed in South America.

The most spectacular examples of stone sculpture are the elaborate megalithic monuments—stelæ, altars, and colossal heads—of the "Olmec" and Maya areas in southern Mexico and Guatemala, the austere stone giants of Teotihuacán and Tula on the Mexican plateau, and the awesome stone deities of the Aztecs. Colossal statuary was also made in Central and South America; there are notable stone seats, slabs, and statues in Panama and Costa Rica and at Manabí in Ecuador. There are also large statues of stone in San Agustín, Colombia, and great obelisks, pillar-like statues, and reliefs in Peru and Bolivia: in Chavín de Huantar, Huaraz, and Tiahuanaco. Curiously enough, megalithic art flourished mainly in the earliest periods of both pre-Columbian Middle and South America (the "Olmec" and Chavín horizons), but it reappears in the Classic and post-Classic periods and the late Mexica and Inca empires.

There are notable schools of small-scale sculpture all over the continent: in bone and ivory in the far north, among the Eskimo and the Northwest Coast Indians; in shell in Mexico, Peru, Venezuela, in the region of Oklahoma, and among the prehistoric Hohokam of southern Arizona, who had developed a technique of etching shell with acid. Small-scale stone-carving was even more widespread; it was highly developed in the Mississippi basin for making effigy pipes, statuettes, and beautiful abstract shapes used as gorgets and as spear-thrower weights, the so-called "banner stones." Small ornaments of stone were extensively made in the Antilles, in Costa Rica, and in northern Colombia and other areas of South America.

The lapidary arts reached their highest level in southern Mexico and Guatemala, and Sahagún refers to the Mexican lapidaries as specialists of high repute. The list of the precious and semiprecious materials they used is impressive: it includes jade, serpentine, amazonite, rock crystal, obsidian, agate, jasper, chalcedony, emerald, opal, amethyst, jet, onyx, alabaster, crystalline hematite, pyrite, turquoise, and malachite. From these they fashioned the most exquisite jewels: figurines, little masks, gorgets, pendants, ear-ornaments, beads, and even vessels and utensils so finely carved and beautifully polished that they often compare with the best Chinese workmanship.

JADE being the preferred material of Middle American lapidary art, and jade-carving one of its most characteristic traits, it is pertinent to elaborate on the problem of its presence on this continent and to discuss the technological development.

Objects of jade have been found abundantly in southern Mexico and in Central America, and the question whether the material itself is native to Mexico, where it is more frequent, has always preoccupied those who believe in the importation of cultural elements from Asia into America. So many are the points of coincidence between China

103

and Mexico on the use, the manner of carving and polishing jade, the artistic styles, and the beliefs in the supernatural powers of the stone that it is difficult not to believe in a common origin, though it has been established by spectroscopic analysis that Asiatic and American jades are two different varieties of the same stone (Norman and Johnson, 1941). This, however, does not dispose of the problem of direct contact at one time or another. Both Chinese and Mexicans attributed magic powers to jade and considered it the most precious of materials. Both carved jade exquisitely, wore it as an amulet, made offerings of it, and buried it with their dead. For the early Chinese of the pre-Buddhist Shang and Chou dynasties, jade had the property of preventing decay; they used to seal the orifices of the corpse, placing a jade cicada inside the mouth of the dead as a symbol of reincarnation. The ancient Mexicans also were in the habit of placing a jade bead in the mouth of their dead, and both Chinese and Mexicans painted their funerary jades with red cinnabar. To complicate matters, the style and decoration of some Chinese and Mexican jades are surprisingly similar: combinations of squared meanders that represent, or are derived from, tigers, dragons, or clouds. To both Mexicans and Chinese, jade was more than a simple jewel; it was worshipped as the symbol of everything precious or divine, perhaps because it was the color of water and of vegetation. The Mexican name *chalchihuitl* and the glyph for jade were synonymous with "jewel" and "precious." Furthermore, medicinal properties were attributed to jade—a belief shared by the Spaniards of the sixteenth century. In fact, the modern name of "jade," and that of one of its varieties, "nephrite," as well, have their origin in the words for the kidneys and the loin pains that jade was supposed to cure. The jade beads first brought to Spain from Mexico were called *piedra de ijar* or *de ijada,* "loin stones," in French *jade,* whence the English word "jade."

Why natural deposits of jade have not been found in Mexico is a recurring question. It is proved that jade is native to America and was mined intensely in ancient times, to judge from the enormous amount of pre-Spanish objects of carved jade known from every middle American period. Jade is not often found in large veins or deposits, however, but generally appears in isolated boulders in riverbeds and ravines, where probably no one has searched for it. Furthermore, only the expert can distinguish between an ordinary stone and a boulder with a heart of jade. In China professional jade prospectors search for the boulders of jade in remote, deep ravines; their methods of identifying these boulders are jealously guarded family secrets. Similar methods were apparently employed in pre-Spanish Mexico, and Bernardino de Sahagún tells of information transmitted to him by his Aztec informants, who had probably obtained it by hearsay: "There are those who know where the precious stones grow, and in fact a precious stone, wherever it is, emanates a subtle vapor or steam, and said vapor arises at sunrise or at sunset, and those who search for such stones place themselves in a convenient place at sunrise and look in the direction of the sun, and when they see the delicate smoke rising, they know there are precious stones there, which have been born there or were hidden in that place. They go to that place, and if they find a stone from which the vapor came they know it contains a precious stone and they break it to find it. If there is no stone there, they dig the earth and may find a stone box containing precious stones, or they find the stones that may be buried or lost in the earth. . . . There is another clue to places where precious stones grow, particularly those called *chalchihuitl;* because wherever they are buried the weeds are always green, because those stones give out a cool and humid exhalation. They dig there and find the stones *inside of which* these *chalchihuitl* grow" (Sahagún, 1938, Volume XI, pp. 277–8).

This reference, however fantastic, is reminiscent of the methods of the Chinese prospectors for identifying native jade, and points to the existence of specialized methods for finding jade among the ancient Mexicans. Jade is found in many parts of the world: besides its traditional home in Asia—Sinkiang and Burma (jade is rare in China proper)—in Siberia, India, central Europe, New Zealand, New Caledonia, and New Guinea. In America it was used in Alaska, Mexico, Guatemala, Honduras, Costa Rica, Panama, and northern Colombia, but it seems to be absent from the rest of South America save for a few isolated trinkets discovered in the Amazon basin. The center of origin of jade-carving and the main source of native jade, however, seem to have been Mexico; I have seen several pieces of unworked jade from the Mexican state of Guerrero and from the bed of the Tesechoacán River in Veracruz, probably carried down from the Chinantla mountains.

The carved jades of the early period of Middle America (generally in "Olmec" style) are predominantly in the varieties of translucent blue-green, bluish gray, and spinach-green jade. They are often carved with surprising sureness and mastery of the technique, but for the present no evolutional steps in the development of this art can be discerned. The masses are of great simplicity and the surfaces are sensuously modeled and polished, often with characteristic secondary lines, precise and finely incised. This style, which is probably the oldest, is in sharp contrast with the styles of the later epochs; in the Classic period, in the Maya zone, in Oaxaca and Veracruz, the carving becomes more baroque, more stylized, and more decorative. Even the taste for the material itself changed; the blue-green and gray-green jade of the "Olmec" period seems to go out of fashion, and the apple-green and emerald-green stone is favored. Of this epoch are the figurines, masks, and earplugs of Teotihuacán style, the ornaments of period III of Monte Albán, and the splendid gorgets and plaques of Classic Maya

106

style from Ocosingo and Nebaj. Instead of the naked fat personages with Mongoloid eyes and thick lips, the personages represented in jades of the Middle American Classic period are carved in shallow relief, richly dressed, with slim, well-proportioned bodies, large, oblique eyes, prominent noses, and full, small mouths. They wear monumental headdresses with fans of long quetzal feathers, as well as necklaces, gorgets, jeweled belts, anklets, and decorative sandals. In this period there was a radical change in the great Indian civilizations of lowland Middle America: great cities of dressed stone and stucco were built, with monuments of an exuberant, almost flamboyant style, which were the antithesis of the serene simplicity of the earlier cultures. All sorts of new elements, such as serpents, spiral motifs, and fans of quetzal feathers, made their appearance. These invaded the monuments, the carved jades, and the pottery. These elements mark the dividing line between the pre-Classic and the Classic cultures of Middle America.

After the long period of decadence that marks the end of the Classic period, about A.D. 900, came the renascentist flourishing of the Toltec and Mixtec periods. This brought another change in the lapidary technique and in the materials used. Probably emerald-green jade became scarce, for most objects of green jade of jewel-like quality from the late period were made of broken pieces of older objects, while white jade mottled in green, and green jade mottled with brown, make their appearance. In the late period mechanization and decadence set in: mass-production methods and carelessness in the execution. Amulets and ornaments of hard stones other than jade were carved in a summary manner by conventional cuts, grooves, circles; and pits made by mechanical saws and tubular drills stand for the limbs, features, and ornaments of the subjects represented, mostly overstylized human beings and animals. The art of carving jade and other hard stones became the province of expert artisans. The inevitable conclusion is that jade-carving was of higher artistic quality in earlier times because it had not yet become an industry.

The techniques used for working stone were also highly developed, and they must have involved a great deal of time and experience. The methods more generally employed for shaping the rough stone were fracture by direct percussion, pressure, heat fracture, water expansion (inserting wedges of dry wood into a crack or groove, then expanding them by soaking), and particularly by crumbling and pecking with hafted or unhafted stone picks or hammer-stones in the manner still employed by the carvers of milling stones and mortars used today in every Mexican kitchen. The masses to be carved were first blocked out accurately in this manner and then were carefully smoothed before the details, such as features and decorations, were carved. This is evident in known unfinished pieces, in which the basic shapes of the carving intended were neatly outlined. This pecking technique undoubtedly made for greater sensitivity to form than that of our method of indirect percussion with hammer and chisel.

Sculptures were finished, particularly in the smaller sizes, mainly by abrading, grinding, whetting, cutting, scraping, drilling, incising, and engraving, and finally polishing. Of these, abrading was perhaps the most commonly employed, wearing away the stone with water and some abrasive powder, or rubbing it against another stone. Sawing, channeling, and dividing were done with an edge, a saw-abrader, a thin blade of hard stone (I have succeeded in cutting a jade bead in half with an Indian flint blade and water), or with filaments with the aid of sand and water. The sawing was done from both sides, and then the thin septum joining the two halves was broken and smoothed. Drilling was done with bow, strap, and pump drills equipped with flint points or with tubular drills of tempered copper, cane, or hollow bird bones, with sand and water as abrasives. An alabaster plate was found in Chalco with a fragment of crane-bone drill in the unfinished perforation (Holmes, 1919). The surfaces were smoothed with sand and leather, and probably with the bark of bamboo, rich in silica, as is still done in the Far East. Sahagún mentions a kind of "precious bamboo," *quetzalotatl,* used for the purpose. He describes the copper instruments the Mexican lapidaries used, the manner of polishing with bamboo, and the fact that the pieces to be worked were mounted in wood. He lists the most precious stones the Indians of his time used, differentiating fine jade (*chalchihuitl yoan quetzaliztli*), green like the Chinese "jewel jade," from the common jadeites and serpentines (called simply *chalchihuitl*), and mentions the "red crystal," amethyst (*tlapaltehuilotl*), and the rock crystal (*iztac tehuilotl*), clear "like a drop of rain."

THE WOODCARVING of the Indians of the Northwest Coast of North America—British Columbia, and the state of Washington—is one of the most remarkable phenomena of world art. These regions are famous for their totem poles, monuments carved out of giant cedars, which reunite the various crests of a chief's clans and are erected to commemorate the greatness of the family lineage. These Indians also carved great "Potlatch statues" of chiefs who ruined themselves but gained great prestige squandering their entire wealth on colossal parties; as well as the fantastic masks with which the spirits of the woods were impersonated. Without doubt, the woodcarving of the Northwest Coast Indians is the finest in America from both the artistic and the technical point of view.

Fine sculptors on a more modest scale are, even today, the Eskimo of southern Alaska, whose favorite material is walrus ivory, but who also carve bone and bits of ocean driftwood into extraordinary masks, thin and flat, in strange shapes, and provided with mobile appendages of wood, whalebone, and feathers. Eskimo masks are masterpieces of abstract synthetism, conceived with surrealist fantasy and humor.

It is unfortunate that only a few examples of Indian woodcarving from the places of great civilization survive, particularly from Middle America, mostly damp jungles and plateaus with abundant rainfall. There is, however, the splendid Maya lintel of hard zapote wood from Tikal in the Ethnographic Museum of Basel, the wooden "Olmec" mask in the American Museum of Natural History of New York, and the statuettes, carved drums, gongs, and spear-throwers in the British and Mexican museums. Although scarce, these woodcarvings testify to the high level of taste and the technical quality of Middle American wood sculpture. On the other hand, on the desert coasts of Peru, where it never rains, everything perishable is admirably preserved and countless examples of central Andean woodcarving are as fresh as when they were made. There are oars, mummy masks, weaving implements, figurines, mirror-handles, boxes, and so forth, particularly from the central and southern coasts of Peru. The favorite motifs here are stylized human beings, birds, fishes, and geometric patterns, used mainly as decoration in a formalized and not too highly developed style.

There are many other interesting examples of ancient Indian woodcarving in scattered places: the delicate, realistic masks and statuettes of animals found in the swamps of Key Marco, Florida; the stylized ancestor effigies, stools, and low chairs of Cuba, the Dominican Republic, and Puerto Rico, well preserved in dry caves, of a style strongly reminiscent of the South Pacific islands; or the contemporary trumpet mouthpieces and clubs of the upper Amazon in Brazil, which seem in a way related to the Antillean carvings. An extraordinary development in America is the almost pure African style of carving of the Djuka, or

Bush Negroes, of Dutch Guiana, transplanted and maintained by runaway African slaves.

POTTERY-MAKING AND CLAY-MODELING. One of the oldest inventions of mankind, the making of vessels and implements of baked clay has always been an outstanding medium of expression among the American aborigines. With few exceptions in the extreme peripheral areas, practically every culture in North, Middle, and South America has a great ceramic tradition. They have all produced an amazing variety of pottery, from the simple pots of daily use for cooking, eating, and storing food, to the most elaborate de luxe wares made to be buried as offerings to the dead. In fact, American Indian pottery is one of the most remarkable in the world because of its abundance and the profusion of its styles, shapes, and means of decoration. Fragile but everlasting, baked clay remains intact for hundreds and thousands of years, even when buried under the most adverse conditions. Pottery is all that remains of many early cultures except for less expressive bone and stone implements.

Pottery is a key element in the study of ancient cultures. For instance, it was always an important article of trade, so that, found in association with local pottery, a pot or a sherd from a known foreign source serves to date a culture and to establish the trade connections of its makers. Pottery sherds accumulated in layers forming refuse dumps, when carefully analyzed, are the most valuable clue for the study of the chronological sequence of, and change in, prehistoric Indian cultures. Thus the characteristic styles of pottery, the shapes and decoration, the clays and slips employed, are indicative of the epoch in which it was made, reflecting the taste of the time and serving as evidence of the artistic temperament of its makers.

It is not known where and how the American ceramic art was born. In almost all centers of high civilization pottery appears in full development even in the earliest times, particularly in Middle America, where no cultures in a pre-ceramic level have been discovered as yet. There are exceptions to this rule, interesting evidences of local development of pottery, in the Basketmaker culture of the southwestern United States and the Archaic Woodland period of the Mississippi basin, as well as in Huaca Prieta on the northern coast of Peru. A claim that any one of these local phenomena was the place of origin of the ceramic art, however, would be untenable. Until it is proved otherwise, we have to assume that the knowledge of pottery came from elsewhere, perhaps from the Old World.

An argument against an Old World origin for American pottery is the fact that nowhere, at any time, did early Americans make use of the potter's wheel, an ancient Old World device unknown in America before the white conquest. This apparent handicap, which has often been pointed out as a shortcoming of Indian civilization, really worked to the artistic advantage of the American ceramists. All pottery was made by hand, without the intervention of mechanical means, and it consequently had a more direct feeling for form and was less bound to the limitations of the traditional shapes determined by the use of the wheel, and therefore produced vessels more expressive and more subject to the potter's creative impulse.

The peoples of the simpler cultures made plain household wares as well as funerary pottery, with or without decoration, geometric patterns, or highly stylized and naturalistic motifs, shaped by every imaginable means: cord and nail markings, incising, carving, scraping, stamping, modeling, and painting in one or more colors, in both positive and negative (batik) techniques. The peoples of the more elaborate cultures made rich and luxurious funerary wares, often beautifully modeled and painted. Outstanding among the finest are the painted pots of the Pueblo Indians of New Mexico and Arizona, both ancient and modern; those of the old Caddo of eastern Texas; the splendid polychromed vases of Cholula and the lacquered vases of Teotihuacán, both from central Mexico; the painted plates and vases of the Maya, with naturalistic scenes of richly dressed priests; the decorative ware of Coclé from Panama; the painted and carved pottery of the island of Marajó in the Amazon delta of Brazil; and perhaps the finest of all, those of the Mochica, Tiahuanaco, and Nazca from Peru and Bolivia. As with the other arts, the artistic and technical quality of pottery is at its peak in the two basic focuses of high civilization—Middle America and the central Andes—dwindling away toward the peripheral areas, until it disappears. Little or no pottery is made in the extreme north and south, where the only peoples without pottery are found: in Tierra del Fuego, Patagonia, eastern Brazil, California, the Plains, the edge of the northern forests, and on the Northwest Coast. Curiously enough, the extremes look alike: the pottery of the Southwest resembles that of the Diaguita of Chile and Argentina; the primitive wares of the Chaco and the pampas are comparable to those of the Archaic Woodlands (Mississippi basin) and of the Algonquians of Canada.

Effigy vessels (pots and vases in human or animal shapes) constitute an interesting link between pottery and sculpture, and were made by nearly all the high cultures. Those of the early Mexican cultures are perhaps the most remarkable from the plastic point of view because of their direct simplicity, inventiveness, and vigorous treatment of realistic, sensual form. In sharp contrast with these because of their decorative stylization are the elaborate funerary urns in human form from the Classic and post-Classic epochs of Monte Albán in Oaxaca, Mexico, in which the ornamentation and the details of dress were exaggerated to the point of submerging both figure and urn. The

113

Peruvians of the north coast made extraordinary effigy vessels, notably the famous Mochica "portrait" pots and the amazing vessels in the shapes of animals, fruits, vegetables, houses, scenes of daily life, and even landscapes.

Clay sculpture, on large and small scale, appears to have been a Middle American specialty, for it reached its highest level of artistic achievement in Mexico and Guatemala. Well known are the expressive and graceful little naked women of clay from the pre-Classic sites of Tlatilco and Chupícuaro; the vigorous humor and uncouth fantasy of the clay statues from western Mexico; and the elegant refinement of the figurines from Teotihuacán, Veracruz, and the Maya island of Jaina, whether they were modeled freehand or cast in molds. Clay figurines are scarcer in North and South America, and they generally appear in cultures that bear certain relationship with those of Middle America. A few figurines have been found in Ohio and Georgia, as well as at the Hohokam site of Snaketown in Arizona, all of which are reminiscent of those from Mexico. Figurines of a similar style were made in the Antilles, Costa Rica, Panama, Marajó in Brazil, Venezuela, and Colombia, and on the Ecuador coast, these last being almost identical with those from the Mexican Gulf coast. The clay-figurine complex extends to Peru, on the Ancón and Paracas regions, and even as far south as northern Chile, among the Diaguita.

Among the most moving examples of the art of freehand modeling were those made, not of clay, but of stucco (fresh lime), by the Maya of Palenque, Uaxactun, Acanceh, and Izamal, heads of an extraordinary realism and reliefs of a refined, almost decadent style. They were used to decorate the sumptuous temples and tombs of these extraordinary people, who seem to have been alone in practicing this unique art.

· · ·

114

INDIAN PAINTING AND DRAWING cover an enormous range of different manners and styles, from the most elementary abstract or decorative designs painted on skins, bark cloth, or the faces and bodies of the peoples of the more barbaric tribes of North and South America, to the fine painted funerary vases of Mexico and Peru and the picture books and the mural paintings, among which stand out the famous Maya frescoes of Bonampak, southern Mexico, showing realistic battles, dances, and ceremonies. It is of course impossible to generalize on the basic character of Indian painting as a whole: in such a wide range of culture types there is every degree of artistic scope and achievement. There is, however, a general tendency in Indian painting for hieratic arrangements of stylized forms, well defined by flat color areas and precise outlines.

The painted motifs in Indian art, whether as decoration of the human body, of articles of dress, and of ceremonial objects, or in funerary pottery, have almost always a religious, symbolic motivation, whether the meaning of the symbols was recognized by the artist or had been forgotten, having become in time simply decoration. Stylization and repetition often transformed a religious motif or a symbol into an abstract pattern or a simple scroll, losing all resemblance to the original subject-matter. On the other hand, certain cultures developed remarkable styles of naturalistic, anecdotal graphic arts: the admirable scenes of daily life or mythology painted on the pottery of the Mochica of northern Peru, the dynamic battles painted on buffalo hides by the Indians of the Plains, or the amusing engravings on walrus ivory of the Alaskan Eskimo, which show lively dances and fishing and hunting scenes in a style reminiscent of our comic strips.

Besides the elaborate painting on the finer pieces of funerary pottery of Middle and South America, ambitious forms of painting are found in Mexico in pictorial manuscripts and in the great mural frescoes decorating temples, tombs, and palaces. The Mexican picture books, generally known as "codexes," were painted on long strips of prepared buckskin or bark cloth, folded like a screen, and bound between two wooden covers. These books, only a few of which escaped the fanatic zeal of the Spanish missionaries, depict in rich and complicated composition of human and animal figures, glyphs, and numerals the religion, cosmogony, calendar, dynastic stories, maps, and accounts of tribute of the Mixtecs, Maya, and Aztecs.

Formal mural painting in true fresco technique, made to last forever, was practiced only in Middle America in the Classic period: for example, in Teotihuacán, Monte Albán, Bonampak, Palenque, Uaxactun, and Tajín, and, in the late or Historical period, in Chichén-Itzá, Santa Rita (Belize or British Honduras), Tamuín (Huaxteca), Mitla, Malinalco, Tizatlán, and so forth. The frescoes of the Classic period are richer, more elaborate, of a higher artistic and technical quality than those of the late period, which are considerably more stylized, more stilted, done predominantly in the so-called "Mixteca-Puebla" style.

Middle American mural painting has an interesting distant relative in North America, in the Southwest, in the subterranean ceremonial lodges (*kivas*) of the Pueblo Indians, the most important of which were found, layer after layer, in the ruins of Awatobi, Arizona. The great plank houses of the Kwakiutl Indians of the Northwest Coast were also richly decorated with stylized painting of mythological and heraldic subjects. There are only two known instances of mural painting in South America: the rather elementary decoration of the tombs of Tierradentro in Colombia, and a painting, which has now disappeared, on the adobe wall in Huaca del Sol, near Moche, northern Peru. Last but not least are the famous dry paintings of the Navajo Indians of Arizona, done to heal the sick, on the floor of the *hogan*, the ceremonial log-house, with sand of different colors to illustrate and underline the magic curative chants. These are masterpieces of concentrated good taste, of delicate harmonies of color, and of balanced, highly stylized design. With typical Indian munificence, the sand-paintings are always destroyed by their makers immediately after the ceremony is over.

Little has been done to analyze the technical aspects of Indian painting, but they all used simple natural colors, mineral earths, and vegetable pigments mixed with a binder soluble in water—the watercolor or *gouache* techniques. Indian frescoes were painted in the classic manner of Europe and Asia, using finely ground, pure pigments mixed with a little water on a fresh layer of lime, into which the color became incorporated when the lime set. This technique, perhaps the most difficult of all, requires a vast chemical knowledge of the permanency of the colors, as well as sureness of hand and intent, as it cannot be corrected and must be finished before the lime sets, within twenty hours after the wall is prepared. The Indians of the Northwest Coast were as original with their painting technique as with everything else; they used oil paints, pigments (black, vermilion, emerald-green, and sometimes blue and yellow) mixed with oil from salmon eggs.

LACQUER. The ancient Americans, like the Asiatics, made lacquer to decorate not only wood and gourd vessels, but even pottery. The technique employed in the most important centers of this craft, southern and western Mexico, consisted in covering the surface to be decorated with a uniform layer of fresh lacquer, made of an inert clay or kaolin and the coloring material, with a binder of animal resin (obtained by boiling a cactus lice of the *cocus* family) dissolved in a drying oil. The lacquer was highly polished with the palm of the hand and allowed to set. Then the intended design, one color at a time, was cut out and scraped away, the next color applied to fill the hollows, smoothed

117

and polished off to the level of the original layer. A variety of this technique was to superimpose a fresh layer of lacquer over the dry one and then cut out and scrape the layer underneath. Both techniques have survived in Mexico and are still intensely practiced, the former in Uruapan, Michoacán, the latter in Olinalá, Guerrero.

The art of lacquering was practiced in Middle America from early times, having originated probably in western Mexico, spreading in Classic times to Teotihuacán and as far south as Kaminaljuyú in Guatemala. Mexican lacquered pottery vessels are remarkable for their rich, harmonious color: various hues of white, gray, black, yellow, ocher, red, rose, orange, and pale turquoise green. The technique seems to have reached the North American Southwest, having been used to decorate stone vessels such as the one found at Pueblo Bonito, New Mexico, and mirror-backs from Snaketown, Arizona. Archæologists have been rather reluctant to accept this technique as true lacquer, and refer to it as al-fresco painting, though recently the more appropriate name of "paint cloissoné" was proposed (Ekholm, 1942). Seen through a stereoscopic microscope, however, the thin layers of color reveal that the manner of inlaying the colors could have been accomplished only by a lacquer: oily, resinous coloring materials inlayed fresh into half-dry layers. Centuries of burial have of course destroyed all traces of the organic binder, leaving only the spongy layer of clay or kaolin and the mineral coloring material. I feel quite justified in considering this unusual way of decorating pottery as true lacquer. There is little doubt that the great bulk of pre-Spanish lacquered vessels was made, like those used in Mexico today, over a foundation of wood or gourd, but no ancient examples have survived. At Cerro de las Mesas, Veracruz, however, the paper-thin layer of lacquer from a tray that had disintegrated was found, and as late as the eighteenth century lacquered trays with pre-Spanish motifs were made in Michoacán.

Lacquer on pottery has also been found in South America, on the Peruvian south coast (in the early culture of Cavernas of Paracas); and the Inca made beautiful wooden cups, called *keros,* decorated with rich lacquered designs. It has not been clearly established whether the lacquered *keros* go back to pre-Columbian times; most of the examples known have representations of personages dressed in colonial European clothes.

NATIVE AMERICAN ARCHITECTURE follows faithfully the cultural pattern of high development and extreme complexity in Middle America and the central Andes, becoming more and more elementary in the areas peripheral to these two centers of civilization. There are thus violent contrasts in house types and ceremonial structures, from the simple windbreak shelters of the Indians of Tierra del Fuego and Patagonia to the elaborate pyramids, temples, and palaces of the Maya and the megalithic mountain cities of the Inca of Peru and Ecuador.

The Indian dwellings of North America are also of the most varied sorts: semi-subterranean *igloos* of the Eskimo, houses built of cut ice blocks and shaped like beehives; *tipis* (tepees), portable conical skin tents of the Plains and the northern forests; the houses of birchbark of the Woodland Indians; the great communal houses of the Northwest Coast, built entirely of great planks, often carved and painted; the multi-storied "apartment" houses of adobe and the cliff towns of the Southwest; and the great pyramidal mounds supporting a temple or a chief's thatched house, reminiscent of Mexico, of the Mississippi basin.

Middle America has a more or less unified complex of ceremonial sites with pyramids, platforms, temples, palaces, and ball-courts distributed around great courtyards and plazas. These are generally faced with dressed and often carved stone, or are built with rubble faced with painted stucco. Notable, and perhaps the oldest structures, are the great earth mounds of Miraflores in Guatemala and Cuicuilco and La Venta in Mexico, all of the pre-Classic period. At a slightly later time, around the beginning of our era, a mysterious race of energetic people built the enormous pyramids of Teotihuacán and Cholula, veritable man-made mountains, most amazing because of the staggering amount of human labor involved in their construction.

Native American architecture reached its highest level of complexity and sumptuousness in the Maya area. The Maya were undoubtedly the most creative architects on the continent, and the cities of the early Classic period, such as Palenque, Tikal, Yaxchilán, Uaxactun, Piedras Negras, and Copán are famous for their elaborate planning, for their pyramids, corbeled roofs and arches, delicately carved roof-combs of stone, imposing stairways, and multi-storied towers. In the late Classic period, in Yucatán, a peculiar local style, known as Puuc-Los Chenes, was developed, rich and original, characterized by elaborate façades of carved-stone mosaic, forming series of rain-god masks, stone latticework, attached columns, corbeled arches, and flat roofs.

A new style of architecture developed in Mexico in the post-Classic or Toltec period, which began around the tenth century of our era. The most important Toltec cities were Tula, capital of the Toltec empire, located to the north of the Valley of Mexico, and Chichén-Itzá, in Yucatán, where Toltec architecture flourished deep in the heart of the Maya country after Tula was destroyed by a great civil war. Peculiar developments of the late or historical period are the pyramids of Tajín and Yohualinchan, on the Gulf coast, with hundreds of stone niches designed to achieve a decorative effect of light and shadow; and the great religious Meccas of Monte Albán and Mitla, in the Valley of Oaxaca, the latter famous because of its unique decoration of mosaics with geometric designs, obviously derived from textiles, made of minute stone blocks admirably fitted together.

120

FACING: left: *memorial statue, about 1.75 meters high;* right: *house panel carved in low relief, the head in the round, with eyes of haliotis shell, about 2.30 meters high. (Both Salish, Thompson River, Washington, AMNH.)*

Architecture flourished along rather different lines in South America; instead of the decorative and elaborate building complexes of Middle America, the civilized Andeans were mostly concerned with massive, awe-inspiring structures built of adobe on the central coast of Peru, of stone in the highlands, not with the delicacy and preciousness of Middle America, but colossal and austere, of the most admirably fitted blocks of stone, some weighing as much as one hundred tons, cut in capricious shapes, built for eternity on a scale designed for giants. Typical of the early megalithic cities of the Andes are the famous Chavín de Huantar and Wilkawain in Peru, and Tiahuanaco in Bolivia, this last remarkable for its colossal monolithic Gate of the Sun and the strange copper clamps to fasten stones in T-shaped slots. Of the later Inca period are such famous cities, often carved out of the living rock of the high mountains, as Machu Pichu and the fortress of Sacsahuaman in Peru, and Coricancha in Ecuador. The Inca achieved further engineering feats, such as terracing whole mountainsides with stone walls for agricultural purposes, and the building of suspension and stone bridges to span the Andean gullies. Equally famous structures of the Peruvian coast are the enormous pyramids of adobe at Moche, known as the Huaca of the Sun and Huaca of the Moon, the terraced pyramid of Pachacamac near Lima, and the great city of Chanchan, near Trujillo, decorated as in Mitla, in Mexico, with designs copied from textiles, delicately cut out of adobe. Chanchan and Mitla were very likely contemporary, as Mixtec pots of this period are decorated with designs obviously copied from Peruvian textiles of the same epoch.

Out and beyond the central Andean area the Indian cultures are simpler, and the structures they built are considerably more elementary. Notable are the beehive houses of mud of the Uro-Chipaya of Bolivia and the great communal houses of wood and thatch of the Brazilian jungle. It seems that the North American pattern is repeated in farther

South America—the conical tepees appear again, among the Caingang of Brazil and the Ona of Tierra del Fuego; and among the Patagonians a simple guanaco skin stretched on a wooden frame served as shelter from the icy winds of the pampas.

METALLURGY. One of the most controversial issues of American archæology is the age and scope of the knowledge of metals among the Indians. It is common to find the experts awed by the artistic achievements of people such as the Maya, who carved splendid stone monuments without the aid of metal tools, the implication being that American Indian civilization stood still in the Neolithic stage. The fact is that hard stone tools, properly used, are quite sufficient to carve stone, and that many metals—copper, gold, and silver, and less frequently tin, arsenic, lead, and platinum (but never iron)—were used at various times and in many places on the continent, often from very early times. They were worked mostly for ornaments, but a great number of tools and implements of copper and bronze was also made by the Indians in North, Middle, and South America. In certain places (Colombia, Ecuador, and Mexico) amazingly complex technologies were developed.

The invention of metallurgy in the Old World is supposed to have taken place in Syria, where beaten copper first appears about 5500 B.C. in the chalcolithic period, whence it was diffused to the farthest corners of Asia and Africa. It was only about two thousand years later that copper began to be smelted and that gold, silver, and lead came into use in Mesopotamia and India. In America, on the other hand, it seems, or at least is so explained, there are many centers of invention and development of metallurgy: (1) eastern North America, the area of hammered native copper; (2) the Amazon basin, the Antilles, and the southernmost tip of Florida, the area of alloys of copper and gold; (3) Colombia; (4) the central Andean zone, Peru and Bolivia with their own typical techniques; and (5) Middle America and on the coasts of Ecuador and Peru, with a common technique that is the result of the mingling of the Colombian and Andean techniques (Rivet, 1926).

Curiously enough, North American metallurgy appears as a completely independent development from that of Middle and South America, and it is quite reasonable to surmise that it had its origins in the Great Lakes region, where native copper in the form of almost pure nuggets is abundant. This is supported by the fact that the earliest metal objects found in North America come from Wisconsin and Minnesota, the implements of the so-called "Old Copper" culture belonging to the Archaic phase of the Old Woodland cultures. To complicate matters, these objects are in typical east Asiatic styles: socketed knives, adzes, and spearheads, often with rivet holes and "rat-tail" stems—enough to make one suspect an early Asiatic infiltration.

The North American style of hammered copper has a sound continuity. In the subsequent period, called by archæologists the Hopewell period, centered in Ohio, it reaches its artistic peak in elaborate ornaments of embossed and cut-out sheet copper conceived with impeccable, sober taste: large gorgets of *repoussé* copper with eagles and eagle-men motifs, hands with eyes on the palm, solar motifs, and so forth. Such ornaments, considerably more elaborate and in different style, continued to be made in the late Woodland period (Temple Mound phase), particularly in Georgia, at the Etowah Site. In southern Florida heavy disks and plumets of beaten gold have been discovered of a technique that belongs in the Antillean and Amazonian traditions.

More difficult to place as to origin and age is the metallurgical tradition of forged copper and even iron of the Northwest Coast, generally regarded as post-historical, brought by the early navigators, though some of the earliest woodcarvings known, from the time of the first contact with Europeans, collected by Malaspina in the late eighteenth century and preserved in the Ethnographic Museum of Madrid, have applications of sheet copper. Captain Cook's statement that the first Indians he saw had iron implements of non-European origin speaks for itself. A few copper bells of Mexican style have been found in the pueblos of the Southwest, but they were probably trade pieces from Mexico. In modern times an important tradition developed in the Southwest, in New Mexico and Arizona, among the Navajo and Zuñi, of jewelry—necklaces, bracelets, rings, and belts—of silver set with turquoise, with strong Mexican (Spanish colonial) influences. Such Indians of the Woodlands as the Menominee and the Iroquois also made ornaments of German silver in the European tradition, but with a strong Indian character.

Metallurgy makes its first appearance in Middle America rather late, not until about A.D. 900, the beginning of the Historical horizon. While early objects of metal are known from North and South America, none has been found in Mexico, Guatemala, or Honduras which could be attributed to the Classic period. Furthermore, there is enough evidence to suppose that the technique came to Middle America from the south in a state of full development and in a style that combines the typical techniques of Colombia and the central Andes. Ornaments of gold and *tumbaga* (gold-copper alloy) from the Isthmus of Panama have been found in Mexico: in Chichén-Itzá, Yucatán, and Coixtlahuaca, Oaxaca, evidence of trade with these remote areas.

Objects of copper, both cast and forged, are abundant in southwestern Mexico, in Oaxaca and Guerrero, and in Michoacán, where the mining activity of the ancient Mexicans seems to have centered; ornaments of gold, and more rarely of silver, cast or *repoussé*, have been frequently found in tombs of the same area; the most famous of such finds, the fabulous treasure of Tomb number 7 in Monte Albán in Oaxaca, included hundreds of fine ornaments of gold and silver, many of them masterpieces of delicacy and technical excellence, besides thousands of pearls, turquoises, and red shell beads, and vases of crystal and alabaster.

For those who heard of the plumed savages of the newly discovered lands it must have been a jolt to gaze upon the loot of gold jewelry sent by Cortés to the King of Spain. The opinion of an artist, the great Albrecht Dürer, entered in his diary after seeing in Brussels the first Mexican works of art, differed considerably from that of his contemporaries, whose heart was only in the intrinsic value of the metal itself: "I also saw the things that were brought to the King from the New Golden Land: a sun entirely of gold, a whole fathom broad; likewise a moon, entirely of silver, just as big; sundry curiosities from their weapons, armor and missiles; very odd clothing, bedding, all sorts of strange articles for human use, all of which is fairer to see than marvels. . . . These things were all so precious that they were valued at a hundred thousand gulden worth. But I have never seen in all my days what so rejoiced my heart as these things. For I saw among them amazing artistic objects, and I marveled over the subtle ingenuity of the men in these distant lands. Indeed, I cannot say enough about the things that were there before me" (Kelemen, 1943, after Thausing, 1888).

The style of Mexican metallurgy is rather uniform; either silhouettes cut out of thin sheets of beaten gold with *repoussé* design, or cast in the "lost-wax" process, in which the object to be cast is first made in wax hardened with white copal resin. Because it had to be hollow, a basic effigy of finely ground charcoal mixed with clay was made first; then this was covered with "sheets of wax thin as spiderwebs" (Sahagún, 1938); then the fillets of the same wax were added, coiled in spirals or in parallel curves, and the whole was covered by a mold of clay. The mold was baked to eliminate the wax, which was replaced by the molten metal; the mold was then broken and the gold object was given a bath

of alum and polished. The objects cast in this manner were faithful re-
productions, even to the smallest flaws, of the original wax model, and
looked, because of the fine filleting, like the most delicate filigree work.

The Mexicans made gorgets, pendants, rings, nail-protectors, nose-,
lip-, and ear-plugs, fan-handles, beads and bells, some quite simple,
others with complicated mythological scenes combining human and
animal subjects with symbolic and decorative motifs. The style of these
is clearly derived from the so-called "Mixteca-Puebla" culture, predominant in southern Mexico a few centuries before the Spanish Conquest. The center of this culture was the Mixteca area of Oaxaca, and
it is reasonable to suppose that the style and the metallurgical technique were developed in this area. There is another important center
for metallurgical activity, with some differentiation from the above, in
the lake area of Michoacán, home of the Tarascan Indians, also famous
goldsmiths. Typically and exclusively Tarascan are certain large copper
bells in the shape of turtles, and elegant copper tweezers, often gilt,
found on the shores of Lake Pátzcuaro.

It is a well-accepted fact that the more elaborate metallurgical
technique originated in South America, where Rivet has defined three
basic areas of different styles and techniques. The first of these, the area
of gold-copper alloy in the Amazon and Orinoco basins and the Antilles,
is known only by a few objects; the second, the area of Colombian metallurgy, had elaborate techniques such as casting, welding, soldering,
forging, and filigree work, with an early period (the cultures of San
Agustín and Tierra Adentro), a flourishing aspect (the Quimbaya and
Sinu cultures), and a late epoch (Tairona, Chibcha). The Colombian
complex extends north into Panama and Costa Rica (Coclé, Chiriquí,
Veraguas cultures) and to the south as far as Ecuador, particularly
around the Esmeraldas coast, where the most highly developed and
complex techniques were known, and in the Manabí-Cerro Jaboncillo

zone of cruder copper and bronze. The third metallurgical complex, the area of the Peruvian and Bolivian Andes, extends far south into the Argentine northwest and northern Chile, with a fourth area, resulting from the mingling of the Colombian and Andean techniques, along the Peruvian and Ecuadorian coasts, where the most elaborate technical developments are found.

Among the representative examples of the great metallurgical tradition of Ecuador and Peru are the splendid objects of *repoussé* gold and silver in the early style of Chavín, found in northern Peru, and—in the same technique—the objects of Tiahuanaco style from the central coast and from the Nazca coast in the south. The elaborate casting techniques in gold, silver, copper, and bronze, developed in later times by the Chimu and the Inca, fully justify the reputation of the ancient Peruvian craftsmen. The Diaguita and Chalchaqui Indians of the southern Andes developed still another separate tradition in bronze-casting, consisting of simple but interesting gorgets, bells, and axes.

South American technology in metallurgy was undoubtedly the most advanced in the separation of metals from ores and in the large range of metals used: besides copper, gold, and silver, it used tin, arsenic, lead, and platinum. Platinum, for instance, requires extremely high temperatures to reach the melting-point (17,550 degrees centigrade), possible only by means of a blast furnace. Platinum was worked nearly pure or alloyed with gold, silver, and copper, and there are gold objects from Esmeraldas plated with platinum (Bergsøe, 1937, 1938). It is significant that the art of alloying different metals was highly developed in South America; in addition to bronze (tin-copper alloy), gold and copper (*tumbaga*); gold, silver, and platinum; and copper, gold, and platinum were used. It is thus evident that the American Indians were far from the Stone Age level of culture.

THE AFTERMATH

THE Spanish and Portuguese conquest of Middle and South America, and the colonization of North America by French and Anglo-Saxons spelled death to high Indian cultures. Ceremonial and religious art automatically ceased to exist upon the forced conversion of the Indians to Christianity. Most of the art techniques died out or were radically replaced by European techniques and ideas. Only in North America and in the more remote and inaccessible parts of Latin America did less organized tribal groups of Indians hold their own and, by avoiding direct contact with European civilization, manage to preserve their crafts and their culture. Practically untouched Indian arts exist today among the Eskimo, on the Northwest Coast, in California, in the Plains and the Southwest, and in marginal South America, in the Orinoco and Amazon basins and the Guianas.

The rapid acculturation of the Indians in the more metropolitan centers of Mexico, Guatemala, Ecuador, Peru, and Bolivia created an American colonial art of European, more specifically Spanish, extraction, often tinged with a strong Indian personality. Such of the ancient crafts as featherwork, lacquer, pottery, and particularly textiles managed to survive. New techniques, new forms, and new ideas were introduced, and a rich and picturesque folk art was born, especially among the Indian population in the neighborhood of the principal urban centers. These folk arts flourished with great vigor and originality from the eighteenth to the end of the nineteenth centuries in the same old centers of high culture—Mexico, Guatemala, Peru, and Bolivia.

It is undeniable that white contact brought doom to great Indian art. Not everything is black in the picture, however: certain cultures, like those of the Eskimo and the Northwest Coast, continued to flourish, and even progressed. The Indians of the Plains and Woodlands created new arts with such new materials as beadwork and ribbon-mosaic, and the Southwest Indians maintained their cultures very much alive. These new arts sometimes reached a high level and became typical of these cultures. Such are the silverwork and weaving of fine blankets of sheep's wool among the Navajo. No such developments of pure Indian art can be credited to Latin America, but the development of extraordinary folk arts makes up in part for what was lost. Furthermore, the Indian heritage is beginning to be felt in the arts of the contemporary peoples of the Americas. An example is the development of the modern Mexican school of painting, strongly influenced by the pre-Spanish art. Moreover, the factors that created the colonial and folk art of America did not come only from Europe: Chinese influence was paramount in certain arts of Mexico from the eighteenth century on because the commercial route from China and the Philippines to Spain passed through Mexico; the African Negro brought to America his innate musical genius, and was responsible for a good part of the folk arts of the southern United States, the West Indies, and Brazil. An interesting development was the importation and elaboration of an almost pure African art in Dutch Guiana, brought by the Bush Negroes, former African slaves, who fought for, and eventually gained, their freedom.

North America:

ALASKA, CANADA, THE UNITED STATES

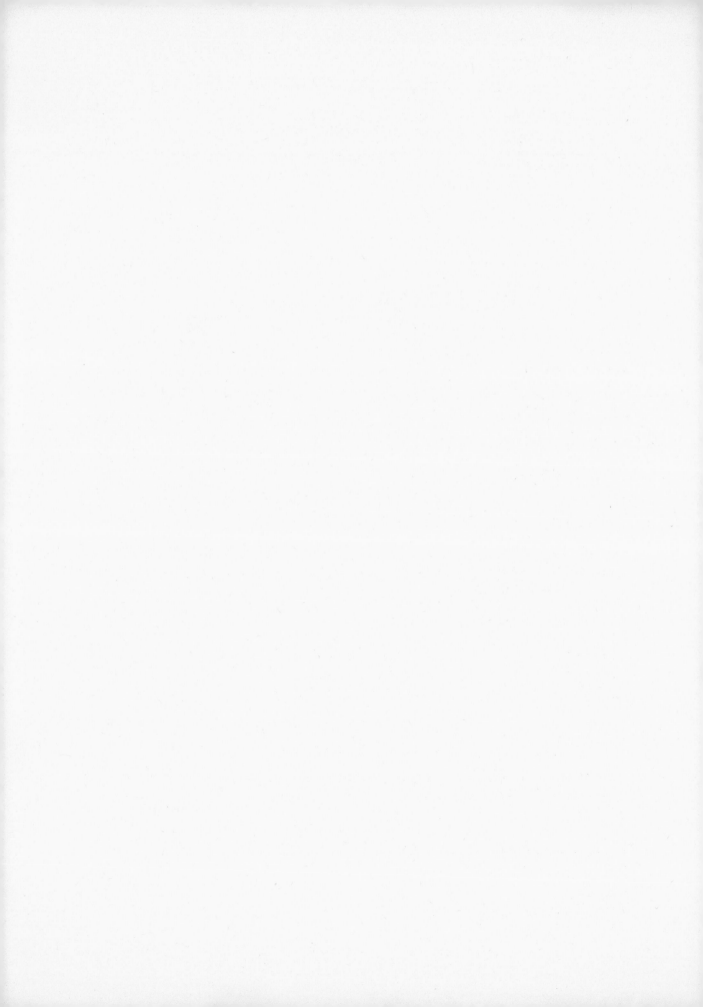

North America

I⊤ is a regrettable fact that even among the art-conscious public a great many people still think of the North American Indian as the broken remnant of the barbaric and romantic "redskins" of the nineteenth century, the noble savages in war-paint who brandished tomahawks and chased the covered wagons of the early settlers. The popular concept of North American Indian art is still a dismal mixture of leering totem poles; dusty garments of beaded buckskin; garish, swastika-decorated rugs fit only for the floor of log cabins; crude silver jewelry; and clay pots with bizarre designs which the tourists pick up as curios from the stolid squaws who sit along the tracks of the Santa Fe Railway.

These childish concepts persist stubbornly, and the general public is unaware of the variety of art cultures, some ancient, some very much alive, which are found from Alaska to Greenland, from California to Florida, and which constitute a rich mosaic of artistic expressions that should be studied as the foundations of the artistic heritage of North America. Some of these cultures are elementary in the extreme, while others show great complexity, unusual refinement, and highly developed technical skills, and are the product of many different peoples whose cultures are conditioned by different economic, social, and, particularly, geographic factors.

133

While the Indian arts of Middle America and many of those of South America are a thing of the past, and those which survive are strongly modified by Spanish influences, many modern and quite pure artistic products of North American Indians—on the Northwest Coast, among the Eskimo, the Pueblos, the Navajo, and the desert dwellers of the Southwest—survive with the style and fine workmanship of five hundred years ago. Undoubtedly, the basic Indian groups have remained in relative isolation throughout their history, resulting in rather clear-cut cultural areas with definite styles and techniques that permit classification into the following art-culture areas, shown here on Fig. 35:

1. THE ARCTIC—the treeless tundra, home of the Eskimo, from the Diomede Islands in Bering Strait to the coasts of eastern Greenland. An area that stands alone for its homogeneous cultures and lively arts, based upon carved ivory, with a continuity of some two thousand years free of outside influences.

2. THE NORTHWEST COAST—the area of the aristocratic sedentary salmon fishermen who live on the islands and in the forests west of the Rockies, from southern Alaska to the state of Washington. This is also a sharply isolated cultural area, with a totemic or, rather, heraldic art of extraordinary artistic quality and technical skill, based upon monumental cedarwood sculpture, and with a complex mentality motivated by obsession with caste and wealth.

3. THE FAR WEST—the area of the simple food-gatherers of California and adjacent parts of Oregon, Utah, and Nevada, the master basket-weavers of the continent.

4. THE SOUTHWEST—a group of agricultural and sheep-herding peoples living in New Mexico, Arizona, and neighboring areas, with characteristic pictorial and ceramic arts of great conservatism. An interesting case of local development and uninterrupted cultural continuity from its beginning to the present.

FIG. 35. *Art-style Areas in North America*

1. The Arctic
2. The Northwest Coast
3. The Far West
4. The Southwest
5. The Woodlands
6. The Plains

5. THE EASTERN WOODLANDS—on the one hand, the ancient, now extinct, cultures of the Atlantic seaboard and the Mississippi basin, characterized by highly developed sculptural, ceramic, and metallurgic arts, mainly of local origin, though with important influences from ancient Mexico and from the far north; on the other, the simpler cultures of the nomadic dwellers of the forests of Canada and the eastern United States.

6. THE PLAINS—the area of the nomadic tribes of bison-hunters and warriors of the Great Prairies, whose art is either graphic or highly stylized symbolism, strongly conditioned by the impermanent character of their restless lives; easily transportable objects made of buckskin, rawhide, beads, feathers, and porcupine quills.

FACING: *"Gift" or "jewel" baskets of feather mosaic, northern California. (a) Pomo, 18 centimeters in diameter; (b) Yuki, Round Valley Agency, Covelo (this extraordinary basket is supposed to be a copy of the basket in which, according to Yuki myth, the sun was stolen from the other world and brought to ours), with shell ornaments representing the sun, the moon, and the stars (USNM); (c) Pomo, Sonoma County (Collection of C. P. Wilcomb).*

CHAPTER I

The Arctic

THE art of the Arctic, the Eskimo area, is one of the liveliest and most dynamic on the entire continent. It possesses a unique personality and a spirited charm that fully reflect the gay and optimistic character of its creators.

The vast treeless tundra, which extends for six thousand miles from easternmost Siberia to Greenland and covers about two fifths of the circumpolar area, is occupied entirely by people of a single stock; it presents the almost unique case of a great cultural unity and uniform artistic style that have survived, practically unchanged, for about two thousand years. In some places, as on Little Diomede Island, in Bering Strait, the Eskimo occupation has been continuous from the beginning of the Christian era to our day (Collins, 1937). In Kukulik, St. Lawrence Island, the accumulation of archæological materials measures six meters (19 feet) in depth and has yielded more than fifty thousand objects covering a period of many centuries (Rainey, 1937).

The Eskimo are quite different from the American Indian, and their culture is in many ways similar to that of northeastern Siberia. They are not recent arrivals from Asia, however; archæology has made it clear that the basic pattern of their culture, with its present-day unity and individual character, was well established over one thousand years ago (Collins, 1940).

The Eskimo are an admirable people. Living in one of the most inhospitable regions of the world, a zone practically devoid of basic raw materials for the development of art and culture, where the climate is unbearable for the greater part of the year, they are thoroughly adapted to an environment in which few men would survive. They have taken full advantage of the limited supply of raw materials at their disposal: walrus ivory, bone, the blubber and skin of animals, whalebone, stone, and some driftwood, developing their inventiveness and technical ability to a surprising level. No other hunting and fishing people possesses such a variety of utensils of its own invention, and no one living in such hostile lands and icy seas enjoys such æsthetic sense, strength, health, and good humor as the Eskimo. Here is a list of some of their inventions:

> tailored clothes of skins, furs, and membranes (bladders and intestines of seals): trousers, blouses, parkas, boots, and gloves; lip-plugs, combs, buttons, and buckles of ivory; skin tents for summer and great semi-subterranean houses of driftwood and whale jawbones; individual skin canoes (*kayak*), and larger canoes for women (*umiak*); dog sleds, snowshoes, visors and goggles to protect the eyes against ice-glare; stone and clay lamps, spoons, ladles, wooden trays, boxes, some pottery, stone pestles, fire-lighters, water buckets, adzes, maces, knives; bows and arrows, harpoons, spears, spear-throwers, pipes, bow drills; games, toys, drums, masks, and maskettes.

We are only beginning to know the cultural history of the American Arctic in the twenty centuries of Eskimo occupation. Exciting discoveries have been made in recent years by archæologists [1] in the frozen islands, bays, and inlets of northern Alaska, the Aleutian Islands, the islands of Bering Strait, the central region northwest of Hudson Bay, and Greenland. In the first place, no evidence has been found of the early Asiatic settlers who supposedly passed across Bering Strait to populate the whole of the American continent; all the remains are Eskimo in character throughout the various levels of human occupation, and no trace has been found as yet of the original, primitive Eskimo, who should have preceded the surprisingly highly developed cultures of the older levels. It is a peculiar fact that the oldest cultures of the Bering Strait area appear fully developed, with an art more refined and complex than that of later times. This is also true of the early cultures of Middle America and the Peruvian Andes. The only possible explanation of the mystery is that the early evolutive stages have not yet been discovered, or that the culture came already developed from elsewhere.

On the other hand, it is clear that the earliest Eskimo came to America at a later time than such primitive Indians as the Folsom man, who hunted the fauna of the Pleistocene—the mammoth, remains of which are found so abundantly in the frozen muck of Alaska, and which the Eskimo apparently did not know.

Eskimo archæology, however young, has already produced spectacular and important results. Many fine examples of early Eskimo art have been recovered, and various roughly dated sequences have been established, from which we can obtain a sufficiently coherent picture of the art history of the area. These sequences have clearly shown the unity and continuity of Eskimo culture for two thousand years, as well as its relationship with the cultures of northeastern Siberia, from those of the mesolithic and neolithic periods, to those of the modern Siberians

[1] Collins, 1926–43; Jennes, 1928; Jochelson, 1925–33; Hotveld, 1944; Hrdlička, 1935–41; Mason, 1930; Mathiassen, 1930–7; Rainey, 1936–42; Wintemberg, 1939–40.

such as the Chukchi and the Koryak. Less clear, though undeniably present, are certain similarities, which may or may not be casual, to the art styles of pre-Buddhist China and Melanesia. This would not imply, of course, the possibility that Eskimo culture came from China or Melanesia, but rather would indicate that it may have received common influences from an Archaic Pacific style that we cannot at present determine. For those interested in the intricacies of Arctic archæology, here are a chart of the approximate age and interrelationship of prehistoric Eskimo cultures (Collins, 1940) and a general description of the most important art aspects.

Four basic periods of Eskimo art can be defined:

EARLY PREHISTORIC (*Old Bering Sea, Ipiutak, Dorset*), *from the beginnings of the Christian era;*
MIDDLE PREHISTORIC (*Early Punuk, Birnirk*), *after* A.D. *500;*
LATE PREHISTORIC (*Punuk, Thule, Inugsuk*), *about* A.D. *1000;*
MODERN, *the Eskimo as of today.*

The remains from Greenland, the central Arctic, and the Aleutian Islands are rather unimpressive implements of bone and ivory, plain or engraved with simple geometric designs (Fig. 37). These belong to cultures called *Dorset*, the earliest, typical of the eastern Arctic, first discovered by Jennes in 1924, at Cape Dorset, Hudson Strait, and Coats Island in Hudson Bay, followed by the *Thule* culture, discovered by Mathiassen in 1923, which belongs in the late prehistoric period. The Dorset culture lacks many basic Eskimo traits such as the bow drill and dog traction. Besides the small bone and ivory carvings, the Dorset people made fine blades of chipped flint, small and delicate. The Thule people, who seem to have come east from Alaska, had a typically Eskimo culture based upon the hunting of seals, whales, and walrus. In Greenland the Thule period is followed by the *Inugsuk* culture, which

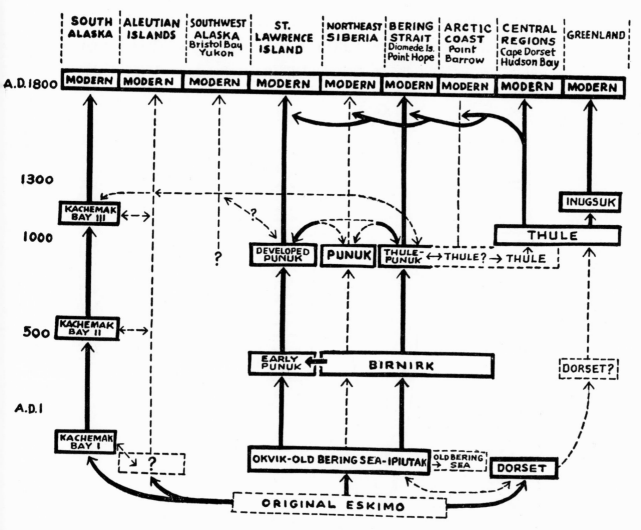

FIG. 36. *Approximate age and interrelationship of prehistoric Eskimo cultures (redrawn after Collins, 1940).*

can be accurately dated because the Inugsuk established contact with the Norse colonists who settled southern Greenland in the thirteenth or fourteenth century.

THE OLD BERING SEA CULTURE

EARLY remains appear scattered all over the American Arctic, but it was in the Bering Strait area and on adjacent coasts that prehistoric

Eskimo cultures flourished. Here were found the finest objects of carved ivory and bone, arts in which the Eskimo have always excelled, but no others are so skillfully carved, so delicately refined, as those of the

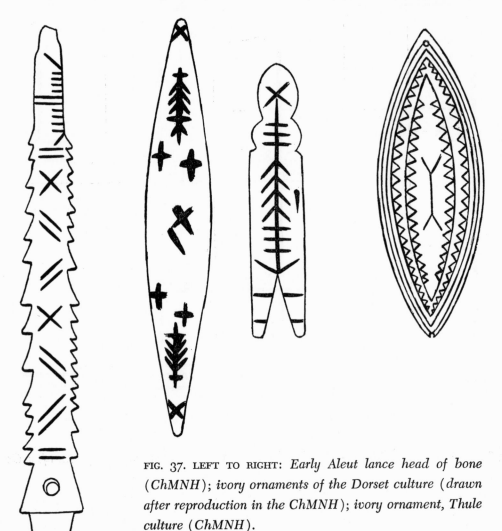

FIG. 37. LEFT TO RIGHT: *Early Aleut lance head of bone (ChMNH); ivory ornaments of the Dorset culture (drawn after reproduction in the ChMNH); ivory ornament, Thule culture (ChMNH).*

earliest cultures of the area, the so-called *Old Bering Sea,* in the Bering Strait islands and on the coasts of Siberia, and the *Ipiutak,* on the Alaskan coast.

It is hard to imagine so advanced a cultural development at such an early age and in an environment so inappropriate, but the evidence indicates a heavy population, an elaborate technology, and a fine art. Near Point Hope, Alaska, was discovered an Ipiutak village of some eight hundred houses arranged in straight avenues, with a population calculated at several thousand. There were also important settlements at Point Barrow, on the St. Lawrence, Punuk, and Diomede islands, and on the Siberian coasts. These points must have had lively contacts by sea. The artistic urge of these peoples is evident in the number and variety of decorated objects they made: among them, handles for stone knives, for drums, and for pails; detachable harpoons; buttons, needle-cases, and figurines. These were made of walrus ivory and even of fossil mammoth ivory, the basic medium used. Because of its great age this ivory is enhanced by a beautiful patina that ranges from greenish gray to brown, mahogany, and nearly black. The prehistoric Eskimo also made objects of wood inlaid with ivory, and pottery lamps and cooking pots of baked clay textured with grooved paddles, a method typical of the early Asiatic cultures. The fact that they made pottery, usually associated with agricultural peoples, would suggest that they had contacts with more southerly, civilized Asiatic peoples.

The art of the Old Bering Sea culture is characterized by complex, streamlined forms, elaborate harpoon heads, winged objects of unknown use, handles and other objects in animal, human, or abstract shapes (Figs. 38, 39). These are decorated with delicately engraved lines in fluid, curvilinear designs: nucleated circles and ellipses, often surmounting low, rounded elevations that suggest eyes; small circles at the inner angle of two converging lines; sweeping parallel lines bristling with minute, nervous spurs or flanked by extremely fine broken or dotted lines. Collins (1937) classifies the Old Bering Sea decorative art into styles 1, 2, and 3, which seem to me to show a clear evolution of the

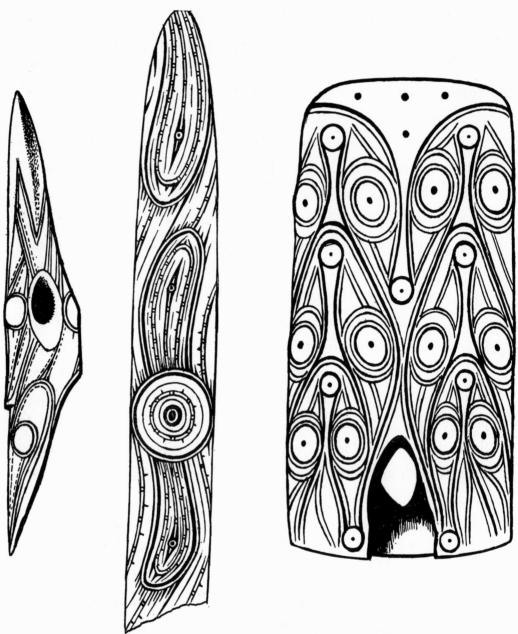

FIG. 38. *Ivory objects of Old Bering Sea style:*
LEFT, *a harpoon head (MAIHF);* CENTER, *a spatula from Wales (Alaska) or Diomede Island;* RIGHT, *carved object (USNM).*

style, though the styles overlap in some single objects. There is, for instance, an early phase, called *Okvik,* found at the lower levels at Gam-

144

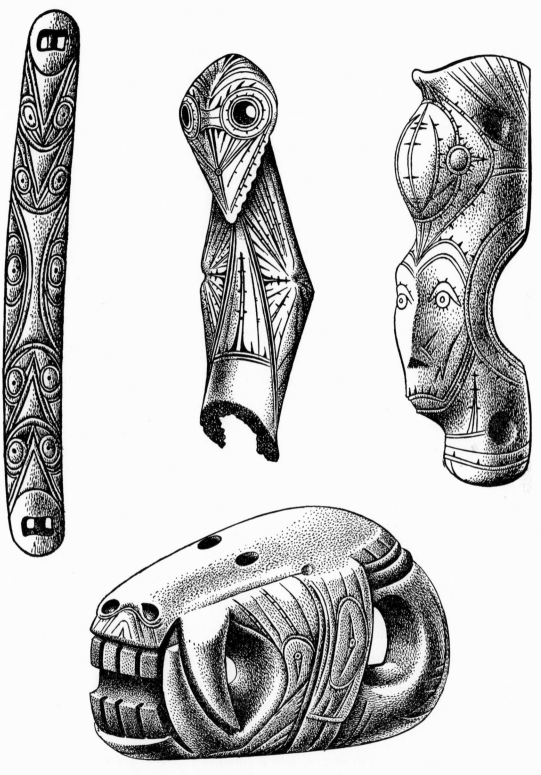

FIG. 39. *Old Bering Sea style carvings:* TOP LEFT, *bone handle, St. Lawrence Island, Alaska;* CENTER, *ivory object, Okvik style, Little Diomede Island;* RIGHT, *ivory drum-handle, Little Diomede Island;* BELOW, *ivory head of a polar bear, Seward Peninsula, Alaska.* (*All from USNM.*)

bell, St. Lawrence Island, which makes exclusive use of style 1, simpler, more nervous and scratchy than the more elaborate style 2 and the frankly flamboyant style 3. Style 1 has a preponderance of straight, radiating lines, short detached spurs, and plain, ovoid circles. Style 2 combines curved lines with nucleated circles, dotted lines, and independent design elements. Style 3 is at the same time an elaboration and a simplification of styles 1 and 2; using a lesser number of elements, it has a rich flamboyancy produced by swirling, flowing curves, flanked by fine dotted lines, around nucleated concentric circles or ellipses over bosses, often arranged in pairs and giving the appearance of eyes (Fig. 40).

When studied carefully, these designs are reminiscent of stylized birds or parts of birds, which would account for similarities with the art of Melanesia, particularly of the Trobriand Islands, New Guinea, and New Ireland, in which a bird is the ever present motif.

THE IPIUTAK CULTURE

A STYLE more elaborate but closely related to the Old Bering Sea culture was discovered in recent years near Point Hope, Alaska (Rainey 1941, 1942). In the ruins of the large Ipiutak town mentioned above, a cemetery was found with tombs of great logs containing sensational burials: in one the skull had been provided with a decorative ivory plaque covering the mouth (Plate 1). The eyes had startling pupils of jet, and two ivory birds (or seals?) were stuffed into the nasal cavities. There were also a remarkable mask of sections of carved ivory, reminiscent of the masks of sections of mother-of-pearl, marble, or bronze from Archaic Chinese tombs; and a number of heavily patined, discolored walrus-ivory objects, among them a beautiful, realistic seal,

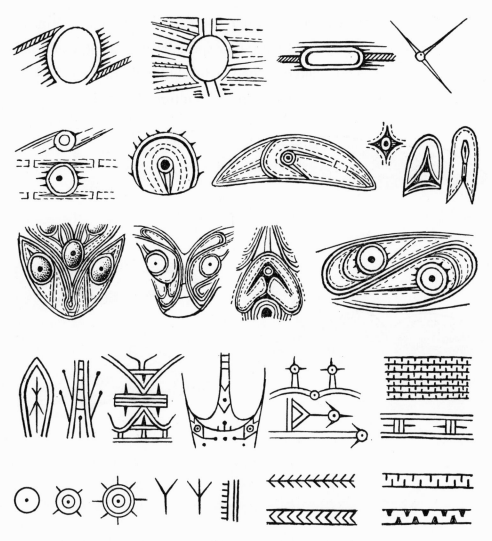

FIG. 40. *History of decorative art of the North American Arctic: some character-istic motifs engraved on ivory, of the Old Bering Sea period, styles 1* (TOP ROW), *2* (SECOND ROW), *and 3* (THIRD ROW); *of the Punuk period* (FOURTH ROW); *and of the contemporary Eskimo* (BOTTOM ROW).

covered with designs of parallel lines and nucleated circles (Pl. 2). Others were puzzling, twisted, pretzel-like objects, chains of various links, comb-like objects, and long-handed back-scratchers (Fig. 41). The significance and purpose of these objects is unknown, but they may well be samples of technical skill in ivory-carving, like the jade chains and ivory spheres, carved one inside another, of the Chinese. Furthermore, making chains of links, a rather specialized concept, could indicate that these people had once had metals but had lost the knowledge of them. The discoverer of the Ipiutak culture, Froelich Rainey, be-

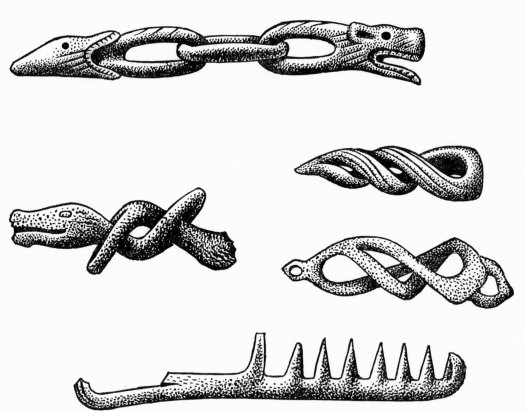

FIG. 41. *Problematic objects of bone and ivory excavated at the Ipiutak site near Point Hope, Alaska (AMNH) (Rainey, 1942).*

lieves it was contemporary with the Asiatic Iron Age and was strongly influenced by it.

The origin of these unique and mysteriously advanced styles—Old Bering Sea and Ipiutak—is supposed to have been a more realistic art, as yet undiscovered. Its Asiatic traits, however, are so persistent that the possibility must be considered that it had some sort of contact with the cultures of early China and thus acquired a style already stylized, without passing through a more primitive, realistic art. The emphasis on the nucleated circle, the "eye" motif, in series or in the body joints of an animal, is reminiscent of the use of this motif in the art of the Ordos River in northeastern Asia, also known as the "Euroasiatic animal style" or "Scythian" (Schuster, 1952), or in the series of eyes of the *T'ao-t'ieh*, the tiger spirit that dominates the early Shang and Chou Chinese carved bones, bronzes, and jades.

THE PUNUK CULTURE

THE middle period of Eskimo cultures already points to the course that modern Eskimo art would follow. In Bering Strait and Alaska this culture was called *Punuk*, after the small island south of St. Lawrence where its most developed phase was first found. The Punuk culture has two epochs: an early one (Early Punuk or Birnirk)—a modified continuation of Old Bering Sea—and Late or Developed Punuk, which no longer resembles the older style. Punuk art consists again of bone and ivory objects engraved with motifs more elemental, more geometric and mechanical than those of the Old Bering Sea style. The flowing curves and fine, sensitive dotted lines give way to sharp, deeply carved, stiff curves and straight lines; the spurs are hard and sparse; the freehand nucleated circles become precise, compass-made concentric circles. The forms of the objects are simpler, losing their streamlined character, and suffering from a poverty of imagination and sensitiveness (Fig. 42).

In this epoch appears a realistic style of human figures, carved in ivory and wood, generally naked women reminiscent of the "Venuses" of the Old World Stone Age. Both styles, geometric and realistic, are perpetuated in the art of the modern Eskimo. The Punuk people also made pottery decorated with curvilinear stamps, another east Asiatic trait. They also used the Asiatic style of plate armor and used engraving implements of iron, probably imported from Asia, as early as one thousand years ago. Thus it is clear that Asiatic traits filtered through Siberia into the American Arctic throughout the prehistoric period and have continued to do so among the modern Eskimo during the last two hundred years. It is assumed that the mesolithic and neolithic cultures of Lake Baikal in Siberia were one of the main sources of Eskimo culture (Collins, 1940, 1943, after Okladnikov, 1941). It is difficult, however, to accept this connection in view of the enormous difference of time and distance between the two. There are three thousand miles between the Angara River in Siberia and Bering Strait, and from six thousand to eight thousand years between the Lake Baikal neolithic and the earliest (Okvik) Eskimo culture.

THE ART OF THE MODERN ESKIMO

MANY of the objects of daily use among the Eskimo are lavishly decorated, either with geometric designs, with descriptive motifs, or with painted representations of ordinary or mythological animals, such as the thunderbird or the sea-serpent Pal-raí-yuk, on wooden bowls or spoons. Frequently these animals are shown with visible internal organs as if they were transparent, the ribs and the digestive system being seen. This concept is found among the Northwest Coast and the Pueblo Indians and, on the other side of the world, among the Australian aborigines. The Eskimo decorate their ivory objects with the traditional geometric motifs derived from the Punuk style and consisting of the same engraved lines, spurs, herringbone borders, and concentric circles drawn with a compass. There is, on the other hand, a rich and entertaining graphic art on ivory or bone, rather like our comic strips, de-

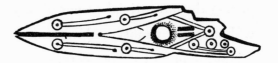

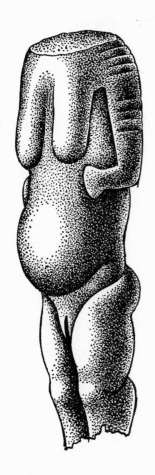

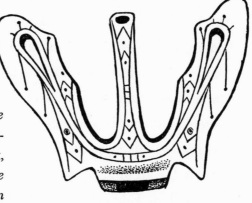

FIG. 42. *Punuk-style objects from St. Lawrence and Punuk Islands:* ABOVE, *fragment of a figurine from Punuk;* RIGHT, TOP TO BOTTOM, *harpoon head, Cape Kialegah, St. Lawrence Island; winged objects; incised object from Punuk. (All from the USNM.)*

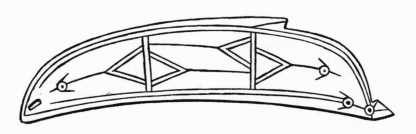

151

picting the most trivial scenes of daily life in minute schematic figures with amazing vitality and movement. This includes whaling episodes, fishing, hunting caribou, ceremonial dances, and happenings inside a winter house (Figs. 43, 44, 45).

The Alaskan Eskimo are extraordinary sculptors in ivory. They carve little figures of men and animals—seals, whales, walrus, polar bears, dogs, and birds—with such realism, simplicity, and concentrated sense of pure form that these objects enlarged to many times their size would make impressive modern sculptures. Some of these miniature carvings have practical uses as buttons, earrings, needlecases, belt-fasteners, cord-attachers, ornaments, and amulets, but most of them are made purely for their own sake, for amusement, with an eye on the traders' dollars. This art is of recent origin, and because it is absent in the prehistoric styles it is possible that it came from Siberia, where it has an identical counterpart in the ivory figurines of the Chukchi and the Koryak. The eastern Eskimo of Labrador have taken recently to making figurines of slate: sleds with their dog teams, igloos, kayaks, whales, and so forth. The artistic activities of the eastern Eskimo cannot stand comparison with that of their Alaskan kinsmen. The southern Greenlanders make some crude wooden masks, and ceremonial dolls and masks of uncured leather of a primitive sort (Fig. 46), though they excel in the art of fine polychrome leather mosaic for boots and belts.

Modern Eskimo art reaches its most stimulating aspect on the lower Yukon and Nunivak Island in the making of fantastic masks from driftwood. They are carved out of light wood, thin and flat, with features in low relief, and painted with areas of white, black, red, and slate blue. The basic form is oval, bristling with feathers and with curious appendages of carved wood, often with thin strips of whalebone attached, which set them vibrating during dances and ceremonies. These appendages are either purely abstract forms or parts or members of

FACING: *Detail of a mural on adobe, found in a kiva, Awatobi, Arizona, Pueblo III period (PMC).*

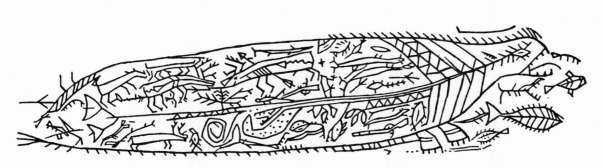

FIG. 43. *Modern Eskimo ivory objects:* TOP TO BOTTOM, *arrow-shaft-straightener (MfVB); needlecase (Collection M. C.); pipestem; a seal design (last two after Hoffman).*

men and animals, such as the wings, legs, and tail of a bird, the fins of a seal, or the arms and legs of human beings. Most often they represent totemic animals—seals, walrus, red and white foxes, and raven—but

153

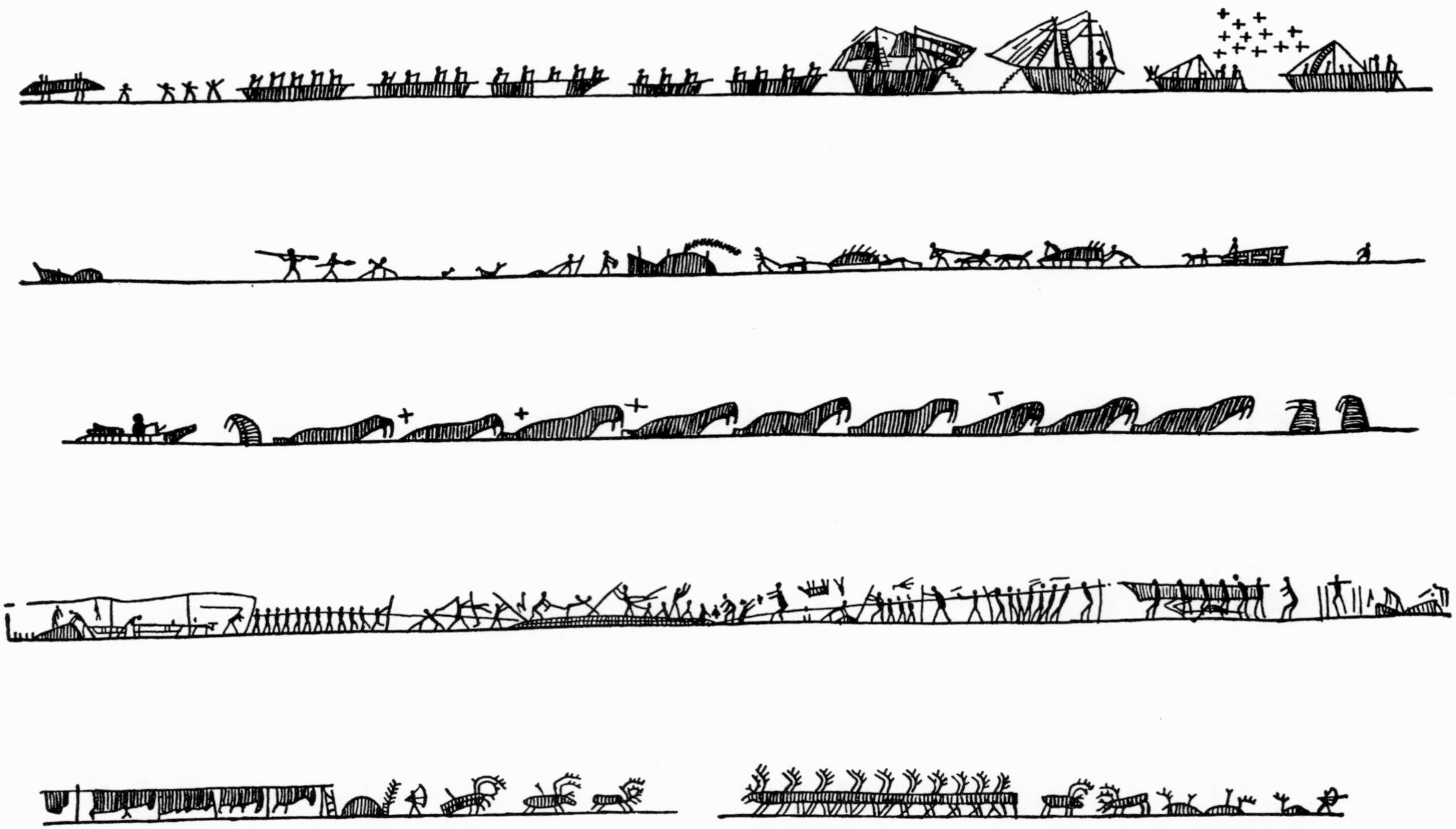

FIG. 44. *Modern Eskimo graphic records engraved on ivory (Hoffman).*

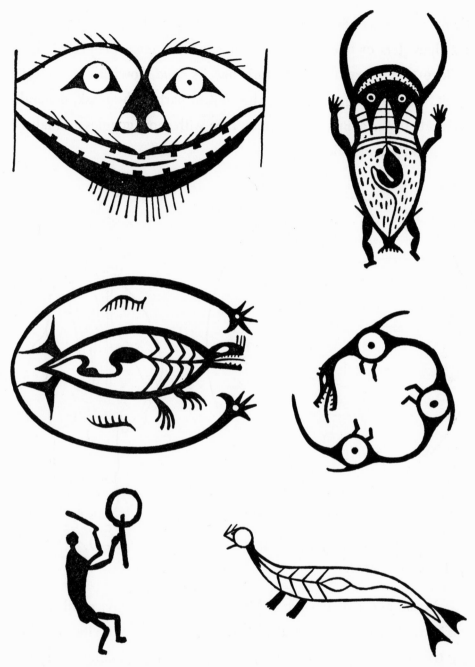

FIG. 45. *Modern Eskimo designs painted on wooden trays and spoons:* UPPER LEFT, *the ghost of the codfish;* RIGHT, *monster showing inner organs;* CENTER LEFT, *a seal and a two-headed serpent;* RIGHT, *the serpent Pal-raí-yuk;* BELOW LEFT, *a shaman playing a drum;* RIGHT, *a seal. (After Nelson, Himmelheber, Douglas, and d'Harnoncourt.)*

155

there are masks of extraordinary fantasy, representing terrifying mythical characters or hilariously humorous, absurd concepts. The Eskimo believe that everything in nature has its *inua*, "owner" or "interior spirit," which is represented in the central part of the mask, generally the body of the animal, as a human face with snow goggles and labrets (Pl. 4 and 5, and Color Plate A).

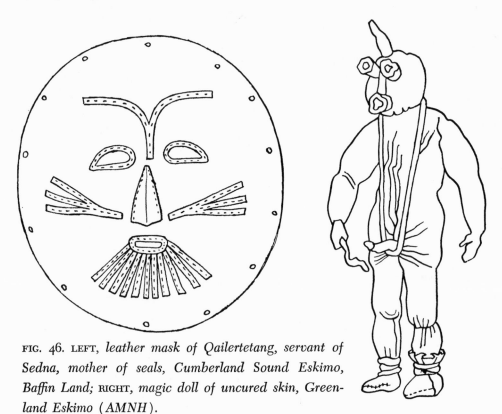

FIG. 46. LEFT, *leather mask of Qailertetang, servant of Sedna, mother of seals, Cumberland Sound Eskimo, Baffin Land;* RIGHT, *magic doll of uncured skin, Greenland Eskimo* (AMNH).

Music and dancing are cultivated among the gay, good-natured Eskimo. They celebrate great festivals, to which they invite neighboring tribes, whom they entertain with magic dances asking the spirits, represented by the masks, the totemic guardians of the participants, for success in future forays. They also celebrate a great festival to honor the dead and provide for their spiritual needs. These dances take place in a great semi-subterranean ceremonial house, and an important part of the festival consists in exhibiting absurd or comic masks with freakish, twisted features to force the guests to laugh. Tradition establishes that the guests should at all times remain dignified and composed, while the hosts may laugh and whoop as boisterously as possible (Hawkes, 1913).

These freakish and fantastic masks are a good clue to the mental agility of the Eskimo artists. They are able to exaggerate and stylize the component units of the face or body of a man or animal, give them new forms, scramble them, and then re-create a new being or an abstract composition from these elements. The resulting fantasy and harmony of style bring to mind the juggling of abstract forms and areas of color by our most inventive cubist or surrealist artists.

THE ALEUT

THE Eskimo share the North American Arctic with the Aleut, a closely related but different people who occupy the western part of the chain of islands forming the land-bridge between Siberia and Alaska. The strategic position of the Aleutian Islands, through which it is taken for granted the original settlers of the Americas passed, makes of Aleutian archæology a promising and fascinating subject. There one should find the skeletons and implements of the first immigrants, solving once and for all the tantalizing problem of the age and origins of man in America.

A review of the reports on excavations in the Aleutians (Jochelson, 1925; Hrdlička, 1938–41) proves a great disappointment; not a trace of the early Asiatic immigrants has been found, and the information obtained is often vague and contradictory. The basic conclusions reached by the archæologists boil down to the following points (Spaulding, 1952):

1. The art and culture of the most ancient Aleutians are vaguely related to those of the Dorset Eskimo of Hudson Bay, and all the evidences indicate that the islands were populated from the east rather than from Asia. Aleut culture is in all respects like Eskimo, however, with some Asiatic traits such as whaling with aconite poison, houses with roof entrance and slat, and rod and plate armor. These could easily have been picked up from such Siberian neighbors as the Koryak.

2. The Aleuts occupied the islands a long time ago, probably at the earliest period of the peopling of northwest America. Excavations in the great shell middens near Dutch Harbor, Unalaska, have revealed two basic periods of Aleut art: an early level at the bottom of the midden containing barbed bone harpoon and lance heads decorated with simple linear designs, deeply cut (Fig. 37), rather like Dorset designs. This period is believed to be contemporary with the Dorset and Old Bering Sea periods (see chart, Fig. 36). The later period, found in the upper part of the midden, resembles the Punuk style—drilled dots, compass-engraved circles, diamonds with central dots, rigid spurs, and so forth. The Punuk style, dated by archæologists at about A.D. 1000, is still cultivated by the modern Eskimo.

The difference between these two periods is really slight, which means that there was no fundamental change in Aleut culture in nearly two millennia. Aleut archæology, however, is still in its infancy, and perhaps some day new finds will reveal unsuspected developments. This is suggested by some interesting wooden masks, larger than life-size and much decayed, which were discovered in burial caves and rock shelters in the Shumagin Islands and Unalaska. These masks, of which next to nothing is known, are totally different from anything in Eskimo or Aleut art; they are quite realistic and vigorous, have great bulbous noses and wide mouths, and are decorated with simple design and curvilinear ornaments (Fig. 47).

The modern Aleut, or rather the few who survived the fur-traders and smallpox, live in communal dwellings, rectangular underground houses, roofed with domes of driftwood and whale jawbones, covered with earth. Like the Eskimo, they used stone and clay oil lamps and made crude pottery, traveled in kayaks, wore extremely well-made clothes of seal intestines, and conical visor hats of bent wood. They fished with harpoons, nets, and composite bone fishhooks. For warfare they used bows and arrows, spear-throwers, and clubs, besides the slat, rod, and plate armor, which is also worn by other Northwest Coast tribes (Tlingit, Shasta, Hupa, and Klamath), and is like that of the Chinese and Japanese. Their language is related to Eskimo and is unlike any language spoken in Asia, and their contemporary art is reduced to the decoration of their characteristic visor hats, the painting and tattooing of their faces with simple straight lines and dotted circles, and their extraordinary basketry.

The Aleut visor hats (Fig. 48) were made by steaming and bending a thin board into a cone, sewn at the back with sinew, the seam covered by a bone plate. They were often richly decorated with painted abstract or representational designs, or with applications of carved bone and ivory in the shapes of seals and fishes, sea-lion whiskers, and feathers. Such hats were extremely valuable; they were worn only by the nobility and were supposed to give the wearer magic powers in hunting.

The women were particularly adept in the making of grass mats, bags, and baskets, as well as the famous little wallets made to sell to the outside world, which used to be much in demand for their exquisite workmanship and finesse, with as many as forty stitches and thirty-eight rows to the inch, so difficult to weave that it took a woman a whole winter to make one wallet. Aleut basketry was made of thin strips of a special grass (*Elymus mollis*), a sort of wild barley, woven in a twining

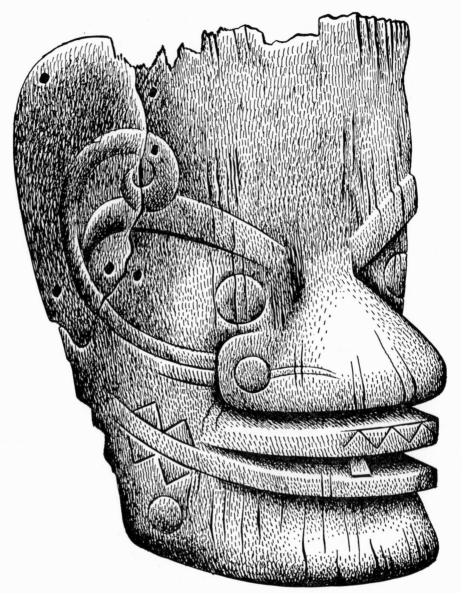

FIG. 47. ABOVE & FACING: *ancient Aleut funerary masks of wood from a rock shelter in the Shumagin Islands (USNM).*

technique and decorated with patterns in colored strips of grass and even silk or wool threads, by the "false embroidery" method; that is, three-strand twined weaving in which one of the elements passes inside the warp so that the design is not visible on the inside. Aleut weaving stands out among the best in the world because of the delicacy and

160

variety of its weaves, produced by the clever manipulation of the warps, to produce extremely fine, gauze-like effects. Such wallets can be seen today only in museums and private collections.

. . .

AN attempt to draw conclusions as to the cultural history of the American Arctic results in a series of problems and contradictions. On one hand, there is no evidence of peoples different from the Eskimo (and the Aleut) ever having occupied the area; the continuity and general

FIG. 48. *Two wooden Aleut visor hats with painted decoration (Ivanov, 1928).*

pattern of Eskimo culture is clear-cut: an early period with a simple art in the central and eastern regions (Dorset), a considerably more complex culture of seafaring people with an elaborate art on the western Arctic coast and the islands of Bering Strait (Ipiutak, Old Bering Sea);

162

a transitional period in the same region (Early Punuk, Birnirk); a middle period with a simpler and more stilted art (Punuk, and, in the central and eastern regions, Thule); and a late or contemporary period, the modern Eskimo, more or less influenced by Punuk and Thule art.

On the other hand, the time and cultural status in which the original Eskimo moved over from Asia are totally unknown; even today the Eskimo straddle the two continents, and they often traveled from Asia and the islands to Siberia and vice versa, at least until political barriers were raised. If we are to believe the anthropologists, the western Arctic should be full of evidences of the many migrations that supposedly took place to populate the Americas; but to date no remains have been found of peoples that preceded the Eskimo; quite the contrary, the trend seems to move from east to west.

Eventually the archæologists will answer these riddles, but there remains a definite positive asset in the art of the Arctic—strong and vigorous, but at the same time refined and delicate in the ancient period, full of realistic charm, originality, and mad fantasy in our days.

CHAPTER II

The Northwest Coast

THE narrow thousand-mile strip of land, countless islands, and fiord-like inlets between Yakutat Bay in southern Alaska and Juan de Fuca Strait in the Columbia River basin constitutes an island of magnificent, spectacular art unlike any other in the Americas. It is the home of a number of Indian tribes who have in common a relatively uniform culture of great complexity, with a unique individuality and surprising technical and artistic achievements, despite the fact that their economy —fishing and hunting—is not generally regarded as conducive to high culture. In fact, in earlier times they lacked the elemental culture traits of agriculture and pottery-making, but possessed the knowledge of metallurgy and textiles. On the other hand, this art has tantalizing similarities to the arts of early Asia and the Pacific islands, but little relation to the arts of the other American Indians. All these factors make the art of the Northwest Coast one of the most challenging puzzles of human culture.

These tribes live in a rather peculiar environment, a sort of warm and luscious virgin Scandinavia. They are literally hemmed in between the sea and the Rocky Mountains, which rise abruptly from the coast to heights of four thousand feet, precluding expansion inland. For such a northerly latitude, the Northwest Coast is a natural paradise with a re-markably mild climate, owing to the warm sea-currents from Japan which wash its length, with an exuberant vegetation produced by con-stant rain and fog. The whole area is covered by forests of giant cedar, fir, spruce, and hemlock, with an undergrowth of ferns, flowers, mosses, and wild berries. Sea food is superabundant; the sea teems with fish— cod, halibut, herring, smelt, candlefish (the oil-yielding eulachon), and particularly salmon, which is caught by the millions and is the staple food and the principal source of wealth. Whales, seal, porpoise, and sea-otter are plentiful, and the beaches are filled with edible mollusks and crustaceans exposed by the tides. The forests have abundant game, but for the Indians it is taboo to eat flesh together with salmon; the forests, furthermore, are populated by dangerous mythical creatures and cannibal spirits.

Most of us are not familiar with the life, customs, and art of the Northwest Coast Indians, but everybody knows their totem poles, their enormous houses of wooden planks, and their great war canoes, sixty-five feet (twenty meters) long, capable of carrying fifty or sixty people. In the old days the men went naked during the summer, but wore fur caps and fiber coats and hats in the winter. The women dressed in gar-ments of cedar-bark fiber and, unlike the majority of the North Ameri-can Indians, went barefoot. They used earrings and lip-plugs of wood inlaid with haliotis shell. Sugar-loaf-deformed heads were a sign of dis-tinction reserved for the nobility. The chiefs wore mountain-goat-wool blankets and elaborate headdresses of carved wood inlaid with shell and ermine skins and crowned with sea-lion bristles or bear-claws. The warriors, whose chief function was to capture slaves, wore plate armor of wooden slats, and brandished sharp daggers of bone, copper, or iron, war-clubs of wood and bone, and pickaxes with jade blades on wooden handles. They practiced strange forms of disposal of the dead: in the north they cremated bodies except for the heart, which they buried; in the south they placed the bodies in wooden coffins on top of high trees or in well-protected caves, but were horrified at the idea of burial in the earth. The Salish placed their dead in canoes raised on logs or trees. Great memorial monuments of cedar carved with the family's crest were then erected near the resting-place of the prominent dead.

To understand the motivating forces behind the sophisticated art and culture of the Northwest Coast Indians it is imperative to review, however briefly, the complicated social and ceremonial concepts that rule their lives. Their society is sharply divided into castes: (1) the wealthy nobility, the best families of the tribe; (2) the commoners, the poor relatives who share the house and do the work; and (3) the slaves, war captives and their descendants, who are a part of a chief's wealth, like his canoes or his blankets. There is neither a concept of tribal unity nor any government. In the old days each village was an autonomous community ruled by the head of the family with the greatest prestige. This led to almost pathological competition and constant clan warfare.

The Northwest Coast Indians had no religion and no gods beyond the belief in spirits of the heavens, the woods, and the underseas. They had no sacred objects, no idols, and no priests except the shamans, or medicine men, who, as spokesmen of the spirits, could perform magic cures. The ceremonial life of the Indians was ruled by totemism, the belief in animal ancestors or, rather, in ancestors of the various clans disguised as animals who became sacred badges or tribal ensigns and gave the clans their surnames. The rich mythology of the Northwest Coast provided the subject-matter for their elaborate art, ceremonies, and dances, which consist in the commemoration or enactment of episodes of their myths, the most treasured property of the clan. Totemism also fixed the degrees of kinship and regulated the marriages, always through the mother's line. The clans were grouped in maternal moieties

166

or "halves," the members of which were forbidden to marry within the clan. For instance, the Haida tribe of Queen Charlotte Islands has, even today, the phratries of the Raven and the Eagle, while the Tlingit of southern Alaska are either Ravens or Wolves, and under no circumstance may a Raven marry another Raven or a Wolf feast another Wolf.

Totemism, the forerunner of heraldry, is the most important trait of the art of the Northwest Coast. The clan's crest is a highly stylized animal that, combined with other individually acquired crests, decorates the property of a clan member. Besides the basic raven, eagle, bear, and wolf crests, there are those of countless sub-clans, such as the beaver, thunderbird, frog, killer whale, shark, salmon, sculpin, hawk, and—less frequently met with—halibut, codfish, skate, seal, sea-lion, owl, gull, goose, auk, mountain goat, starfish, and even the moon, the stars, and the rainbow. These crests have the same function and significance as the rampant lions, two-headed eagles, and unicorns of European heraldry.

Further factors in the development of the artistic culture of these Indians are the superabundance of food, the surplus of which, together with the accumulations of fish-oil, canoes, blankets, and slaves, created an unprecedented wealth; the accumulation of this wealth in the hands of an aristocracy; leisure, which, during the long winter after the summer months of fishing, is used for the production of works of art and in celebrations and dances inside the great smoke-blackened houses by the light of the fires on the central hearths. The most important factor in the development of the art of the Northwest Coast, however, was the aristocracy's immoderate desire, bordering on insanity, for ostentation and competition. Its social standing depended upon prestige and "face," acquired by showing a grandiose contempt for wealth, by giving away or deliberately destroying property to embarrass and discredit a rival chief, who also had to destroy goods of equal or greater value if he wanted to retain his position. This urge reached its grand climax in the *potlatch* festival, given by a chief upon any pretext to distribute his wealth among the hundreds of guests. These gifts were rather invest-ments, for they had to be reciprocated with at least one hundred per cent interest. Furthermore, because clan membership generally fol-lowed the maternal line, children could not inherit their father's prop-erty. In some cases the rivalry among chiefs led to mad extremes: they engaged in catastrophic wars waged with speeches and the destruction of valuables; enormous quantities of salmon oil were poured into the flames of the hearth inside the house, and even set it on fire; canoes were smashed to bits; slaves were killed; and the monetary units called "coppers" were broken and thrown into the sea.

The most important tribes, or those particularly distinguished by their art styles, are, from north to south: the *Tlingit, Tsimshian, Haida, Kwakiutl,* and *Nootka* (see map, Fig. 35). Although they speak dif-ferent languages, their arts and cultures are so similar that only a spe-cialist can tell them apart. Southward and toward the interior plateau, on the Frazer, Thompson, upper Columbia, and Clarke rivers, live the *Salish* tribes, whose art shows marked differences from that of the Northwest Coast Indians proper. Specifically, the following charac-teristics can be detected in the art of these peoples, differences caused by specialization and personality rather than by cultural factors:

Tlingit and *Tsimshian:* refined art, naturalistic and subtle, with great sensibility in the manner of carving. The Chilkat branch of the Tlingit makes unique textiles of mountain-goat wool and cedar-bark fiber. Tlingit women weave baskets of excellent design. The Tsimshian have carved some of the finest totem poles.

Haida: more hieratic, conservative art within the traditional style. They are distinguished by their monumental sculptures in cedar, great totem poles, and mural paintings. Only the Haida carve slate.

Kwakiutl: a vigorous, daring, and inventive art, with a great dramatic sense, expressed in impressive masks of mythical personages and fantastic animals, often provided with mechanical contraptions so that they move. The line and forms of Kwakiutl art are bold, sharp, and dynamic, and their sculptures show great freedom and liveliness in execution, leaving the marks of the carving tools visible.

Nootka, the most southerly group: a simpler, more mechanical art, with little developed sculpture. The lines and forms are sharp and precise, making a liberal use of paint in bright colors on flat boards. Typically Nootka are the wolf-mask helmets.

Salish: fine imbricated baskets and mantles of fiber and dog's hair, with simple geometric designs. Their sculptures in wood and clubs of bone are in a more primitive style, without the characteristic rounded forms of the other Northwest Coast tribes. They are strongly reminiscent of Polynesian and Melanesian art rather than North American. They have in common with the cultures of the South Pacific other tantalizing points that will be discussed later.

AMONG the basic motifs of Northwest Coast art the human figure is of paramount importance, in images either of chiefs or of spirits such as Tsonoqua, the Wild Woman of the Woods, and Nengase, the Bear Woman, or animal spirits like Wasco, the wolf-shaped sea monster, and Sisiutl, the double-headed serpent. Equally important are representations of the totemic animals used as crests by the nobility, often extremely stylized and with their component parts juggled in a way that renders the animal unrecognizable. Sometimes only certain identifying features are represented. They are further distorted and rearranged to fit into any shape: circular, to decorate a hat or a round dish; rectangular, for the sides of a box; lance-shaped to fit a paddle. Often the animals are humanized and can be differentiated from men only by their

animal ears. The animals most often encountered are the bear, recognizable by its large nostrils, paws, teeth, and often protruding tongue; the beaver, sometimes shown gnawing a stick, with large incisors, a hachured wide tail, and hat of rank; the wolf, identified by a longer muzzle, elevated snout, and long tail; the raven, eagle, hawk, and crane, clearly differentiated by the shapes of their beaks; the killer whale, in-

FIG. 49. *Heraldic motifs of the Haida Indians:* FACING, *a sea monster and a shark;* ABOVE, *thunderbird (Mallery, 1893).*

dicated by its prominent dorsal fin; the frog, by its toothless mouth; the shark, by its downward-curved mouth full of sharp, triangular teeth and rows of crescent-shaped gill-slits; and the sculpin or bullhead, by its large head, mouth turned up at the corners, and two spines over the nostrils. Such more ambitious compositions as totem poles show these motifs combined to relate an episode in a myth.

A characteristic feature of this art is the concept of bilateral representation: splitting an animal into halves and laying it open to show both sides; two profiles facing to make a full-face mask (to represent mammals), or united by the back with two profiles facing away from each other (to represent birds) (Fig. 49). A shark is dissected and the pieces rearranged; first the body without the head is split along the spine, and the halves placed on each side of the head, which is seen from underneath. The eyes are moved to the underside and new nostrils added, while the true nostrils become purely decorative, on each side of a row of gill-slits. The principle of showing animals as if dissected makes more logical the fact that, like the Eskimo, the Northwest Coast artists represent animals sometimes as if they were transparent, with parts of the skeleton and digestive system visible (Fig. 50).

An ever present motif in flat carvings, painted on skins and boards, or woven in textiles, is a squatting figure of a man, bear, or beaver, shown in front view with arms and legs outstretched on each side of the body in frog fashion (Figs. 51, 52, 53, 54, 55). This fascinating figure, which shows up throughout this book, is characteristic of many ancient arts, particularly in eastern Asia, Indonesia, and the South Seas,

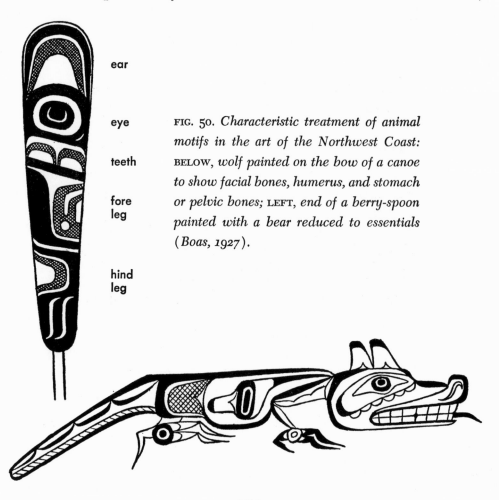

ear

eye

teeth

fore
leg

hind
leg

FIG. 50. *Characteristic treatment of animal motifs in the art of the Northwest Coast:* BELOW, *wolf painted on the bow of a canoe to show facial bones, humerus, and stomach or pelvic bones;* LEFT, *end of a berry-spoon painted with a bear reduced to essentials* (*Boas, 1927*).

as well as along the Pacific coast of the American continent. It would be premature to state either that its appearance on the Northwest Coast is owing to diffusion or that it is simply the bilateral representation of an ancestral squatting figure seen in profile.

FIG. 51. *Beaver crest on a flannel shirt* (WSM).

These motifs are carved in high and low relief or incised or painted on flat surfaces. The Northwest Coast artists show a masterful sense of handling the complicated, irregular, rounded shapes, building them up with a careful regard for their relative values of form, relief, and color.

173

FIG. 52. *Bear crest with multiple human faces, woven in a Chilkat shirt of mountain-goat wool and cedar bark* (MfVH) (*Fuhrmann, 1922*).

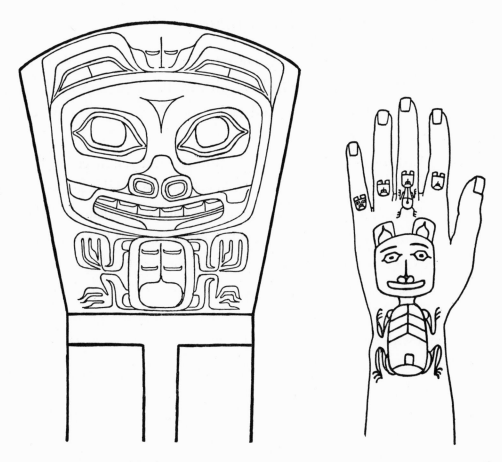

FIG. 53. LEFT: *Grizzly-bear crest engraved on a copper (PMV) (Ravenhill, 1938)*;
RIGHT: *hand of a Haida Indian tattooed with the bear totem (Mallery, 1893).*

FIG. 54. *Haida slate pipe (Fuhrmann, 1922).*

They are able to carve a seventy-foot totem pole and the handle of a horn spoon only three or four inches high with the same sense of balance in forms and proportions, and with a peculiar, surging, upward vitality.

The basic material used is the plentiful red and yellow cedar, the carving of which, in technical skill and in magnitude, reaches unprecedented heights of importance in the range of native American art. The Indians were, and still are, unexcelled carpenters, able with only wedges and adzes to obtain great boards for the construction of enormous houses. Out of single giant trunks they carved graceful canoes with fore and aft prolonged upwards, decorated with mythical serpents, and with sails of matting like the great canoes of Asia. They devised a unique manner of making square boxes out of a single board, which was bent by steaming, after the corners were thinned by a beveled groove. These boxes are often beautifully carved and painted with totemic motifs (Fig. 56).

In wood the Northwest Coast peoples carved all sorts of objects: oil and food dishes of every size and design, as large as canoes or small as card-trays, either in the shape of animals or carved in low relief in the traditional style; ceremonial rattles used by the shamans to call the spirits, of which the most characteristic type is intricately carved with a scene of the Raven Who Stole the Sun Myth (Pl. 20); the amalaid, the frontal ornament of the chiefs' headdresses of ermine skins and sealion bristles, carved out of wood with some totemic motif, painted and inlaid with plaques of iridescent haliotis shell (Color Plate D).

Also of wood were carved masks of the most varied types, realistic or fantastic, used in ceremonial dances to enact the episodes telling when ancestral totemic animals came down to earth and took off their masks to become men. The Tlingit and Tsimshian carved naturalistic masks with sensitive features, lightly decorated with designs painted

FIG. 55. *Carved flat section of cor-
ner house-post, Haida, from Queen
Charlotte Islands* (USNM).

177

FIG. 56. *Food box of painted bent wood, Tlingit (WSM).*

with red cinnabar, turquoise blue, and black. The Kwakiutl carried realism to the extent of giving the impression of cutting a man's head

178

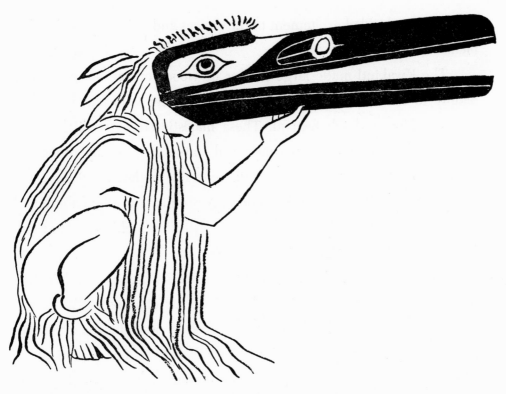

FIG. 57. *Raven dance, part of the Hamatsa (cannibal spirit) ceremony of the Kwakiutl. The articulated mask is of wood, the dress of white cedar bark.*

in view of the public, using a wooden mask with real hair and with a gruesome deathlike expression. The fantastic masks represent mythological characters, cannibal spirits, great birds of prey (Fig. 57), bears, wolves, sharks, and even mosquitoes, conceived with a dramatic, truculent imagination calculated to evoke the supernatural and cause awe. The Kwakiutl have a genius for mechanical contraptions to make trick masks with movement controlled by weights, pulleys, and strings: fantastic birds that snap their beaks, or split through the middle revealing a human face hidden in the interior (Pl. 16); masks that open and close their eyes, with removable mouths, or with telescoping noses; and double masks representing a chief in a placid and in an angry mood. They also make headdresses and puppets with parts animated by strings to give added excitement to the dances and to introduce the element of surprise.

The Kwakiutl made large statues of wood for various purposes, mainly to commemorate the greatness of a chief who had given an epoch-making potlatch festival. These majestic statues, which often have the dignity of European medieval statuary, generally represent the chief holding a large copper (Pl. 12). The potlatch statues were placed on top of the chief's own house. A peculiar variety of these are the "ridicule" statues or poles, made to order for a chief whose rival has not measured up to the circumstances.

The art of colossal woodcarving reaches its highest level in the making of totem poles, equivalent to the coats of arms of European nobility, monumental heraldic crests erected to proclaim the ancestral aristocracy of the family, showing the symbols of its component clans and relating its totemic myth. Great and imposing, a totem pole cost a fortune to erect, for famous carvers were hired and entertained during the long months it took to carve the pole. Often the prospective owner of the pole had to wait until he had saved enough wealth to invite the prominent families for the inauguration. The carvers worked in secrecy, perhaps to increase the expectation of the festival given to inaugurate the pole. Should the master carver feel he lacked the skill to make a pole worthy of his generous employer, he reserved the right to call in someone else, keeping, however, all the credit for himself (Barbeau, 1930).

There were famous totem-pole carvers in the nineteenth century. Barbeau (1930) mentions the greatest: Haesem-hlyawn, a Tsimshian who died in 1868, and his pupil Hlamee, who supposedly introduced paint to complement his poles, and who died in 1900. They are the creators of some of the best poles on the upper Skeena River in British

Columbia, where some of the tallest, oldest, and most beautiful poles still stand. The Haida Indians of the Queen Charlotte Islands have a reputation as the best carvers of totem poles, and the art is usually associated with them, but since they became Christians they have ceased to erect poles and the majority of the old ones have been sold, stolen, or destroyed. Fine sculptors are living today, however; in 1938 the eighty-year-old Haida sculptor John Wallace, with his son Fred, went to the San Francisco World's Fair and after months of work carved the thirty-foot totem pole now in the Museum of Modern Art in New York.

The carvers plan the design carefully, subordinating it to the cylindrical form of the tree trunk, and begin to work with well-sharpened iron adzes, finishing with knives and chisels. In the north the surface is smoothed with sharkskin used as sandpaper, but the southern Kwakiutl like to preserve the hammered-copper texture left by the adze-marks.

There are various sorts of totem poles: (1) those which constitute the central post of old-style Haida houses, with an oval opening cut out to serve as a door (Pl. 9); (2) the tall, slender memorial poles carved with legendary and genealogical motifs (Fig. 58); and (3) the "grave fathers," funerary monuments of two types. The first type is a pole supporting a carved coffin, a variety of which has two columns and a coffin large enough for two or more bodies; the second type is a sort of vertical coffin, a single pole channeled in the back to receive the corpse, which is sealed in with boards. From these "grave fathers" it could be inferred that the totem-pole concept evolved from its funerary function to a purely heraldic one during the nineteenth century, when the culture of the Northwest Coast flourished. The importance attached to the size and magnificence of totem poles in the days when the chiefs prospered by the fur trade is well illustrated by the story of Hladerh, chief of the Wolves, who had Sispegoot, chief of the Finback Whales, mur-

181

Raven, the culture hero who released the
sun and the moon to their places in the
sky and made daylight ——————————————→

The Woman Mother of Frogs holding her child —————→

Her Frog Husband ——————————————————→

Mink, the companion of Raven —————————→

Raven again ——————————————————→

The whale in whose stomach lived Raven
and Mink, eating the fish it swallowed.
The whale holds a seal in its mouth and
its blow hole is indicated by a small
face over the head ——————————————→

"Raven-at-the-Head-of-the-Naas," the
grandfather of Raven and mythological
chief of the Raven clan ————————————→

FIG. 58. *The famous Seattle Totem Pole, carved in the mid-
nineteenth century and erected in the Tlingit village of
Tongass, southeast Alaska, in memory of a woman of the
Kininook family of the Raven clan. It was brought to Seattle
in 1899 and stood in Pioneer Square until 1938, when it was
damaged by fire. A modern replica of the pole was then
erected in its place. (Viola E. Garfield; The Seattle Totem
Pole, University of Washington, Extension Series, 1940.)*

dered for his attempt to erect a pole higher than his. Later Hladerh compelled another Wolf chief to shorten his pole twice, much to his humiliation (Barbeau, 1930).

The question of whether the Indians of the Northwest Coast had an art in stone is relevant because enough isolated individual examples exist to establish the fact that they did carve stone. Many museums own fine pestles and mauls, stone bowls, and palettes decorated in the traditional style. There is a fine stone totem pole from Vancouver Island in the Royal Ontario Museum of Archæology in Ottawa; a green serpentine pipe in the shape of a frog, from Kluckwan, Alaska, in the Museum of the American Indian in New York; and a beautiful stone mask from the river Naas in the Musée de l'Homme in Paris. Perhaps more such stone-carvings will be discovered in the future and the scope of stone-carving better established. The antiquity of this art of stone-carving is suggested by the objects of stone in the British Museum, brought by Captain Cook in 1778 (Fig. 59).

An interesting style of slate-carving is practiced only by the Haida. This slate is a compact carboniferous shale of intense black color, called argillite, capable of taking a high polish, and is found only in the Queen Charlotte Islands. Of this the Haida make totem-pole models, elaborate pipes, boat models with oarsmen, carved platters, and boxes with lids. The art of slate-carving dates from about the middle of the past century, and since that time it has been practiced chiefly for export. Many early examples show a strong Russian influence. Despite the commercial purpose of these carvings, they are always good examples of the masterful technique and austere good taste of the Haida. Some, like the famous Bear Mother, carved in 1883 by one Skaowskeay, now in the United States National Museum in Washington, reach the level of great works of art. Slate-carving is still practiced, and the last of the old Haida sculptors, Louis Collingson, of Skidgate Mission, Queen Char-

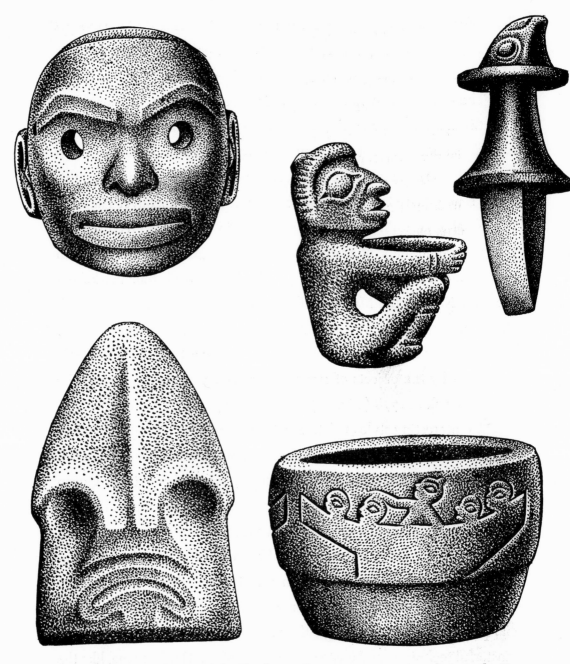

FIG. 59. *Stone sculpture of the Northwest Coast:* ABOVE LEFT, *mask from the Nass River (Ml'H);* BELOW LEFT, *pile-driver, Kwakiutl (Collection of W. C. Arensberg);* CENTER, *figure holding a bowl (BrM);* ABOVE RIGHT, *"slave-killer" from British Columbia collected in 1778 by Captain Cook (BrM);* BELOW RIGHT, *ancient bowl from Bella Bella, Kwakiutl (PMV).*

184

lotte Islands, at the age of sixty, was still carving fine model totem poles (Harryngton, 1949).

Other materials used for carving are bone, walrus ivory, and horn, out of which the Indians make personal ornaments and implements as beautifully carved as the finest objects of wood. Out of horn, which is softened by boiling to give it the proper shape, they make delicate bowls and fine, elegant spoons, the handles of which are often as elaborate as the most complicated totem poles.

Metallurgy has long been practiced on the Northwest Coast, perhaps since pre-European times. The Indians made all sorts of objects out of native hammered copper from natural nuggets: daggers, masks, rattles, bracelets, and particularly the so-called "coppers," which are oversize monetary units symbolic of a chief's wealth. These coppers are simple but harmonious forms of heavy sheet copper, averaging two feet in length, and are decorated with engraved and painted designs in the classic style. There are famous coppers known by their individual names and histories, and coppers worth as much as four thousand blankets are mentioned. The Haida still make bracelets, engraved with fine designs, out of copper or of silver obtained from dollars hammered out.

Painting was practiced extensively to decorate the great wooden boards inside and outside the houses (Pl. 18), canoes, skin garments, and drum skins, and in general to finish all works of sculpture. The motifs employed were the usual totemic and mythological subjects, painted with precise lines and areas of flat color in black (soot), red (cinnabar), turquoise blue (copper salts), and, more recently, commercial orange, yellow, and green. The technique was that of oil paints, the colors being mixed on a stone palette with oil from chewed salmon eggs. The wood surface was given a coat of this oil, and the paint applied with a brush of cedar provided with bristles.

All the arts described above are reserved for men only. The women may only make the skin garments and weave baskets, hats, mats, and the famous Chilkat blankets. The baskets are made of spruce roots and the inner bark of cedar, and are decorated simply with well-balanced, sedate, geometric designs, an art at which the Tlingit women are masters. There are some examples of basketry with representations of totemic animals, canoes, whales, and so forth, particularly among the Haida and Nootka. The Wasco, an inland Salish group, weave baskets in a style strongly reminiscent of the South Pacific islanders (Pl. 22).

A most extraordinary development for a people so far removed from the American area of textiles is the art of weaving elaborate garments of wool and fiber. The Chilkat branch of the Tlingit weave mantles, shirts, aprons, and leggings out of cedarbark fiber and mountain-goat wool. These are done in a simple tapestry technique with the fingers and without a loom. They are decorated with heraldic motifs copied from models painted on boards, with the various elements of design guided by patterns cut out of cedarbark. These motifs—human faces and parts of totemic animals—are used as decorative elements for the sake of design alone and are often scrambled so that they have no specific meaning. They are excellent examples of composition, however, and show an innate sense of balanced design, in contrasting masses and lines of white, the natural color of mountain-goat wool; black, dyed with hemlock bark; golden ocher from wool moss; and blue-green from copper salts (Pl. 19). Chilkat blankets are still being made, and they fetch high prices in the limited Alaskan market. At the turn of the century the Indians took to making effective mantles of commercial blue or black broadcloth with applied designs cut out of red broadcloth and decorated with dentallium shells and mother-of-pearl buttons.

The age and origin of the art of the Northwest Coast are a deep mystery. The Indians had their first contacts with Europeans during the middle of the eighteenth century, with the Russian expeditions of Bering and Chirikov, and later with such Spanish explorers as Malaspina and Moziño, who sailed from Mexico, the English captains Cook, Dixon, Mackenzie, and Vancouver, and the French La Pérouse. The nineteenth century ushered in a boom with the establishment of advanced commercial outposts in Alaska and British Columbia. Iron tools became plentiful, and the Indian chiefs profited from the new sources of income, with the result that the art of the Indians flourished. The boom did not survive into the twentieth century; the Indians soon lost their rights over the timberlands and fishing grounds and had to fish for the canneries. Their culture finally received a death-blow when the Canadian government, for good or evil, forbade their potlatches, around which their social organization was built. There are still fine old artists left on the Northwest Coast, but it is only a question of time before their art will fall into the realm of archæology.

A lively controversy has raged over the antiquity of totemic art, and the most cautious anthropologists date it as post-eighteenth-century. The evidence hinges on whether the early explorers did or did not see totem poles or other woodcarvings, and almost every author jumps to the conclusion that the golden age of woodcarving was the result of the introduction of European iron tools among the Indians. Archæology, which usually settles such questions, has given to date only negative results, which is to be expected because the explorations have been conducted on too small a scale and because an art in wood leaves no trace of its existence in a rainy, humid climate. The established duration of a totem pole is from forty to seventy years, for it is abandoned to the ravages of the weather from the time it is created.

The early explorers were not much concerned with Indian art, and only a few left drawings of objects identical with those of today.[1] Objects of carved wood and stone, collected by the captains Cook, Dixon, and Malaspina, and preserved in the British Museum and the Ethnographic Museum of Madrid, are identical to those made today. This would mean that one hundred and fifty years ago the style of the Northwest Coast was already in existence, fully developed and with its present character. Such a complex and peculiar style cannot possibly develop overnight without passing through a long evolutive process, and it is left to the reader to guess whether it took another hundred and fifty years or five hundred or even a millennium to reach maturity. Boas (1927) is inclined to believe that the more elaborate forms of totemic art developed from the idea of exalting a rank and had their origin in north British Columbia, while the more geometric arts of Vancouver Island and of the Salish represent an older style. The use of geometric designs in the basketry of the northerly Tlingit supports this theory, but leaves unexplained the source of the super-stylized totemic motifs, made of curves and irregular rounded shapes, more reminiscent of the arts of pre-Buddhist China and the Marquesas Islands than of the arts of the American Indians.

The introduction of iron tools by Europeans is often advanced to explain the flourishing of this art. Abundant iron tools must certainly have intensified the artistic production, but the experience of other peoples—the Melanesians, Polynesians, and ancient Mexicans, all excellent sculptors who worked with tools of stone, bone, and shell—teaches us that metal instruments are not essential to, and do not im-

[1] Such as Bartlett's naïve sketch of a Haida house with a gigantic totem pole (1791), the carved house-posts in Cook's atlas (1785), the colossal bear tomb and the decorated Nootka hats in the Mexican engravings of Malaspina (1789) and of the anonymous author of the *Voyage of the Schooners Sutil y Mexicana* (1792), Dixon's carved dish from Queen Charlotte Islands (1789), and so forth (Paalen, 1944).

prove, the quality of sculptures. In New Guinea, for instance, the carvings made with metal instruments are inferior to those made in the old manner. The explanation for the apparently contradictory statement that decadence often coincides with the introduction of modern technical means is simply that along with these means come negative factors that undermine the traditional culture in general and are subsequently reflected in the quality of artistic production. Furthermore, even if knowledge of metal tools were indispensable to fine woodcarving, there is good reason to believe that the Indians of the Northwest Coast had iron before the Europeans brought it to the area. Captain Cook observed that they had iron tools not of European make and was amazed at the dexterous use of them, which only the "longest practice" could provide. He concludes that from the abundance of such iron tools it must be inferred that they obtained them from other Indian tribes, who were in turn in contact, directly or indirectly, with Europeans (Paalen, 1944).

The problem of the origin of the art of the Northwest Coast is complicated by the extraordinary number of traits from Asia and the Pacific and the paucity of traits common to other North American Indian cultures. A list of the most obvious of these traits will serve better to illustrate this fact:

1. Great houses of wood with central totemic posts like those of the Maori of New Zealand, the Naga of Assam, the Bataks of Sumatra, and other peoples of Asia.

2. Totemic posts with figures of men and animals arranged in series, such as are found in New Zealand, New Ireland, New Guinea, Luzon Island in the Philippines, among the Bataks, and elsewhere (Figs. 11, 12). The principle of heads arranged in series is found in the Shang bones of early China and among the Maya in the great stelæ of Quiriguá and the temple of Kabah in Yucatán.

189

3. The principle of bilateral representation of mythological or heraldic animals, characteristic of the Amur River area in Siberia and of archaic China (Fig. 10).

4. Eyes or human faces in the joints of arms and legs (Fig. 8), an idea typical of the Scythians of the Ordos River in Inner Mongolia and of the Polynesians and Melanesians, as in the tattooing of the Marquesas Islanders, whose art bears other striking resemblances to that of the Northwest Coast. Eyes in the joints also appear in the shell gorgets of Oklahoma.

5. The squatting figure, single or multiple, with arms and legs in frog fashion, typical of early China, southeast Asia, Polynesia, Melanesia, and even primitive Australia, as well as Central America, Colombia, Ecuador, the Amazon basin, Peru, and down to Patagonia (Figs. 51, 52, 53, 54, 55).

6. The system of excentric curves adapted to rounded rectangular shapes, typical of the art of early China, of the Ainu of northern Japan, of the Marquesas Islands, New Britain, and—in America—of "Olmec," Maya, and Chavín art.

7. The use of bell-shaped pestles or mauls with peculiar handles, which spreads from New Guinea across the whole of Polynesia. In America they reappear on the Northwest Coast, in California, Mexico, the Antilles, and Costa Rica (Fig. 30).

8. Use, among the Salish, of stone and whalebone clubs identical with the *mere* and *kotiate* of the Maori of New Zealand. Some examples in the United States National Museum are identical in every respect with the Maori clubs, and it is guessed they were obtained by the Salish from whalers who came from the South Seas.

9. The extensive use of haliotis shell for inlay in wood, typical of New Zealand and other South Pacific islands.

Considering the fact that migration across the Pacific is not so impossible as was formerly thought (the records of the past one hundred and fifty years show that more than fifty Asiatic junks have been driven to the American coast), it becomes more and more difficult to believe that this great art is purely a local development. It is at present impossible to determine the exact connections among the Northwest Coast, Asia, and the Pacific, or the time when such elements came across the ocean. The simultaneous existence of two basic styles, totally different in concept and origin, is plain, however, on the Northwest Coast: (1) the simple geometric designs of the Salish, the Nootka, and the Kwakiutl, and those which survive in Tlingit basketry, rather like those of the Californians, Athapascans, and Algonquians, probably representing the original native styles, and (2) the elaborate totemic art with its rounded complex shapes, elaborate symbolism, and technical mastery in woodcarving, textiles, and metallurgy. This latter was perhaps imported in a more archaic form by a foreign people of higher culture, later undergoing an intensive development alongside the increasing predominance of an aristocracy suffering from megalomania. These factors, helped by the relative prosperity, technical skill, and fantasy of its creators, produced a vigorous, sophisticated art that stands alone on the American continent.

CHAPTER III

The Far West

THE countless tribes that formerly owned California and parts of Oregon and Nevada are among the most timid and primitive on the continent. They are extremely interesting because they represent some of the most backward examples of human culture—seed-gatherers on a pre-agricultural, pre-ceramic level—with, however, a fine art and a highly developed technology. Some, like the Chumash, Gabriellino, Fernandeno, and Juaneno, of the Los Angeles area, have become extinct; the pitiful remnants of others lead a precarious life in a modern world that is not theirs; others, like the Pomo, who live north of San Francisco, are famous as the makers of the finest baskets in the Americas.

The peoples of the Far West lived in isolation and apparently developed independently, having little or no contact with their neighbors of the Northwest Coast, the Plains, or the Southwest, and possessing a unified culture and a characteristic art despite the fact that their linguistic affiliations are varied and show intrusive groups of remote origin.[1]

[1] Linguistically they belong to two basic groups: the *Hokan* (Karok, Shasta, Pomo, Salina, Chumash, Yuma, Mohave); and *Penutian* (Wintun, Maidu, Miwok, Yokut, etc.).

Their economy could hardly have been simpler: their staple foods consisted of acorns (the flour of which they baked into a sort of bread), wild chestnuts, piñon nuts, roots, and tubers, which they collected and stored in beautifully woven baskets. They also gathered mollusks and fished with hooks of mother-of-pearl and haliotis (abalone) shell identical with those used by the Polynesians. Pottery-making was unknown to them, and the only means they knew of cooking their food was to boil it in waterproof baskets or in stone bowls into which hot stones were dropped. They lived in simple shelters or semi-subterranean huts, round or rectangular, covered with grass.

In former times they went naked, their bodies painted or tattooed, the men wearing only a short skirt of buckskin, the women a simple fringe of fiber in front. Some tribes wore a small basketry skullcap to protect their foreheads from the strap with which they carried their great baskets. The tribes of the Sierra wore mantles of rabbit skin during the winter, and in the American Museum of Natural History in New York there is a Californian feather mantle that resembles the feather capes of the Polynesians. For their festivals they wore necklaces of haliotis and dentallium shells, headdresses of buckskin and feather mosaic, and a short bar through the septum of the nose. Their ceremonial ornaments show tantalizing resemblances to those of certain South Pacific islands.

Their religion consisted in the cult of the spirits of nature, with ceremonial sacrifices of eagles to consecrate their feathers. Magic dances of fire-walking were performed by dancers intoxicated with *toloache*, a drug-plant. They practiced shamanism and ceremonial initiations with dry (sand) painting, and cremated their dead. They were

There are some intrusive linguistic groups in the area: *Algonquian* (Wiyot, Yurok); *Dene* (Athapascan, Hupa); *Shoshonean* (in the Great Basin: Nevada, Idaho, Utah); and *Yakon* (on the Oregon coast: Coos, Takelma, etc.).

extremely docile toward the whites, and were quickly Christianized. They were the Indians most deeply affected by contact with Europeans: their number, which in 1770 was around 133,000, had dropped to 16,350 by 1910.

Little is known of the antecedents of these peoples; on the islands and coast of Santa Barbara and Los Angeles, burials have been found of the ancient inhabitants, the ancestors of the Chumash and Gabriellinos, with stone vessels, pipes, and amulets of steatite (soapstone)

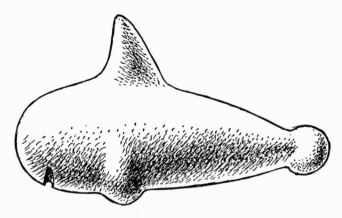

FIG. 60. *Steatite whale from St. Nicholas Island, southern California (MAIHF).*

ornamented with little disks of shell glued with asphalt. These amulets are often surprisingly realistic or fantastic sculptures of whales (Fig. 60) and fish, and constitute the only naturalistic art manifestation of the entire area. The contemporary Hupa of northern California make great blades of chipped obsidian for use as ceremonial insignia, and conical or bell-shaped stone pestles for crushing nuts, the shape being characteristic of Polynesia and Melanesia (Fig. 30). It is impossible not to mention the fact that parallels between the cultures of the Californians and those of the South Sea islanders are closer than those with other American Indians; they have in common such characteristic traits as feather mosaics on basketry, feather capes, bell-shaped stone pestles, fishhooks of shell, shell money, fire-walking, gorgets of iridescent shell, pendants of abalone, cut-out feather ornaments, wooden pillows (used in the sweat-houses by the Yurok and Hupa), net bags, bamboo flutes (Mission Indians), boomerang (rabbit-killing sticks of the Diegueño), and anular stone mace-heads.

The art for which the California Indians are specially distinguished is basketmaking, in which they have maintained undeniable supremacy, not only because of the high technical quality, but also because of the elegance, simplicity, and good taste of their baskets and designs. Every known technique of basket-weaving is used in the area: the imbricated double strand predominating in the north (a technique typical of the Northwest Coast), the spiral weave technique typical of the south, with a mingling of both techniques in the center. The raw materials employed are fibers, roots, fern stems, always in their natural colors: cream, yellow, light brown, sepia, and black. The Pomo Indians, master basketmakers, use the roots of sedge, willow, spruce, nut pine, and bracken; the bark of shoots of redbud and hazel, and California flax stems and grapevines. The general shapes of the baskets are conical or semi-spheric bowls, but there are also oval and spheric ones. In the south the Tulare and Kern River Indians make vase- and bottle-shaped baskets.

The decorative motifs are generally geometric, of great simplicity, predominantly combinations of triangles, rectangles, and zigzags, admirably composed, though some use is made of stylized designs of men, animals, or plants. The geometric designs have identifying names, such as the following recorded among the Maidu: fish teeth, earthworm, flying geese, quail, duck's wing, millipede, grasshopper leg, raccoon, feathers, eye, flower, pine cone, vine, flint arrow points, and mountains and clouds (Dixon, 1900).

The most famous basketmakers are the Pomo Indians of the coast north of San Francisco, but other fine artists are the Klamath of Oregon,

the Paiute of Nevada, and the greater part of the California tribes—
Yurok, Karok, Hupa, Shasta, Miwok, Maidu, Yokut, Washo, Kern
River, Tulare, and the Mission Indians (Luiseño, Cahuilla, Serrano,
Cupeño, Diegueño, etc.).

The Pomo make baskets in all sizes, from minute ones the size of
a pea to great baskets over a yard in diameter, both extremes as technical *tours de force*, without ever losing the sense of proportionate design. The Pomo are also the authors of the famous "gift" or "jewel"
baskets covered with feather mosaic, made as wedding gifts. These
baskets are among the objects of Indian art most highly prized by
collectors. They are small, shallow or jar-shaped bowls totally covered
with brilliant feather mosaic in yellow, red, orange, black, and metallic
green,[2] with additional ornaments of small shell disks and pendants of
haliotis or mother-of-pearl (color plate facing page 136).

The names of famous California basketmakers were at the turn
of the century well known among collectors, and their works fetched
high prices. There was, for instance, Mary Benson, a Pomo Indian
woman who made the finest baskets known to date, and the noted
Washo basket-maker Datsolalee, or Luisa Kayser, who gave names
to her baskets (Fig. 61). One of her most beautiful works, a coiled
bowl only five inches high, now in the University Museum of Philadelphia, was called "Slaying of the Snow Birds," and commemorated
a famine during which the Washo Indians were forced to feed on their
beloved birds. It is decorated with a rhythmic pattern of black triangles
on cream ground. It was woven in the spring of 1904 in thirty-nine days.
Someone calculated that twenty thousand stitches (twenty-five to the
running inch of coil) went into its making.[3]

[2] The red feathers come from the throats and scalps of woodpeckers, the yellow
from the breast of the meadowlark, the green from the scalp of mallard ducks, the
orange from orioles, and the black from quail.

[3] *University of Philadelphia Museum Bulletin*, Vol. III, nos. 3–4 (1932).

FIG. 61. ABOVE, *Washo baskets made by Datsolalee (the middle one has the meaning "clear sky, good weather")* (*UMP, USNM, after Mason, 1904*); BELOW, *great coiled Paiute storage basket made by Lucy Tellez (IACB).*

Minor artistic manifestations of the Far West Indians are, besides the rather magnificent feather and fur mosaic headdresses and dancing wands of the Hupa, the shell-money banks and spoons of elkhorn, carved wooden spatulas, and head-scratchers of bone, often decorated with simple incised geometric designs (Fig. 62).

The Indians of the Far West present the curious case of fossilization of a rather primitive stage of cultural development, probably taking place at least two or three thousand years ago. Ancient remains

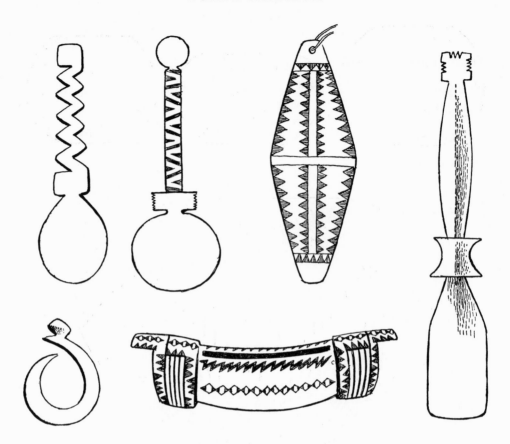

FIG. 62. *Californian implements:* ABOVE, *elkhorn spoon, Maidu (AMNH); elkhorn spoon, Hupa (USNM); head-scratcher of bone, Hupa (USNM);* BELOW, *shell fishhook, southern California (AMNH); elkhorn bank, Hupa (after Kelly, 1930);* RIGHT, *wooden spatula, Maidu (AMNH).*

have been found all over California—on an island in Humboldt Bay, in the Buena Vista Lake (upper San Joaquin River valley), in the Santa Barbara region and the Channel Islands, in the Sacramento Valley, near San Francisco Bay, on the San Dieguito plateau, at La Jolla, in the desert, on the former shores of dry Lake Mohave, and in the Pinto Basin. Skeletons of longheaded people have been found in some places, as have animal-shaped stone clubs (Humboldt Bay), steatite tubular pipes and charms, fishhooks of shell and bone, harpoon points of antler, and well-made points of obsidian, slate, and flint. These remains, however modest and unimpressive, not unlike the implements of the modern California Indians, form a rather continuous archæological sequence, which, it is calculated, goes back to at least the second millennium B.C. or even earlier (Martin, Quimby, and Collier, 1947).[4]

[4] For chronological chart and bibliography of the archæology of California see pp. 440, 441, of work cited.

CHAPTER IV

The Southwest

THE Indians of the Southwest are today restricted to small parts of New Mexico and Arizona, but formerly they occupied these states in their entirety and spread over most of Utah, parts of Colorado and Nevada, and far south into Mexico. The zone is a high mountainous plateau, with forests of pines, cedars, juniper, and piñon among vast stretches of desert, with cactus, agave, and sagebrush. It can be made fertile by irrigation and can sustain a large population. The Southwest is inhabited today by many peoples with a rather homogeneous artistic culture despite the fact that there are among them enormous differences of physical type, material culture, economy, and language. Some, like the Pueblo Indians, are sedentary agriculturists with an ancient and highly developed cultural tradition; others are nomadic shepherds like the Navajo or hunters like the Apaches (both Athapascans originating in the far, sub-arctic north), ferocious warriors much feared by their neighbors. There are also peaceful, primitive agriculturists, hunters, and gatherers, who live in the desert, in the basins of the Colorado and Gila rivers; these include the Pima, Papago, Maricopa, Yuma, Mohave, Walpai, Havasupai, and Yavapai (see map, Fig. 63).

Even among the Pueblo group there are so many different lan-

FACING: *Central motif of a painted elkskin from the Central Plains, Sioux or Arapaho. This was certainly painted by the artist-author of the famous skin in the Collection of Miss Amelia White of Santa Fe (Plate 47). (Drawn from scattered data in Cosío Pijoan, 1941.)*

guages that they use Spanish to talk among themselves. For instance, the Hopi (one village excepted) are Shoshone; those of Acoma, Cochiti, Santo Domingo, San Felipe, Sia, and Santa Ana are Keres; the Taos, Isleta, Picuris, and Sandia are Tigua; the Jemez and Zuñi are isolated groups without known linguistic connections; and the Nambe, Tesuque, San Ildefonso, San Juan, Santa Clara, and the Hopi of Hano are Tewas. All these peoples live in a restricted zone and are close neighbors, presenting the remarkable situation of many peoples of the most varied ethnic affiliations having a common artistic culture.

THE ARCHÆOLOGY OF THE SOUTHWEST

THE oldest traces of early man on the American continent have been found in the Southwest. The best-known are the stone spear points of Folsom, Yuma, and Sandia, which already show an advanced technique and characteristic styles (Fig. 1). These points have been found in caves associated with bones of extinct animals of the Upper Pleistocene, which gives them an age of ten thousand or fifteen thousand years, or more. The points from the cave of Sandia in New Mexico were found in a geological level below one that contained Folsom points, which makes the man of Sandia the oldest known to date in the New World. No other remains than these points have been found—no bones that would reveal the physical type of their makers, no other artifacts that might indicate an art beyond the manufacture of these utensils.

In southeastern Arizona there has been discovered an extremely elementary culture, called Cochise after an Apache chief, which could be regarded as the "Southwestern Archaic" because of its local character and because it fills the gap between the Folsom man and the later, more elaborate cultures of the Southwest. The Cochise culture

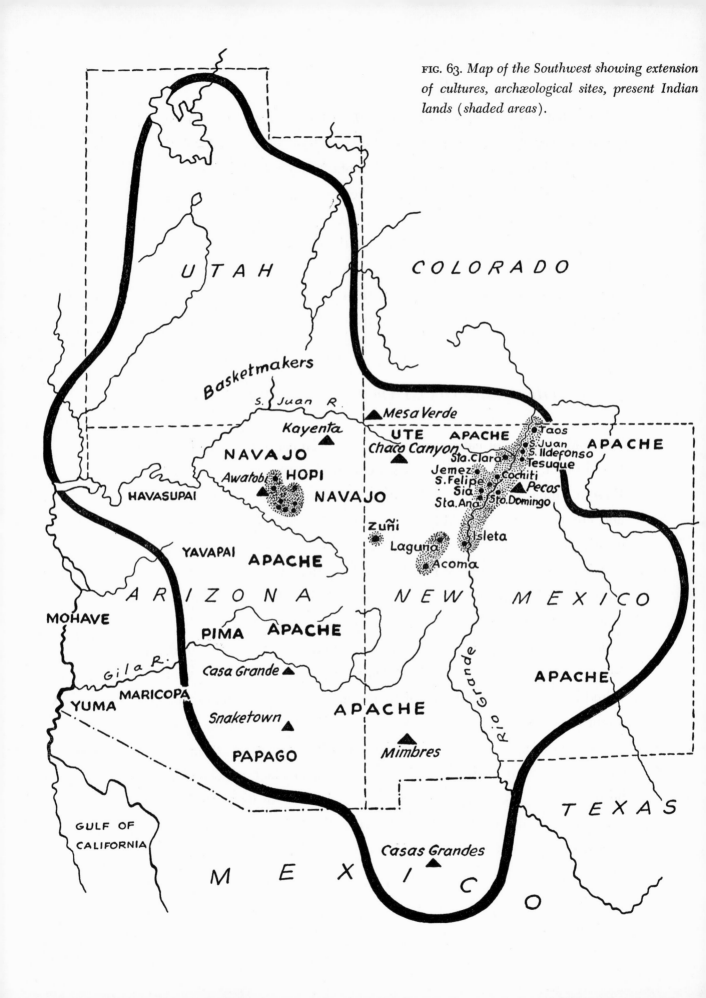

FIG. 63. *Map of the Southwest showing extension of cultures, archæological sites, present Indian lands (shaded areas).*

stretches over an amazingly long period of time and has three phases, which show only slight changes in the crude stone tools these Indians made: the Sulphur Springs phase, estimated at between 13,000 and 8000 B.C.; the Chiricahua period, between 8000 and 3000 B.C.; and, last and most advanced, the San Pedro period, 3000–500 B.C., when they made axes, blades, knives, and scrapers of quartz, chert, and obsidian. There is no other evidence of artistic endeavor in the whole range of the Cochise culture. From the earliest period these Indians used stone grinders, which indicates that they were gatherers of wild vegetable foods as well as hunters (Martin, Collier, and Quimby, 1947).

Basing their studies upon the most minute changes in pottery styles, the archæologists have grouped the ancient inhabitants of the Southwest into three different branches, each with its own roots. One comprises the ancestors of the modern Pueblo Indians; it is a clearly defined culture of high artistic achievement, with an uninterrupted continuity of some two thousand years. It has been named Anasazi, which in Navajo means "ancient people." The second branch corresponds to the culture of the ancestors of the Pima and Papago Indians of the arid zone of southern Arizona, and it is called Hohokam, which means "ancient people" in the Pima language. This culture is characterized by buff-colored ceramic decorated with lively motifs painted in red, as well as by small-scale sculpture in stone and shell. The third branch is the simple, unassuming Mogollon culture, which later blooms into the fine, Classic period of Mimbres Valley, and has a late aspect in the Casas Grandes culture of Chihuahua in northern Mexico.

Each of these basic cultures has its own character. For instance, the Anasazi is essentially a plateau culture, Hohokam is of the desert, and the Mogollon belongs in the mountains. Each has various successive periods, which, however, merge into one another, and each of

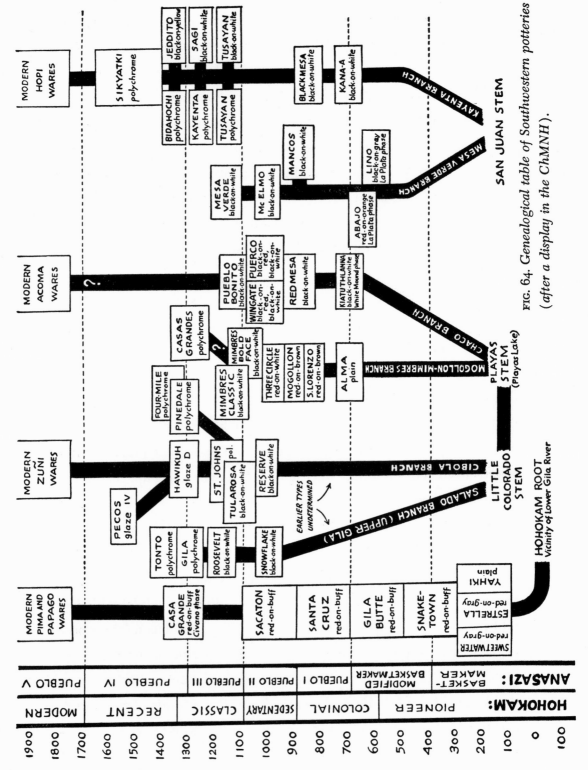

FIG. 64. *Genealogical table of Southwestern potteries (after a display in the ChMNH).*

204

which has a distinguishing name. Furthermore, each of these periods has a variety of pottery styles, each in turn bearing a name, all of which makes Southwestern archæology a complex science that only specialists can understand. It is the object of this book to present each culture in its most condensed form, and the hairsplitting designation of ceramic styles of the Southwest will not be discussed here except in general outline. However, for those interested in following the complicated archæological sequences, here is a genealogical tree of Southwestern ceramic arts drawn after an illuminating display prepared by the specialists of the Chicago Museum of Natural History.

THE ANASAZI CULTURE

TOWARD the end of the past century there was discovered in Grand Gulch, Utah, a culture dating from the beginning of the Christian era. It was baptized Basketmaker culture because in its early stages its creators did not know pottery-making, but made fine baskets, coiled and twilled, and textiles of yucca fiber decorated with geometric motifs in black—triangles, diamonds, interlocking zigzags, and rows of small spurs—already in the characteristic style of the later cultures of the Southwest, showing clearly the textile origin of its decorative art. To satisfy their need for food the early Basketmakers probably had corn and pumpkins, besides other wild seeds and nuts and the flesh of small game. Their burials contain skeletons of individuals, generally long-headed without artificial deformation, wrapped in mantles, and with offerings of food in baskets. For hunting they used dogs and spear-throwers. Interesting rock paintings, such as that of Barrier Canyon in Utah (Pl. 26), are attributed to this period. This great mural shows large, stylized figures probably representing deities, and realistic silhouettes of men and animals in animated poses reminiscent of the Stone Age rock paintings of Africa and Spain.

About A.D. 500 the Basketmaker culture began to develop: textiles and baskets became more elaborate, the designs acquired a bolder, more mature style, and red was added to the black-and-cream scheme of the previous period. The Basketmakers began to make pottery: sun-dried, unfired pots made on basket molds first, but later baked, tempered with sand or crushed rock, and even decorated with painted geometric motifs in black on gray or white and in red on orange. The Indians of this period made permanent houses, raised turkeys, beans, and several varieties of corn, acquired the bow and arrow, made notched axes, and wore ornaments of turquoise. This period is now called by archæologists Modified Basketmaker.

After the Basketmakers come the direct ancestors of the Pueblo Indians. These were predominantly roundheads who deformed their skulls. They probably came from Mexico about A.D. 700, the time when the southern Mexican civilizations were at their height. This is the formative period of the Pueblo culture, and comprises the phases called Pueblo I and Pueblo II, up to about A.D. 1050. These Indians added the growing of cotton to their economy and gave new impetus to the art of pottery-making. For everyday use they made simple corrugated jars and bowls built up of rolls of clay in spiral, pinching the rolls so that they would adhere, sometimes obtaining decorative effects that obviously imitate basketry designs. They also made smooth pottery in an exuberant variety of forms, decorated with designs consisting of fine parallel lines, interlocking scrolls, stepped terraces, checkered boards, and hatchings, painted in black over a white, or sometimes red, slip (Fig. 65). There is some discrepancy of opinion on the origin of the

Southwestern pottery: some authorities consider it a logical development of basketry, a local invention, while others suppose it to have been imported from Mexico. This problem is complicated by the fact that similar pottery shapes and designs spread from the Southwest to Argentina, particularly among the Diaguita Indians of Chile and Argentina, whose pottery bears a strange resemblance to that of the Pueblos.

The Classic Anasazi period, called Pueblo III, lasted from about A.D. 1050 to about 1300. To this period belong impressive ruins such as the famous "Cliff Houses," towns built in great caves, of Canyon de Chelly in Arizona and the palaces in Mesa Verde, Colorado, or great semicircular towns built in the open on top of high mesas. All the other arts progressed alongside architecture: turquoise mosaic, textiles, basketry, and particularly pottery-making, which reached its highest point of technical excellence and restrained good taste, decorated always in geometric motifs in black on white, or sometimes in black and red on white, particularly in three sites on the San Juan River basin: Chaco Canyon, Mesa Verde, and Kayenta (Fig. 66). For unknown reasons the Indians abandoned their villages toward the end of period III. Many theories have been advanced to explain this exodus: (1) pressure from barbaric neighbors, presumably the Navajo; (2) epidemics; (3) droughts and failure of crops (Dr. A. E. Douglass has found, by the system of tree-ring counting, that a severe drought afflicted the zone between 1276 and 1299); and (4) the disintegration of the social system because of intertribal conflicts. It is likely that a combination of all these four catastrophes caused the collapse of the Classic Pueblo culture. A parallel collapse of the great Toltec civilization of the Mexican central plateau took place about one hundred years earlier, and it is not unlikely that the Southwest reflected the situation there.

FIG. 65. *Early Anasazi artifacts:* ABOVE, *woven carrying-band, Basketmaker period;* CENTER LEFT, *Lino black-on-gray pottery bowl, Modified Basketmaker period;* RIGHT, *Kana-a black-on-white jar, Kayenta area, Pueblo I period;* BELOW LEFT, *Red Mesa black-on-white jar, Chaco Canyon district, Pueblo II period;* RIGHT, *Black Mesa black-on-white olla, Oraibi, Arizona, Pueblo II period (final three after Martin and Willis, 1940).*

FIG. 66. *Anasazi pottery of the Classic period (Pueblo III):* UPPER LEFT, *White-water, Arizona (Roberts, 1940);* RIGHT, *Mancos Canyon (BM);* CENTER LEFT, *Tularosa (Martin and Willis, 1940);* RIGHT, *Jeddito black-on-orange, Homolobi, Arizona (Martin and Willis, 1940);* BELOW LEFT, *Tularosa (AMNH);* CENTER, *Pueblo Bonito, Chaco Canyon (Pepper, 1920);* RIGHT, *Chaco Canyon (Roberts, 1940).*

FIG. 67. *Design on a "Four-Mile Polychrome" bowl (Pueblo IV),
Homolobi, Arizona (ChMNH).*

PUEBLO IV

AFTER the mysterious vanishing of the Classic Pueblo III culture, there
was a total readjustment in the Anasazi area. The subsequent period,

Pueblo IV, eventually ushered in an artistic renaissance (Fig. 67). Despite the long stretch of time attributed to this phase, 1300 to 1700, and the great size of its cities, some covering ten or twelve acres, this is the least-known period in the Southwest because the results of the most systematic exploration (at Awatobi in the Hopi country) have not yet been published fully. Two salient facts, however, are known: there was a definite tendency to move southward, and there was a radical change in the art styles.

The best-known sites of this period—Sikyatki and Awatobi—are located in the Hopi country in the lower Little Colorado River valley.[1] Sikyatki is famous for its polychrome pottery, which best illustrates the change in personality of the Pueblo IV period: new painting techniques, concepts of design, color, composition, and even subject-matter make their appearance. Gone were the austere geometric black-and-white designs of the Classic Pueblo pottery; at Sikyatki there are daring, dynamic designs, mostly representing birds, reptiles, insects, and masked deities, so stylized as to become merely abstract composition, painted with sweeping brush strokes in black, red, rose, and white over a background of yellow or orange clay. Often parts of the design are stippled and the backgrounds spattered to produce contrasts in texture (Fig. 68). The central or excentric placement of a motif to fill most of the interior area of a bowl is also a characteristic of this period, leaving large empty spaces that would have made a potter of the Classic period itch with the desire to fill them with all-over patterns.

The most spectacular artistic achievement of the Pueblo IV pe-

[1] There are five sub-areas of the Pueblo IV period: (1) The Hopi area (lower Little Colorado River valley), with Sikyatki polychrome and Jeddito black-on-yellow wares; (2) the Salado area (upper Gila and Salt rivers), with Gila and Tonto polychrome wares; (3) the Zuñi or Cibola area, with Heshothauthla polychrome and Hawikuh glaze-on-white wares; (4) the Rio Grande area (central New Mexico), with many types of polychrome and glaze wares; and (5) the Chihuahua area, discussed under the Mogollon-Mimbres culture.

riod is also a novelty in the Southwest: great murals painted in bright colors on the clay walls of the kivas, the semi-subterranean ceremonial houses used as temples. Such murals have been found at Awatobi and Kawaika-a in the Hopi area of Arizona, and at Kuaua, near Albuquerque, New Mexico. Of these, the finest are those of Awatobi, which represent deities, animal spirits, and offerings, already in the style of the modern Pueblos (Pl. 31). Particularly charming is the humanized squash transformed into a dancing girl. These murals show the fine sense of color, of harmonious flat masses of color combined with careful and even line designs, which is the most laudable characteristic of Anasazi painting.

The Southwest Indians first came in contact with the Spaniards in 1540, when Coronado conquered and plundered the Zuñi towns. The Indians firmly resisted all efforts to Christianize them, though they permitted the friars to build Catholic churches within their towns, some of which were eventually abandoned when the friars' failure became obvious. Such a church, now an archæological ruin, exists at Awatobi, and excavations at the site have shown that the Indians reused the remains of the church walls to build their own houses. The Spaniards had established a wedge in the Southwest by 1609, when the town of Santa Fe was founded, and by 1699 they had conquered the Pueblo Indians, thus ending the Pueblo IV period. The following period, Pueblo V, is that of the Indians down to our day, and will be described after a parenthesis dealing with the two other basic cultures that shared the Southwest with Anasazi: the Mogollon-Mimbres and the Hohokam.

THE MOGOLLON-MIMBRES CULTURE

THE Mogollon is a conservative, timid continuation of the primitive Stone Age Cochise culture, with a few such additional elements as the

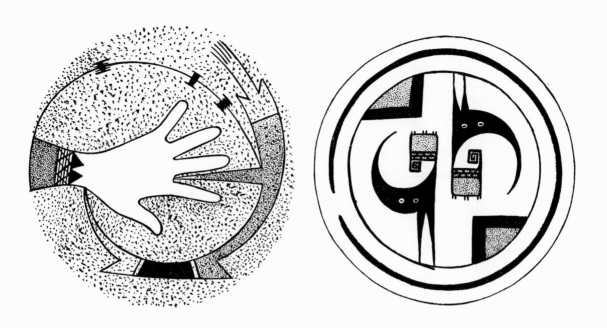

FIG. 68. *Late Anasazi pottery designs from Sikyatki, New Mexico (Pueblo IV):* ABOVE LEFT, *design on a bowl painted in black and red on a spattered beige ground (USNM) (Fewkes, 1896);* RIGHT, *reconstruction of a bowl (PMC) (Douglas and d'Harnoncourt, 1941);* BELOW, *man-eagle design on a bowl (USNM) (Fewkes, 1896).*

making of simple brown or red undecorated pottery, the introduction of agriculture, and the building of semi-subterranean pit houses. Important as these elements of culture are in indicating a regulated sedentary life, the Mogollon people apparently did not have much of a ceremonial life, and as a result apparently no artistic urge, no examples of Mogollon art being known.

However simple, the Mogollon culture is important because it was ancestral to a style of pottery which is without doubt the outstanding artistic achievement of Southwestern ceramic art. About A.D. 900 (in the so-called Tree Circles period) a new pottery began to be made in the Mimbres Valley in southern New Mexico: bowls decorated with geometric designs, interlocking spirals, and wavy parallel lines painted in black on a white ground with a bold and flowing brush, whence its name of "Mimbres Boldface Black-on-White." This style shows influences from both the Anasazi and Hohokam cultures, retaining, on one hand, the elegance of the Classic Anasazi black-on-white designs, the sense of spacing of black, gray (hachured), and white areas in combination with designs in pure line, and, on the other, the loose, free brushwork of the Hohokam and their preference for naturalistic representations. In about one hundred years the Mimbres Boldface style developed into the famous Classic Mimbres pottery, which is extraordinary not only for the technical skill of its makers and the amazingly steady hand and accuracy of the brushwork, but also for its rich and varied motifs—no repetition of designs can be found in the 741 examples illustrated from the Swarts Ruin (Cosgrove, 1932).

Classic Mimbres pottery consists chiefly of bowls (which were "killed" before they were buried with the dead, a small hole being knocked out at the bottom of the bowl) magnificently decorated with elegant, delicate designs of fine black lines, concentric or parallel, as well as with solid areas of black, painted with amazing precision and spaced with the most distinguished taste. Besides the typical geometric designs of Southwestern art, the Mimbreños decorated their bowls with naturalistic figures of men and animals of a humor and liveliness unprecedented in Indian art: mythical and human figures in events of their life, masked dancers, antelope, deer, mountain sheep, badgers, coyotes, wildcats, rabbits, opossum, buzzards, turkeys, quail, ducks, herons, small birds, fish, turtles, frogs, lizards, horned toads, crawling and flying insects, and so forth (Figs. 69, 70), a sort of catalogue of Southwestern zoology painted on pottery. We have to agree with Kidder (1924) that the unique style of Mimbres is the result of the work of "some forgotten individual genius, whose work so stimulated her [pottery is invariably made by women] contemporaries and successors as to result in the founding of a local school or tradition in pottery design."

The cities of the Classic Mimbres period were abandoned, as in all of the Southwest, about A.D. 1200, with all evidence indicating that the exodus took place gradually and peacefully. It is not clear what became of the excellent Mimbreño draftsmen. There is a continuation of this culture, however, in the last archæological period (corresponding to Pueblo IV, 1200–1450) farther to the south, in Chihuahua around the remains of a great adobe town called Casas Grandes. The typical pottery of the Casas Grandes area consists of gracefully shaped jars of yellow-ocher color with elaborate geometric decoration of parallel lines, solid triangles, stepped motifs, and scrolls in black and red. The lines are clean and precise, and in many ways this style shows its relationship to its ancestors, the Classic Mimbres style. Naturalistic motifs are often presented in the decoration: parrots, other birds, serpents, and human faces (Fig. 71). Effigy vessels representing men and women are com-

FIG. 70. *Mimbres bowls (Cosgrove, 1932).*

mon in the style of Casas Grandes. They are ably modeled, often with a peculiar sense of humor, and decorated with red and black geometric designs (Fig. 72).

THE HOHOKAM CULTURE

ANOTHER important Southwestern culture grew in the desert around the junction of the Gila and Salt rivers in southwestern Arizona. Its discoverers named it Hohokam ("Ancient Peoples," literally "Those Who Have Gone" in the Pima language) because it is believed that the modern dwellers of the desert, the Pima Indians, are its direct descendants. The Hohokam culture is quite different from others in the Southwest, not only in its pottery shapes (they made a characteristic large jar with a shoulder near the base, Fig. 73), but also in its style of

FIG. 69. (FACING PAGE) *Motifs from Mimbres pottery bowls (Cosgrove, 1932).*

FIG. 71. *Vase from Casas Grandes, Chihuahua, Mexico (Lumholtz, 1902).*

decoration: naturalistic motifs of schematic human figures and animals, as well as geometric designs, painted in cursive style with a free and agile hand, invariably in red on buff-colored clay (Fig. 74). The gay and amusing rows of naturalistic little men, dancing holding hands or bent over a cane, of birds eating fish, lizards, snakes, or turtles, are a welcome relief from the formalized, austere geometric designs, Mimbres excepted, of ancient Southwestern pottery.

Unlike the other peoples of the Southwest, the Hohokam were sculptors on a small scale, and made clay figurines (Fig. 75) as well as objects and ornaments in soft stone and shell. From stone they carved bowls, small images of animals, and rectangular palettes with raised borders decorated with incised designs. These palettes are often shaped

218

FIG. 72. *Effigy vessel, painted in black and white,*
Casas Grandes, Chihuahua, Mexico (USNM).

like such animals as lizards or horned toads and show traces of paint, probably used to paint the body (Pl. 29). From shell the Hohokam made beads, bracelets, rings, and pendants in the shapes of birds, frogs, coyotes, and so forth, which show a strong resemblance to similar objects found on both coasts of central Mexico (Fig. 73). A unique shell was found, decorated with a fine geometric design etched with acid, probably acetic acid, obtained from fermented saguaro fruit, the raised part of the design protected by a resistant gum or pitch (Fig. 73).

The ancient Hohokam were extraordinary agriculturists, and have been justly called the "master farmers" of North America (Haury, 1945). By A.D. 700 they had built a most elaborate system of canals, covering some 150 miles, to irrigate the wastelands of southwestern Arizona, around the Salt River. Thus they cultivated maize, their staple food, and cotton, complemented with some game, mesquite beans, and saguaro cactus fruits, which they gathered from the desert.

From the earliest times the Hohokam lived in large rectangular

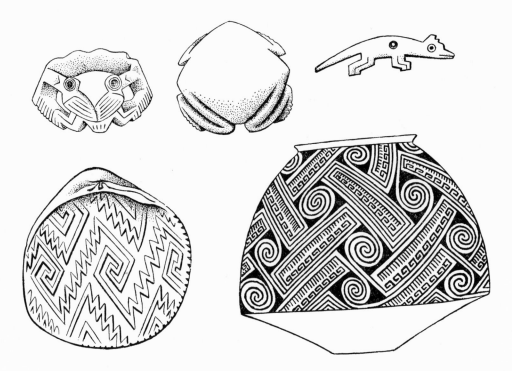

FIG. 73. *Hohokam art, southern Arizona.* ABOVE: *finger ring of shell carved with two buzzards (LACM); shell frog (LACM); shell coyote (ASM).* BELOW: *shell ornament with design incised with acid, Sedentary period (ASM); large jar of the Sacaton red-on-buff style, Sedentary period (GP).*

pit houses, but no known structures indicate an intensive ceremonial life, though they cremated their dead and built courts, great oval sunken areas, to play the Mexican ball game (a rubber ball was found inside a jar). Other clues point to Mexican influences: the making of clay figurines, vessels with three and four legs, stone- and shell-carving, and copper-casting by the "lost-wax" process (a single bell was found, the only known case of Indian metal-casting in North America). The Hohokam were, of course, excellent at weaving and basketmaking, this last an art that has survived among the descendants of the Hohokam, the Pima Indians of today.

The Hohokam culture is as old as any in the Southwest, and the

FIG. 74. *Styles of decoration of Hohokam pottery:* UPPER LEFT, *Pioneer period,*
Snaketown red-on-buff phase; RIGHT, SECOND ROW & THIRD LEFT, *"Colonial" period,*
Santa Cruz red-on-buff phase; THIRD ROW RIGHT, *"Colonial" period, Gila Butte*
red-on-buff phase; BELOW LEFT, *Sedentary period, Sacaton red-on-buff phase;*
RIGHT, *Classic period, Civano phase, red-and-white-on-black* (Clarke, 1935).

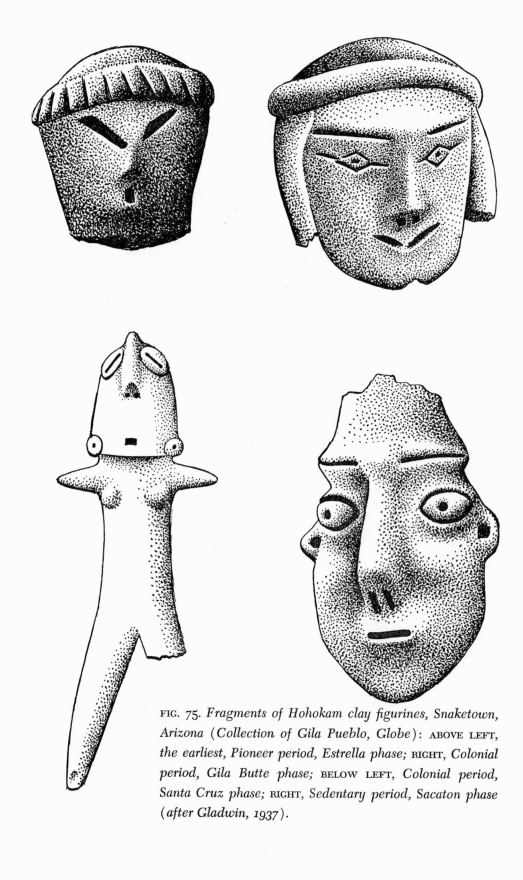

FIG. 75. *Fragments of Hohokam clay figurines, Snaketown, Arizona (Collection of Gila Pueblo, Globe):* ABOVE LEFT, *the earliest, Pioneer period, Estrella phase;* RIGHT, *Colonial period, Gila Butte phase;* BELOW LEFT, *Colonial period, Santa Cruz phase;* RIGHT, *Sedentary period, Sacaton phase (after Gladwin, 1937).*

archæologists who have studied it have been fortunate enough to establish four well-defined periods. These have been dated accurately
by the correspondence with tree-ring chronology of the Pueblos, with
whom the Hohokam exchanged pottery:

PIONEER *period:* 300 B.C.–A.D. 500. At this early stage the
Hohokam culture was already well defined; the Hohokam
made stone tools, bowls, and palettes, shell ornaments, and
simple clay figurines with long, slanting eyes. The pottery of
this period has four phases: Estrella red-on-gray, Sweetwater
red-on-gray, Sweetwater polychrome (red-and-yellow-on-
gray), and Snaketown red-on-buff.

COLONIAL *period:* A.D. 500–900. Irrigation-canal system well
developed; intensive cultivation of maize and cotton; ball-
courts; effigy vessels, bowls, and palettes of polished, carved,
and incised stone; shell ornaments, and better-finished clay
figurines with coffee-bean eyes. Pottery phases: Gila plain,
Gila Butte red-on-buff, Santa Cruz buff and red-on-buff.

SEDENTARY *period:* A.D. 900–1100. The really Classic Hohokam
period, characterized by the fine Sacaton red-on-buff, Sacaton
red, Santan red, and Gila plain. Clay figurines are realistic and
well made; ball-courts grow in size. Contact with Mexico is
evident in this period: vessels with supports, copper bells, etc.
Most important site: Snaketown.

"CLASSIC" *period:* A.D. 1100–1400. Misnamed because it is
the period of frank decadence: ball-courts became smaller
again and pottery styles lose much of their personality (Gila
plain, red, and smudged; Casa Grande red-on-buff). About
A.D. 1300 an Anasazi people, the Salado, moved in with Hohokam and lived peacefully with them, each people retaining its

culture and making its own pottery and kind of house. New elements appeared then: Pueblo style adobe buildings, burial of the dead instead of cremation, and the new pottery styles (Gila and Tonto polychromes) of the Salado people. At the end of the period the Salado appear to have moved away (Haury, 1945; Martin, Collier, and Quimby, 1947).

THE CONTEMPORARY INDIANS OF THE SOUTHWEST

THE historical period lies between the Spanish Conquest of the Southwest at the beginning of the eighteenth century and our own day, and is characterized by the growing influence of Western traits on the life and culture of the Indians. For instance, the modern Hopi cook their food in iron or aluminum kettles, but make beautiful painted pottery to sell; the modern Navajo drive jalopies all over the desert to assist at a magic ceremony for curing a sick member of the tribe, enlivening the long ride with rhythmic chants, as they did when they galloped on their ponies. The cultures of the Southwest Indians, however, retain great cohesion and extraordinary continuity. No sudden changes occur in the long development of their culture as a whole, and there are not, as elsewhere, cultures in full bloom that appear and disappear suddenly. Their art is always sober, formalistic, and conservative, essentially pictorial, with a fine sense of values in the masses as well as in line and choice of colors. Their motifs began with basketry and textile designs, and later took inspiration from such religious subjects as abstract representations of spirits, maize, clouds, and rain, becoming more and more decorative with time.

The Pueblo Indians are even today extremely eager to keep all matters concerning their religion out of the hands of the whites. They tolerate visitors at some of their ceremonies, but photography and sketching are strictly forbidden, and no one would sell a mask or other ceremonial object. This resistance to the penetration of the whites into their spiritual life has preserved the Indian cultures of the Southwest in an astonishing purity; it is not without reason that it has often been said that the culture of the Pueblos is a case of "living archæology."

THE PUEBLO V PERIOD

THE modern Pueblo Indians live the uneventful sedentary life of their ancestors, cultivating corn, beans, squash, and cotton. They eat rabbit, deer, and mutton. Their villages consist of rectangular houses of adobe or stone, with flat roofs supported by beams, forming recessed conglomerates of various stories like great apartment houses. Formerly they wore homemade cotton short skirts, loinclothes, and sashes, and moccasins of buckskin, but today they wear shirts, dresses, and trousers of silk, velvet, and wool. Wool has been in use among them since the Spaniards introduced sheep. The horse was used by the Pueblos only in a limited way, and today they travel by foot or automobile.

The religion of the Pueblos is centered in the cult of the deities of the heavens, of maize, and of the Makers of the Rain, as well as of their spokesmen or messenger spirits, called katchinas. These spirits are represented, among the Hopi and the Zuñi, by little statues of carved wood, some amusingly realistic, others in abstract geometric shapes, painted in bright colors (Pl. 32). The katchinas are made for certain annual ceremonies, and after they have served their purpose they are given to the children to play with or (only among the Hopi) sold to white visitors.

The katchinas are also impersonated by dancers wearing masks

225

made of cylinders of leather painted with distinguishing marks of the specific katchinas, and with additions of gourd, wood, cloth, feathers, and branches of pine, in well-designed and admirably conceived abstract structures. These masks and the geometric headdresses of wood which top them (*tablitas*) are sacred, and under no circumstances can be sold (Pl. 33). The Zuñi retain the cult of a feathered serpent as a celestial deity, a clue to the Mexican origin of certain elements of their religion. Their temples are semi-subterranean clubhouses called kivas, entered at the top through a ladder. No stranger is ever permitted in them.

Even in our highly commercialized world the old arts of the Pueblos have held their ground and new ones have been created: pottery-making maintains a high æsthetic and technical standard; the traditional styles of weaving have not been abandoned altogether; turquoise mosaic is still practiced by the Zuñi, combined with black jet and red and white shell to cover ornaments of shell or bone, or as fine pieces of jewelry set in silver. The silver bracelets, rings, earrings, and pins set with turquoise made by the Zuñi have delicacy and lightness in contrast with the massive silverwork of the Navajo, which will be discussed later.

The Pueblo Indians are particularly distinguished by their admirable ceramics, which in some cases continue prehistoric styles. The process of manufacture remains what it was fifteen hundred years ago: a loaf of clay tempered with sand is gradually hollowed on a dish or a round basketry tray. The walls of the vessel are built up with coils of clay smoothed with a fragment of gourd. When finished, the vessel is dried in the sun and polished. Next it is coated with a slip of white clay and polished again. The decoration is then painted with a brush of yucca fibers, the motif being drawn directly. The painter has the de-

FIG. 76. *Modern Zuñi jar with rainbird motif (Mera, 1937).*

signs clearly defined in her head, and she does not use models of any sort. The vessel is then baked in a pile of burning sheep dung.

Each Pueblo has its own style. The Hopi make beautiful squat jars and bowls of orange clay decorated with dynamic, unsymmetrical, super-stylized bird motifs used by their ancestors. These are painted in black, red, and white on orange. This pottery, a true revival of an old style, was started by a woman named Nampeyo about 1859 after she saw the pottery dug up by archæologists at Sikyatki (Underhill, 1945). The Zuñi make large jars decorated with elegant designs of stylized birds (Figs. 76, 77), deer with the heart visible, and rosettes painted in black on white, with occasional touches of red. The potters of Acoma and Zia paint their jars with realistic birds and plant forms in red and black. In

227

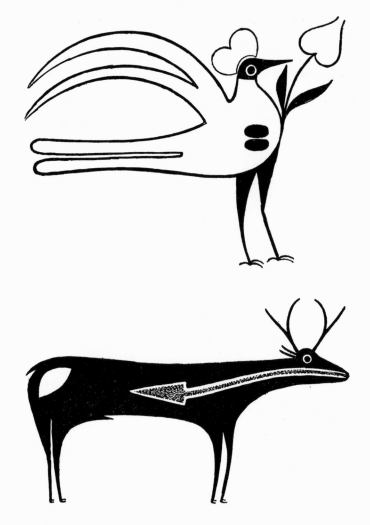

FIG. 77. *Painted designs on modern Pueblo pottery:*
ABOVE, *a Sia bird* (DAM); BELOW, *a Zuñi deer* (TMCS).

Santo Domingo they use large geometric designs in black on cream, with a fine sense of spacing. In San Ildefonso and Santa Clara they make a beautiful shiny or dull black pottery, the black color being obtained by smothering the fire before baking is completed. This style is quite recent; at San Ildefonso a woman potter of genius, Maria Martinez, began to experiment with black pottery about 1919; she was helped by her husband, Julian Martinez, one of the few men ever associated with

228

pottery-making. This famous couple has turned out quantities of pots and bowls of black burnished clay of great elegance and technical perfection, decorated with motifs in flat black. These are only a few of the styles of pottery made by the Southwest Indians, showing that the art is very much alive and is undergoing a constant transformation. This clearly illustrates how pottery phases developed in prehistoric times.

The Southwest Indians are essentially painters with an ancient tradition. The early Basketmakers painted on rocky cliffs, and in prehistoric times covered the clay walls of their kivas with layer upon layer of mural painting. They developed the art of painting on ceramics to a high level, and they invented the art of dry painting, done with colored sands on the floor of the kivas during religious ceremonies, an art the Navajo later appropriated and developed.

Today a new school of painting signed pictures for sale among the whites has grown in the Southwest,[2] especially among the Pueblos, but has also spread to the Navajo, the Apache, and even the Plains Indians. These are painted on paper with watercolors. The subjects are from daily life or are mythological scenes, dances, and wild animals, some highly stylized, others amazingly realistic, but all composed and executed with an elemental simplicity of mass, line, and color in a refined and expressive style that often combines traditional elements with the decorative delicacy of East Indian and Persian miniatures.

Collectors today pay high prices for these pictures, particularly if they bear the signature of the most famous Pueblo artists: Awa Tsireh, Fred Kabotie, Oqwa Pi, Velino Shije, Ma-pi-wi (who painted some fine murals in 1938 in the Department of the Interior at Washington), Otis

[2] The movement started at the beginning of our century when two Hopi artists painted a series of katchinas in watercolors for J. Walter Fewkes for his paper on "Hopi Katchinas" (1903). Isolated drawings in pencil and crayon were made at various pueblos, but it was not until about 1917 that the movement caught fire, from its center, San Ildefonso, under Awa Tsireh, Oqwa Pi, and Julian Martinez.

Polelonema, and—perhaps the most famous of all—Tonita Pena, the first woman to invade the manly art of painting naturalistic human figures.

THE NAVAJO

THE meek and peaceful Pueblo Indians lived in constant fear of their neighbors, the Navajo, originally a wild and hardy tribe of nomadic immigrants from the far north, who raided the Pueblos systematically for plunder and slaves. The Navajo were easily adaptable, and the tribe grew rapidly; even today, despite adverse economic conditions, the Navajo constitute the largest Indian group in the United States. From their perennial enemies, the Pueblo Indians, the Navajo learned to cultivate corn, beans, and squashes, and from the Spanish invaders they obtained two basic elements of their nascent culture: the horse, which enabled them to move freely over their vast but arid land, and sheep, which provided them with their staple food and with wool for the development of weaving, which they learned from the Pueblos and of which they were to become undisputed masters.

The oldest Navajo textiles known were found on the bodies of a group of Navajo murdered in 1805 in the Cañon del Muerto in Arizona. These are simple mantles decorated with plain bands of brown and white across the width of the blankets. Navajo textile art progressed with the introduction of the red Spanish cloth called *bayeta*, which they unraveled to weave their mantles, combining the brilliant red thread with wool dyed with Mexican indigo and with natural white and brown wool. Curiously enough, the art of weaving, which was among the Pueblos a man's pastime, became a women's province among the Navajo.

From these modest beginnings the Navajo blanket soon developed into one of the most spectacular manifestations of the characteristic Indian sense of color values and of bold, well-spaced design. During the nineteenth century, beautiful blankets were made in a variety of styles; some, like the so-called "Chief blankets," have horizontal stripes of various widths in red, white, and blue-black, sometimes interrupted by oblong blocks or diamond- or lozenge-shaped areas with fine serrated concentric designs in various colors. Others have diamonds, triangles, zigzags, and chevrons spotted against a plain or striped background; many consist of large serrated zigzags defining zones. A radical departure from the geometric style is found in blankets with pictorial designs of human figures, horses, cattle, birds, and even houses and railroad trains. Another variety of pictorial blanket reproduced designs from sacred sand-paintings, but these were frowned upon by the Navajo elders, and the makers tried to offset the sacrilege by making deliberate errors in the design.

Eventually the Navajo obtained commercial yarns, some permanent and some dyed with anilines. "Indian" blankets became fashionable in the early twentieth century, and the Navajo had to satisfy the questionable taste of their customers, often having to copy designs from second-rate Near Eastern rugs. The style degenerated, and abominable blankets were made around 1910. A few well-intentioned collectors, however, succeeded in reviving the fine old styles, and blankets of high quality and artistic merit are still made, relegating the making of the so-called "Indian blankets" to factories selling their merchandise through mail-order catalogues.

Navajo sand-painting is perhaps the most interesting and original of Southwestern arts. For the Navajo, however, it is not an art or an ordinary expression of the individual, but a powerful magic performance, the making by a medicine man, under divine guidance, of the illustrative episodes of the sacred "chants" used to cure a sick or an injured person. Disease and bodily injury are supposedly caused by an offended spirit whose magic has to be neutralized by a more powerful magic. Consequently, if the chants performed are of no avail, others are tried, until the patient recovers or dies. There are various sets of sand-paintings for each chant, and the designs employed, of endless variety, are full of abstract symbolism, with every form, line, or color having a specific meaning. According to the legend, the sand-paintings were given to the Navajo by their gods, painted on skins, but the medicine men of old, fearful that the powerful pictures would fall one day into strange hands, memorized the designs and destroyed the originals.

In making sand-painting the earth floor of a ceremonial hogan (an octagonal house of logs) is spread with a two-inch layer of fine, clean sand over an area about ten feet square. The medicine man and his assistant work from the center outward, sitting crosslegged or kneeling with five bowls of colored sand in front of them. The colors employed are: black (sand mixed with powdered charcoal from piñon twigs), white, red (a mineral earth), yellow (natural ocher), and "blue" (really gray, charcoal mixed with white sand). The medicine man begins the design after carefully smoothing a section of the sand with a long wooden paddle from a weaving loom. He takes a handful of the required color and lets a fine stream of colored sand run between the thumb and forefinger, producing amazingly accurate lines and wedge-shaped patches or filling in flat areas of color, developing the design without a model of any sort. The sensation of the Indian Art Show of the Museum of Modern Art in New York held in the spring of 1941 was the seventy-three-year-old Navajo medicine man Charlie Turquoise, who astonished New Yorkers by his skillful, sure hand.

The medicine man has the design, proportions, and composition

FACING: *Katchinas, "Messengers of the Gods," painted by a Hopi artist. From upper left to lower right they represent: Sio Humis, Tiwenu, Tawa (Sun katchina), Patun (Squash katchina), Coto, and Tetañaya (Wasp katchina) (Fewkes, 1903).*

clearly established in his mind, and the sureness with which he dashes a line, draws a delicate feather, or pinches off a dot or a spot of color is evidence of his masterful technique and great power of concentration. The motifs used in the sand-paintings are mainly katchina-like deities with oblong bodies, long necks, round heads for the male, rectangular heads for the female, and small angular arms and legs. These are combined with symbols for the sun, moon, stars, lightning, clouds, mountains, cornstalks, buffalo, horses, birds, serpents, and so forth. Frequently the painting is protected from evil influences from the north, west, and south sides by a *natseelit,* the personified rainbow, with an extremely elongated torso, represented by a long tricolor band (red, white, and "blue") framing three sides of the painting, with head and arms on one end, kilt and legs on the other (Pl. 34). The opening toward the east is sometimes protected by other figures, such as the Messenger Fly, the Bat, the Bear, or the Sun and Moon.

When the sand-painting is finished, and after certain ceremonies, the medicine man places pinches of corn meal and pollen on key places —the heads, hands, and feet of the figures. Songs are chanted and prayers muttered; the patient is seated on the sand-painting and is given an infusion containing corn meal, pollen, and sand from the painting. The ceremony over, the painting is systematically destroyed: the medicine man shuffles over each section, obliterating the design. The sand is then collected and deposited in a deserted place lest its magic harm someone.

The Navajo have another variety of magic dry paintings serving the same curative or protective function, but done on buckskin, with the designs executed in pollen from corn or other flowers (yellow and red), corn meal (white), dried powdered larkspur blossoms (blue), and charcoal (black) (Oakes, 1943).

The Navajo are supposed to have learned the art of dry painting

from the Pueblo Indians, who make simple dry paintings with corn meal and colored earths on the floors of their kivas. The concept of dry paintings is rather rare in the world; in the Americas it is practiced only by the Navajo, the Pueblos, and in an elementary manner by some Californian and Plains tribes; it is found, strangely enough, also, among the Mandalas of Tibet and among some of the primitive Australian tribes (Wheelright, 1942).

The Navajo are also famous for their excellent silverwork. Old-style *concha* belts, bracelets, rings, wrist-guards, necklaces, and bridle ornaments are among the most sought-for collectors' items in the Southwest. Navajo silverwork is distinguished by its massive simplicity and good taste. It is either plain or set with large chunks of turquoise.[3] They obtained the silver from old Mexican pesos, which they hammered or cast in sand molds. In fact, they learned the art of silverwork from Mexico, supposedly about 1853, when a Captain Henry Smith took a Mexican silversmith to Fort Defiance. Many a Mexican motif was incorporated into the Navajo style of silver jewelry. For instance, the popular "squash blossom" ornament of Navajo necklaces is a copy of a Mexican pomegranate flower; the motifs stamped with dies were those of the Mexican workers of tooled leather. Today the Navajo use dies with such local motifs as arrows, feathers, swastikas, and thunderbirds. These are simply decorative, without any special significance. In recent years the Navajo have had to compete with manufactured "Indian jewelry" for the curio market, and the quality of their work has suffered a frank decadence. Fortunately in 1938 the Indian Arts and Crafts Board went to the rescue and created a market for more expensive, authentic Navajo jewelry of high quality made in the vigorous simplicity of the old pieces.

[3] The use of turquoise in Navajo silverwork is also of recent date, not earlier than 1885.

In closing, I must mention the lesser groups of Southwest Indians, whose arts differ considerably from those of the Pueblos or the Navajo. These are the Apache of the mountains of New Mexico and Arizona and the dwellers of the deserts of southwestern Arizona, notably the Papago and Pima, both makers of fine baskets.

The Apache are known for their warlike past and their ferocious resistance to white domination. They are divided into four groups: Mexcalero, Jicarilla, Chiricahua, and San Carlos Apache, and they constitute a sort of link between the hunters of the Plains and the simple Indians of California and of the Arizona desert. The Apache led a reckless life and dressed like the wild Indians of the Plains. They were constantly on the warpath in garments of buckskin, decked with feathers, and brandishing painted shields of leather. There are three important aspects of Apache art: basketry, magic designs painted on buckskin (Fig. 78), and vigorous and dramatic "devil" dances. The Apache baskets, particularly those of the San Carlos group, are often masterpieces of technique and of bold, elegant design. They make large shallow trays with swirling patterns, and great basket granaries shaped like jars, decorated with ample geometric designs defining zones filled with animated motifs of men and animals (Pl. 30).

The desert-dwellers have quite primitive material cultures and make simple pottery on a small scale; such are the polished red vessels, decorated in black, of the Maricopa, and the crude but lively effigy vessels and figurines of buff clay, painted in yellow and red, of the Yuma and Mohave (Fig. 79), which carry over, however faintly, the Hohokam tradition. The climax of the art of the desert-dwellers is found in the basketry of the Papago and Pima, who weave shallow, circular trays like those of the Apache, decorated in black or sepia with geometric motifs consisting of dynamic, rhythmical lines that zigzag and radiate from the center (Fig. 80). These trays are true works of

FIG. 78. Apache painted skin, a mantle of invisibility (USNM).

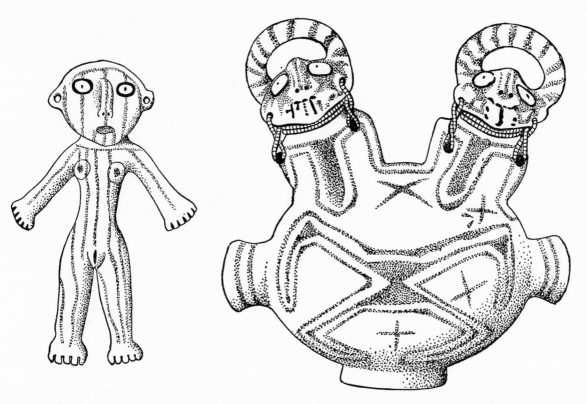

FIG. 79. LEFT, *Mohave clay doll* (USNM); RIGHT, *Mohave clay jar* (DAM).

art, which have solved in the most admirable manner the problem of combining mechanical precision with disciplined, yet expressive design, to decorate, most successfully, the round area of the tray.

FIG. 80. *Pima coiled basketry trays:* ABOVE LEFT, *a labyrinth (Collection of Artie Shaw);* RIGHT, *eagle (after Breazeale, 1923);* BELOW LEFT, *three-petal squash blossom (Collection of René d'Harnoncourt);* RIGHT, *swastika (AMNH).*

CHAPTER V

The Eastern Woodlands

THE eastern part of the United States possesses a rich and fascinating culture, or, rather, a mosaic of more than eighty known cultural units that flourished at various times and different places. Of particular interest is the fact that the art of these cultures is totally different from all others in North America, though it shows, in many instances, a remarkable relationship with the art of ancient Mexico. These cultures seem to have developed locally, from primitive paleo-Indians of the region, with such evolutive steps as more or less elaborate stone tools, pottery-making, agriculture, mound-building, fine stone-carving, metallurgy, and textiles. Many of these elements were invented locally; others obviously came from Mexico, and perhaps even from South America by way of the West Indies; still others found their way from northeast Asia, having been brought directly or introduced perhaps by the ancestors of the Eskimo or by the ancient Algonquians of the northern forests.

The creators of these cultures are popularly known as "Moundbuilders," but archæologists frown upon this title because not all these Indians built mounds, and instead call them and their culture "Old Woodland." The construction of mounds and gigantic earthworks, however, is one of the spectacular features of these cultures. There are many funerary and effigy mounds, enormous man-made hills in the shape of animals, birds in flight, and—most famous—the Serpent Mound in southern Ohio, a great winding serpent measuring 1,400 feet (430 meters) in length (Fig. 81). Later mounds are really truncated pyramids and platforms of earth, which served as foundations for temples or chiefs' houses. Some of these are gigantic structures, evidences of a highly developed social structure capable of carrying out great communal works: Monk's Mound, the central unit of the Cahioka Group near East St. Louis, Illinois, one of the largest earthworks in the world, has a height of one hundred feet and covers sixteen acres.

The area of the Old Woodland cultures includes almost the whole of the eastern half of the United States. Its borders to the north are beyond the Great Lakes and New England; to the east, the Atlantic coast; to the south, the Gulf of Mexico; and to the west, a line from north to south about one hundred and fifty miles west of the Mississippi River.

The zone coincides exactly with the heavily wooded areas of the eastern United States, whence the fitting name "Woodland cultures" for the entire complex, which has in turn well-defined sub-areas: (1) the Northeast (New York and New England); (2) Ohio; (3) Illinois; (4) Wisconsin and Minnesota; (5) the Plains; (6) the Ozark plateau; (7) middle Southern; (8) lower Mississippi Valley; (9) Georgia; (10) Florida; and (11) Caddo (eastern Texas and southeastern Oklahoma) (Martin, Quimby, and Collier, 1947). It is not yet clear whether all of these culture areas are really separate entities, for no exhaustive comparative study of them has been made, though certain sites stand out for their characteristic techniques and art styles. For instance, one of the most important sites—Hopewell, in Ohio—is famous for its

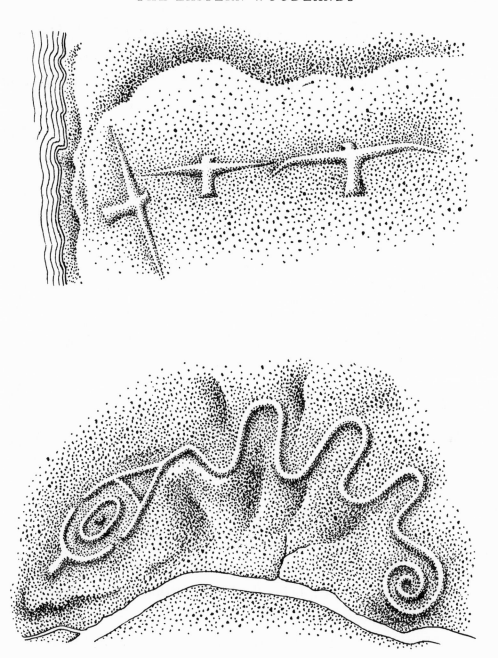

FIG. 81. *Two famous effigy mounds:* ABOVE, *the Lower Dell Bird Mound group, Sauk County, Wisconsin, near Madison (the largest bird having a wing span of 240 feet);* BELOW, *the Great Serpent Mound in southern Ohio (following the curve, it measures about 1,400 feet in length).*

realistic pipes of carved stone in the shapes of animals, stylized ornaments of cut-out copper sheet, ceremonial silhouettes of mica, and fine
designs incised on bone. Adena, also in Ohio, is the home of a stone
pipe carved with a human figure which is one of the masterpieces of
American art. Etowah, in Georgia, has human and animal figures on
repoussé copper plate; Key Marco, in Florida, has yielded beautiful
carvings in wood; Spiro, in Oklahoma, is characterized by its carvings
in shell; the northeast area—New York and New England—has beautiful streamlined objects of abstract shapes, made of banded slate and
other attractive stones. Everywhere, but particularly in the Mississippi
Valley, the Indians made simple but elegant pottery decorated with
geometric curvilinear and naturalistic designs, notably the decorated
pottery of the Caddo area and the polychromed clay bottles and effigy
vessels of Arkansas.

Woodland archæology has a long and romantic history. The early
settlers were already concerned with the ancient remains, and by the
time of the Revolutionary War there was considerable controversy as
to what superior race—Chinese, Phœnicians, Egyptians, Welsh, or
even the ten lost tribes of Israel—was responsible for the mounds. Ben-
jamin Franklin, Thomas Jefferson, and William Henry Harrison were
among the first to fall under the spell of Indian archæology. Jefferson
actually explored burial mounds in his native Virginia and published
his observations in 1801, being the first to attribute the archæological
remains to the ancestors of the Indians of the region.

Many later studies have been made by distinguished specialists,
but there are still many unknown factors, particularly in the chronology
of these cultures. Until recently the tendency was to regard the Woodland cultures as rather young, but there is new evidence of their continuous development from the paleo-Indian horizon, represented by
flint artifacts of the Folsom and Yuma types, dating back to the Upper

Pleistocene 8,000 B.C. or earlier, from which developed a localized Archaic period. As new elements of culture developed or were introduced from elsewhere, the cultures of the Woodlands became more complex and acquired local characteristics, a process that continued uninterrupted until the eighteenth century, when the white conquest put an end to the Indian manner of life.

In the last few years the knowledge of the cultures of the Eastern Woodlands has made great strides toward some semblance of order in the chaotic situation of chronology, multiplicity of cultures, and lack of comparative studies. Archæologists have now established three basic periods for the prehistory of the Woodlands: an "Archaic" or developmental period, followed by a florescent or "Burial Mound" period, comparable to the Classic period of Middle America, and ending with a late renaissance or "Temple Mound" period. These were hypothetically dated rather conservatively, partly because all Indian culture was formerly regarded as a late development, partly because tools and ornaments of hammered copper are typical of the Woodland cultures and metals only began to be in use in Middle America after A.D. 900. There is every indication, however, that the technique of hammered native copper was in use in the Woodlands in much earlier times, independently of Mexico, and the typically Middle American technique of mold-casting was apparently never known in the Woodlands. Recent tests of radioactive-carbon content of Woodland materials have yielded surprisingly ancient dates—nearly three millennia earlier than had been guessed before (Libby, 1950).

Because a chronological scale must be provided here, and because the previously suggested dates for the Woodland cultures have become unacceptable, I have prepared the following chart, showing the relative position of the various periods and their most important cultures and sites, based upon recent archæological publications (Griffin, 1952), with the new chronology suggested by the radioactive-carbon tests, supported by the possibility of correlating certain general aspects of the Middle and South American chronological pattern—that is, the sequence of early farming communities, developing from pre-ceramic, pre-agricultural peoples, followed by a well-organized theocracy of master craftsmen, and ending with feudal city-states.

The Paleo-Indian Period: the antecedents for the ancient cultures of the Eastern Woodlands lay in sporadic and often vague finds of artifacts, mainly of spear points of flint, such as the Folsom and Yuma points, known to have been associated with animal remains of the extinct fauna of the Upper Pleistocene (see Fig. 1), at least eight to twelve thousand years old. The Folsom culture is best represented by the finds at the Lindenmeier Site in northeastern Colorado; those of Yuma style are found at various places: in Guilleford in North Carolina, in Georgian Bay (northern Lake Huron), and at the bottom of shell heaps in Kentucky.

The Early Archaic Period: for which a rough date of 3000 B.C. is guessed, is the formative period of the Woodlands, developing from the simple hunters, fishers, and gatherers of the paleo-Indian period. It consists of a number of homogeneous complexes of stone artifacts with some differentiation in the later phase: flaked projectile points, awls, needles and scrapers to make skin clothes, fishhooks, shallow stone mortars and pestles, the so-called "gorgets," rectangular stone tablets with perforations, and simple "banner stones" used as spear-thrower weights. Typical Early Archaic sites are Frontenac and Lamoka in New York, Plainview in Texas, the remains of Browns Valley from Minnesota, early Macon from Georgia, Suwannee from Florida, and so forth.

The Late Archaic Period: roughly dated at about 1000 B.C., is an elaboration of the former, with a considerably greater artistic activity

244

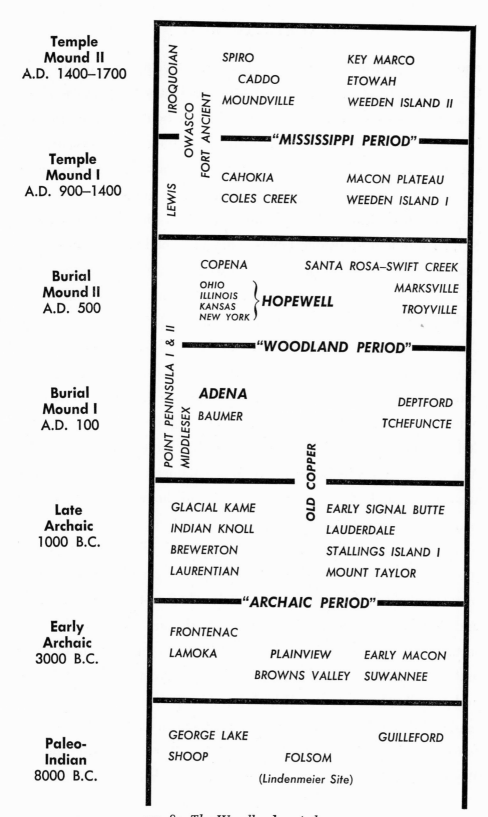

Temple Mound II A.D. 1400–1700	SPIRO CADDO MOUNDVILLE	KEY MARCO ETOWAH WEEDEN ISLAND II
	"MISSISSIPPI PERIOD"	
Temple Mound I A.D. 900–1400	CAHOKIA COLES CREEK	MACON PLATEAU WEEDEN ISLAND I
Burial Mound II A.D. 500	COPENA OHIO ILLINOIS KANSAS NEW YORK } HOPEWELL	SANTA ROSA–SWIFT CREEK MARKSVILLE TROYVILLE
	"WOODLAND PERIOD"	
Burial Mound I A.D. 100	**ADENA** BAUMER	DEPTFORD TCHEFUNCTE
Late Archaic 1000 B.C.	GLACIAL KAME INDIAN KNOLL BREWERTON LAURENTIAN	EARLY SIGNAL BUTTE LAUDERDALE STALLINGS ISLAND I MOUNT TAYLOR
	"ARCHAIC PERIOD"	
Early Archaic 3000 B.C.	FRONTENAC LAMOKA	PLAINVIEW EARLY MACON BROWNS VALLEY SUWANNEE
Paleo-Indian 8000 B.C.	GEORGE LAKE SHOOP	GUILLEFORD FOLSOM (Lindenmeier Site)

(Vertical labels: IROQUOIAN, OWASCO, FORT ANCIENT, LEWIS, POINT PENINSULA I & II, MIDDLESEX, OLD COPPER)

FIG. 82. *The Woodland periods.*

and some surprising features, such as the development of the Old Copper culture of Wisconsin and Minnesota, where copper tools of Asiatic style were made one thousand years before metallurgy was known in Middle America. The implements of the early Archaic period continued to be made, but they became more elaborate and beautiful: celts, full-grooved axes, gouges, gorgets, "banner stones," "boatstones," tubular and conical "pipes," plummets or sinks for fishing nets (Fig. 83), steatite and sandstone bowls. They also made copper and shell beads, barbed harpoons, pins and combs of bone, often decorated with incised geometric design, cups and gorgets from human skulls, and antler headdresses. In the northern area, particularly in New England, there is a most interesting complex of extremely well-made tools of ground slate: spear points, knives, semilunar knives, and so on, finished with extraordinary precision and surprisingly similar to the slate tools of the ancient Eskimo (Fig. 83). Most puzzling of all is the mysterious "Old Copper" culture of the Great Lakes area. Here again the ghost of Asiatic origin rears its head: the tools of hammered copper—socketed spear points and adzes, some enormous, with holes for rivets; knives and lance heads with tangs and notched stems, crescent-shaped knives, harpoon heads, chisels, etc. (Fig. 3)—are exact replicas in copper of tools used by the ancient (Dorset) Eskimo, and are identical with the metal implements from northeastern Asia. The "rat-tail" stems, sockets, and rivet holes are unique in the New World and are indicative of a metal tradition rather than of the suggested local replacement of stone and bone implements by those made of copper. Another eastern Asiatic and Woodland (as well as Eskimo) trait is pottery with the surface marked by a cord wrapped around a mallet, which makes its appearance toward the end of the late Archaic period. Throughout the various Woodland periods, types of pottery were made that resemble the pot-

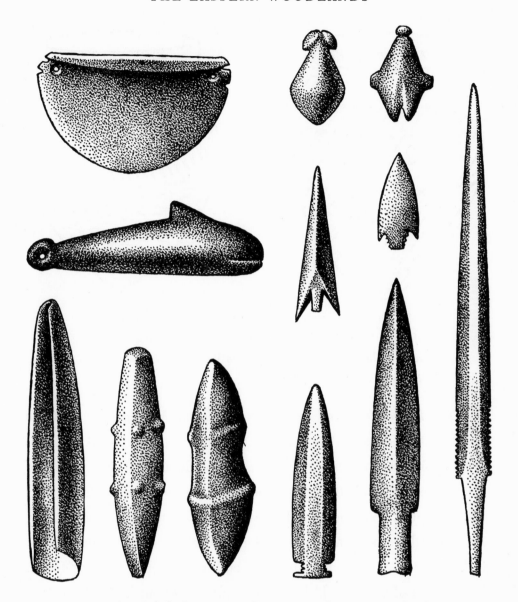

FIG. 83. *Polished stone implements of the New England Archaic period, from Maine and Massachusetts: a semilunar knife, plummets, a whale-shaped pendant, spear points, chisels, and gouges (after Willoughby, 1935).*

tery of the early Bronze Age of the Lake Baikal and Yenisei Valley in Siberia (Fig. 84).

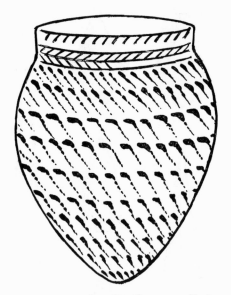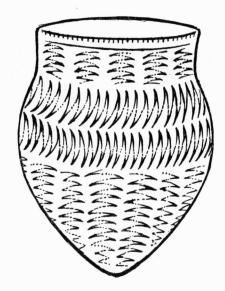

FIG. 84. *Similar vessels from Siberia and Maine:* LEFT, *early Anafasiev, Yenisei Valley, Siberia, dated about 2000–1500* B.C.; RIGHT, *middle Woodland period, from Waterville, Maine* (PMC) (*after Willoughby, 1935*).

The Early Woodland Period (called *Burial Mound I* for the Ohio area): rather conservatively dated (Griffin, 1952) at about A.D. 100 (radioactive-carbon tests give dates around 1000 B.C.), is a period of clear transition, with the appearance of important new traits, such as the building of great mounds, fine textiles, mica ornaments, and pottery. Although there is no absolute evidence of agricultural knowledge, it is difficult to believe that such a new cultural impetus, through such a long period of time, could have taken place without agriculture. It is taken for granted that agriculture came from the south, from Mexico or from the Southwest by way of Texas (Griffin, 1952), bringing maize, beans, tobacco, and squashes, as an addition to the local crops—sunflower, pigweed, gourds, etc. The impression one receives is that shifting agriculture was practiced during this period as a secondary source of food and did not become intensified until the middle Woodland period. It is curious that pottery and agriculture did not appear simul-

FACING: *Navajo sand-painting representing male (round heads) and female (rectangular heads) gods framed by a rainbow (Stevenson, 1891).*

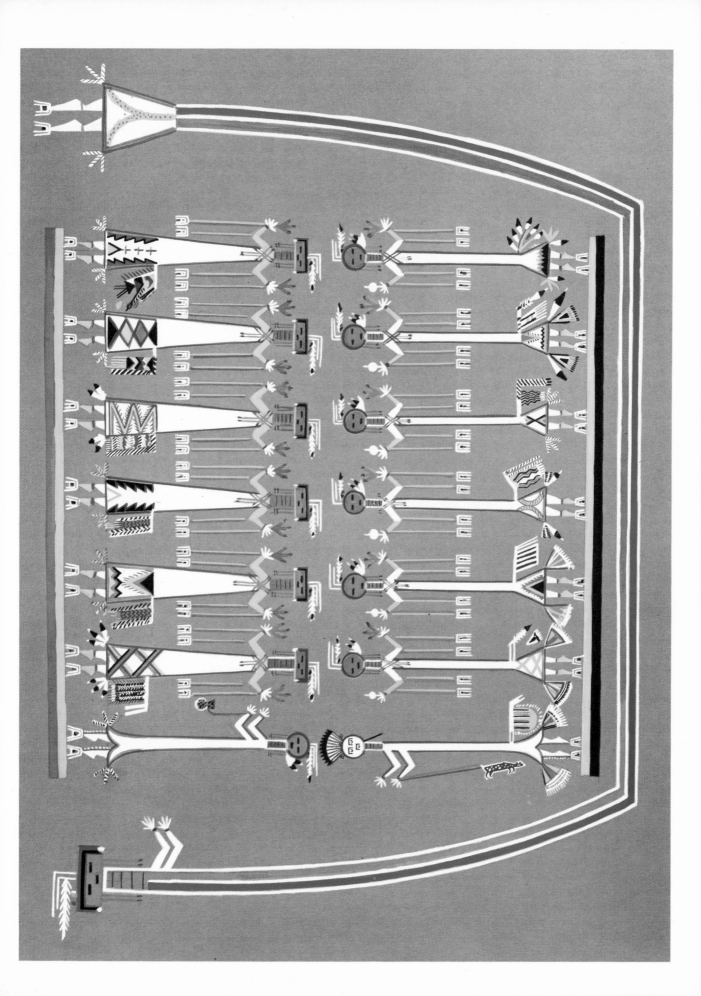

taneously; the early pottery is fiber-tempered, with forms derived from stone vessels, plain or decorated, smoothed, stamped, cord-marked, or textile-impressed in the north (Adena in Ohio), with punches along the border (Baumer in Illinois), or punched, incised, pinched, and stamped in various ways (Tchefuncte in Georgia). It is still debated whether the knowledge of pottery-making was a local development or was imported from Asia or Mexico. It is my guess that it first came from Asia by the northern route and later received some Mexican influences. Eventually the two styles merged and many new styles developed.

The late Archaic art in stone persists strongly in the early Woodland period. The old forms for spear-thrower weights and gorgets continued to be made, but considerably more elaborated in form and finish, and naturalistic stone sculpture made its appearance. One of the finest sculptures of ancient Woodland art is the famous Adena pipe, carved with a realistic human figure made in the early ("Olmec") Mexican tradition (Pl. 37). Adena, where this fine sculpture was found, is a site in the central Ohio Valley, which from this time on becomes the most important center of culture of the whole of the Woodland area. The Adena culture, elusive and mysterious, is characterized by its great mounds, effigy pipes, reel-shaped gorgets, copper bracelets, incised stone tablets with curvilinear designs (Fig. 85), and other traits clearly antecedent to the great classic culture of the Woodland period, that of Hopewell. Despite all evidence that the Adena culture antedates and is the antecedent of Hopewell, the radioactive-carbon tests have given dates considerably older for Hopewell (350 B.C.) than for Adena. This has shaken the scientists specializing in the archæology of the eastern United States, and the problem lurks as to whether it is carbon 14 or themselves that are wrong. Of course, a comfortable way out of the problem would be to postulate an earlier beginning for Hopewell and a considerable persistence for the Adena culture.

FIG. 85. *Early Woodland designs on stone tablets:*
ABOVE, *from Adena, Ohio (Griffin, 1952);* BELOW, *from Waverly, Ohio (CiMA).*

The Middle Woodland Period (Burial Mound II): A.D. 500. The Classic Woodland period is really an elaboration of the preceding epoch, but with a well-defined character, a spectacular and well-integrated civilization, with intensive farming, religion, art and commerce, and with a social structure capable of carrying out great communal enterprises, such as the building of gigantic earthworks and effigy mounds. The most important site is Hopewell, in central Ohio, definitely the focus from which this great culture spread far and wide, eventually all over the Eastern Woodlands; there are subsidiary Hopewellian cultures in New York, Michigan, Tennessee, Indiana, Illinois, Wisconsin, Iowa, and Kansas. There is a southern variety of Hopewell culture in Marksville and Troyville in the lower Mississippi Valley, and the Santa Rosa–Swift Creek culture in Florida and Georgia (Fig. 86). Because the skeletons found in Hopewellian burials show marked ethnic differences, it is inferred that different peoples shared the same culture.

The problem of how and where these great cultural developments originated has hardly been explored. The evidence at hand points in two directions: toward the north, and beyond to Asia; and to the south, toward Mexico. Both clues are slight and elusive: the bear cult, bilateral patterns, pottery styles, costume, projectile points, etc., are northern traits; mounds, flake knives, obsidian, earspools, pearls, etc., are typical of Middle America.

Trade and commerce must have been carried out with the most intense activity, obtaining raw materials like copper, mica, sea-shells, obsidian, grizzly-bear teeth, coal, and pearls from places as remote as the Rocky Mountains, the Atlantic coast, and the Gulf states. The Hopewell Indians cremated their dead and buried the remains with elaborate ceremonial under enormous funerary-mound complexes with systems of earthen walls. They also built, for unknown purposes, great effigy mounds in the shape of animals.

During this period the arts reached a climax of technical excellence and sedate, classic good taste. The Hopewellians made unpainted ceremonial pottery of special shapes decorated with curvilinear incised designs, simple decorative or naturalistic birds, notably the roseate spoonbill, with areas differentiated by punctate patterns or stamped with

251

FIG. 86. *Prehistoric pottery from Florida:* UPPER LEFT, *Alligator Bayou rocker-stamped, Santa Rosa–Swift Creek period;* RIGHT, *Indian Pass incised, Weeden Island period;* LOWER LEFT, *Crystal River zoned red, Santa Rosa–Swift Creek period;* RIGHT, *Alligator Bayou early stamped, Swift Creek period (all after Willey, 1949).*

zigzags made with a characteristic rocker-stamp (Fig. 87). Fine clay figurines of a style that archæologists have called "mayoid," perhaps because it is refined and realistic, were found in the Turner Mounds,

FIG. 87. *Hopewell-period pottery:* TOP, *from Hopewell, Ohio
(Moorehead, 1922; Shetrone, 1930);* BOTTOM, *Marksville-style
pottery, a variant of Hopewell, from Crooks site, La Salle Parish,
Louisiana (Ford and Willey, 1949).*

Hamilton County, Ohio (Pl. 43). These are modeled freehand, and the
fact that the Indians used no molds such as were prevalent in Mexico
at the time is a sign that Hopewell received no further influence from
the south or is considerably older than archæologists surmise.

Characteristic of Hopewell are the small stone pipes (Fig. 88)
carved with exquisite delicacy, often in the shapes of animals—bears,
dogs, wildcats, beavers, opossum, otters, ducks, hawks, owls, turtles,
frogs, etc.—and showing a deep knowledge of realistic forms. These

253

Fig. 88. *Platform pipe of polished stone, with incised design on the bottom, middle Woodland period, from Revere, Massachusetts (PMC) (after Willoughby, 1935).*

pipes are made of "Ohio pipestone," a soft but compact conglomerate capable of taking a high polish. They have a flat, curved base or pedestal, perforated to let the smoke pass, the body of the animal forming the bowl. Many such pipes have been found in Ohio; in Temper Mound, Scioto County, one hundred and forty-five pipes were found in a single cache, ninety of them in the shape of animals (Pl. 39).

Metallurgy had a peculiar development in Hopewell times. Natural copper nuggets were hammered into sheets and cut out to make all sorts of elaborate ornaments; the Hopewell Indians also knew how to work silver and to forge meteoric iron. They had no knowledge, however, of casting metal, an art highly developed in South America and later in Mexico. Sheet copper was used to make helmets with antlers, spoon-shaped earplugs, oblong gorgets, and all sorts of cut-out ornaments to be sewn on clothing. These last were in the shape of birds, serpent heads, fish, and bear-claws, as well as in simple, austere decorative shapes (Fig. 89).

A unique art found in the Hopewell sites is that of the beautiful stylized silhouettes of mica with sharp, precise edges. They represent headless human bodies with dismembered arms and legs, human hands (Pl. 38), heads, eagle-claws, duckbills, bear-teeth, spear-throwers, and replicas of stone spear-points. Undoubtedly they were votive offerings to be buried with the dead, perhaps more elegant substitutes for the real thing, made of a material that must have been rare and precious. Another trait of Hopewellian art is certain ornaments made of human or animal bone, engraved with delicate curvilinear designs, with hachured or crosshatched areas, representing cats, birds, and serpents, and with complicated motifs composed of various superimposed elements (Fig. 90). Stone-chipping was highly developed: masterfully made ceremonial blades of obsidian and colored flints too large for actual use were buried with the dead in the mounds. Besides all this gorgeous regalia, pearl necklaces and pendants of grizzly-bear teeth, often set with large pearls, were worn.

A holdover from early times is the complex of "problematic" objects carved out of various unusual or beautiful stones such as banded gray and green slate, marble, steatite, granite, jasper, and colored quartz: the already mentioned "banner stones," believed to have been weights for spear-throwers, perhaps developed in time into symbols of rank; the so-called "boatstones"; and highly stylized little birds. These objects are true abstractions of pure and elegant form, comparable in their plastic conception to the modern sculptures of Brancusi (Pl. 36, Fig. 91).

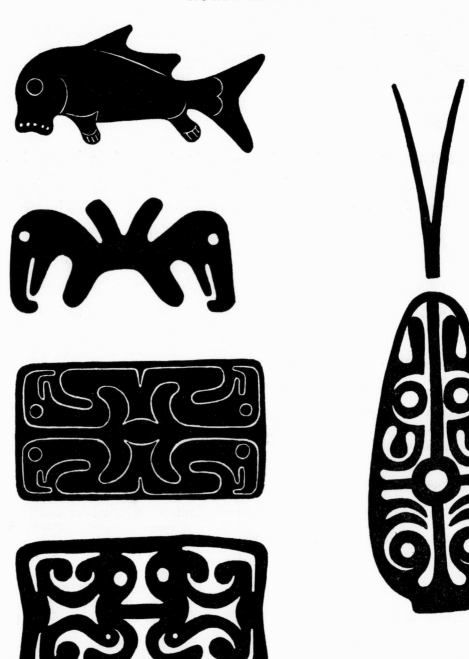

FIG. 89. *Hopewell cut-out and* repoussé *ornaments of copper.* LEFT, TOP TO BOTTOM: *a manatee; double bird motifs;* RIGHT: *a serpent head, from Ross County, Ohio. (From Shetrone, 1930, and ChMNH.)*

FIG. 90. *Hopewell designs incised on bone:* ABOVE LEFT, *a cat,
bird, and serpent composition on a disk of the parietal bone of a
human skull;* RIGHT, *a human head wearing antlers and a roseate-
spoonbill mask;* BELOW LEFT, *an albatross;* RIGHT, *an ocelot. (All
from the Hopewell burial mounds, Ohio, after Willoughby, 1935;
Moorehead, 1922.)*

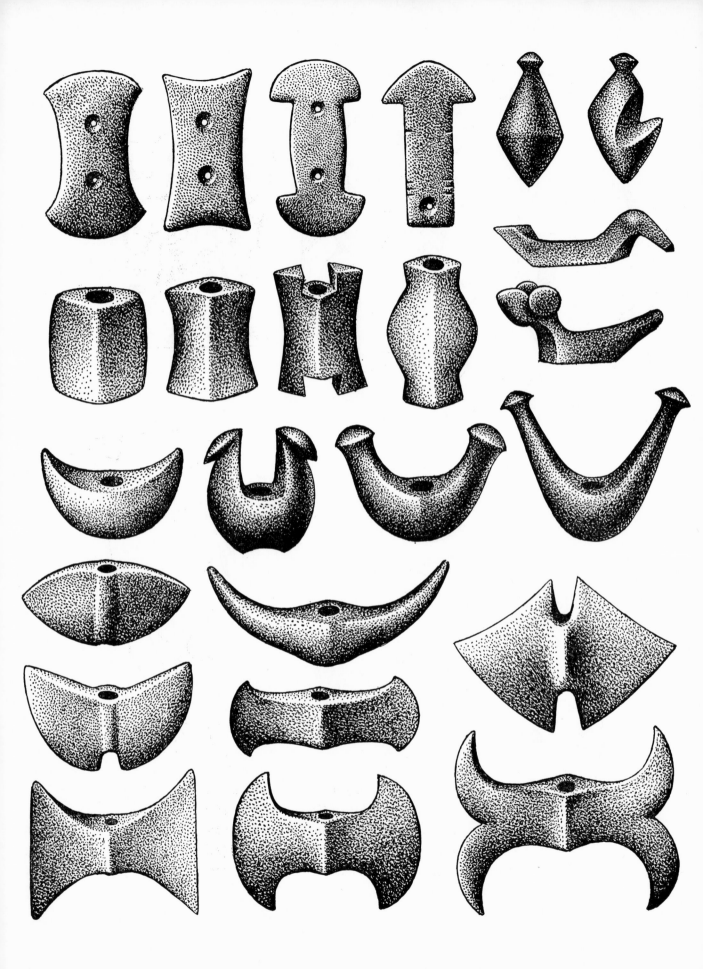

The Mississippi Period: A.D. 900–1700. The great Hopewell culture passed away suddenly like the Classic cultures of Middle America, leaving no traces of the causes of its disappearance. What came next in the eastern United States was a renaissance that flourished in the central and lower Mississippi Valley (Arkansas, Mississippi, Tennessee, and Louisiana), from where it spread to Georgia (Macon Plateau), Florida (Weeden Island), and Ohio (Fort Ancient), to name a few of its representative aspects. It reached the Great Lakes in the north, the Atlantic seaboard to the east, and the Plains to the west, with, however, the middle south holding pre-eminence.

The Mississippi period has also two phases: early and late, called by archæologists "Temple Mound I" and "Temple Mound II." These names, devised for the Ohio area, are particularly appropriate, for the most characteristic trait of this period is the introduction, probably from Mexico, of mounds that were no longer burial places, but substructures for temples and chiefs' houses.

The towns of the Mississippi period were built after the Mexican pattern: fortified city-states with neighboring vassal villages, each built around a central plaza with truncated earth pyramids surmounted by thatched temples and chief's houses reached by stairways (Fig. 92). These mounds were built in successive layers, reminiscent of the Mexican custom of adding a new layer to enlarge the structure every cycle or "century" of fifty-two years. Mexican influence did not end there; during the Temple Mound II period a new religious cult, supposedly based upon the Mexican death cult, made its appearance in the Mississippi Valley and spread rapidly, bringing new elements that strongly

FIG. 91 (FACING). *Characteristic problematic stone objects of the northeastern Woodlands: gorgets, plummets, sinkers, "birdstones," and "banner stones," made of banded slate, quartz, steatite, diorite, and porphyry (drawn after Knoblock, 1939; Willoughby, 1935; and Lilly, 1937).*

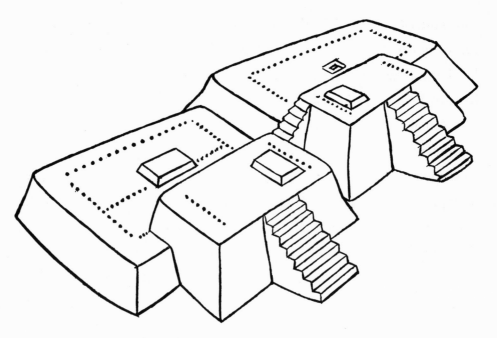

FIG. 92. *A complicated substructure mound of the Mississippi period, showing postholes, from Miwassee Island (after Griffin, 1952).*

influenced the arts. These elements—human skulls, trophy heads, eagles, warriors, solar disks, crosses, the so-called "weeping eye" in the palm of a hand, rattlesnakes, spiders, woodpeckers, monolithic axes, stone clubs, etc.—constitute a complex called by archæologists the "southern (death) cult." The former tendency to date Indian cultures as late developments led archæologists to believe the southern cult was introduced somewhere between the sixteenth and seventeenth centuries, supposedly brought by Mexican Indians who came with the Spaniards of the Tristán de Luna expedition of 1559–61. It was also attributed to a fatalistic psychosis of fear induced by crisis such as crop-failures, and to the impending threat of Spanish atrocities (Martin, Collier, and Quimby, 1947). These concepts have perhaps become obsolete in the face of the new chronology, and it is more likely that the southern cult, if it came from Mexico at all, must have been in existence since A.D. 1200, the time of the collapse of the Toltec empire. Because the similarities between the southern and the Mexican death cults are rather general, it is more likely that the Mississippi death cult is of local origin, with some basic Mexican concepts received indirectly, perhaps by hearsay and without actual Mexican contact.

Among the arts of the Mississippi period stands the prolific development of pottery in many new styles, forms, and decorations. The most spectacular pieces come from the middle southern and lower Mississippi Valley areas, where beautiful bottles, jars, and bowls have been found. Some are painted in red, white, and black or sepia on yellow clay, incised or stamped on gray, red, or black clay, with simple geometric motifs or with dynamic, swirling, interlocking spirals or curvilinear swastikas; others are decorated with naturalistic designs of the death cult—eagles, skulls, bones, hands with eyes on the palm, solar disks, and so forth—while still others are modeled in the shape of human figures, squatting hunchbacks, human heads, birds, frogs, and fish (Figs. 93, 94).

Stone-carving also flourished in a style reminiscent of Mexico, quite different in spirit from that of the classic Hopewellian effigy pipes. The pipes of this period are massive, realistic human figures (Pl. 38), generally made of handsome stones such as red bauxite or translucent yellow-green fluorite, with the bowl concealed in the back; the orifice was probably fitted with a reed stem. Another style, typical of Tennessee, consists of large tubular pipes in the shape of birds made of steatite or serpentine. Also carved in the Mexican tradition are certain large human figures of limestone and a few human heads, found in Kentucky and Alabama, without apparent practical use. Typical of the stone-carving of the period are magnificent bowls in the shape of birds, such as the masterpiece of graceful and harmonious design of polished diorite found in Moundville, Alabama, representing a crested wood duck (Pl. 40); and sandstone disks, believed to have been palettes, one of

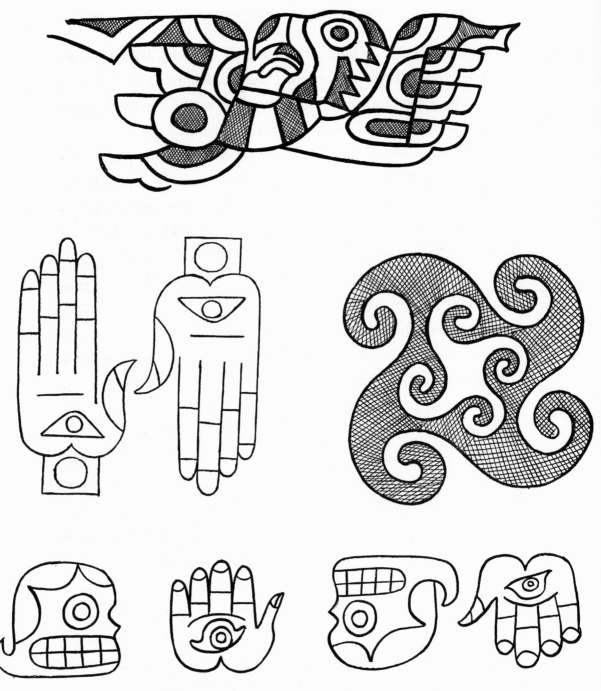

FIG. 93. *Typical motifs of the Mississippi-period pottery:* TOP, *eagle incised on a pot from the Tombigbee River, northwest Florida coast;* LEFT CENTER, *decoration on a vessel from Moundville, Alabama;* RIGHT, *swastika incised on a vessel from the Ouachita Valley, Louisiana;* BELOW, *skull and eye-on-hand motif on a bowl from Moundville, Alabama. (All after Moore.)*

FIG. 94. *Mississippi-period pottery: (a) effigy-head vessel, Arkansas (USNM); (b) bottle in red and white on yellow, Arkansas (Moore, 1908); (c) bottle painted in red and white, Arkansas (PMC); (d, e) incised bottles, Ouachita Valley, Louisiana (Moore, 1909); (f) Caddoan-style incised black bottle with red paint rubbed into the designs, Arkansas (MAIHF); (g) gray clay frog effigy-jar, Arkansas (MAIHF).*

which, found in Mississippi, was decorated with an incised design representing two interlocked feathered rattlesnakes (Fig. 95). There are also representations of hafted axes carved out of a single piece of stone, a form typical of South America and the West Indies.

Shell-carving is another art characteristic of the Mississippi period: circular gorgets, funerary masks, and engraved conch-shells. The gorgets are particularly interesting for the motifs that decorate them, all representative of the southern cult, and for the fact that similar decorated shell gorgets (and earplugs) were the fashion in the Huaxtecan region of the Gulf coast of Mexico. The motifs of the Mississippi Valley shell gorgets, either incised, carved in low relief, or cut out, represent warriors carrying trophy heads, human faces with the "weeping eye" motif, rattlesnakes, spiders, woodpecker heads, crosses, and solar symbols (Figs. 96, 97). The most elaborate specimens come from the Spiro Mound, Le Flore County, Oklahoma, from Sumner County, Tennessee, and from New Madrid County, Missouri.

Large and elaborate cut-out plates of copper with *repoussé* design from the Etowah Mounds near Cartersville, Georgia, are indicative of a continuation of the Hopewellian metallurgic tradition. They represent elaborately dressed and winged warriors, sometimes carrying a severed head, spotted eagles, eagle-men, and the tantalizing human hand motif, with an eye in the palm, under a solar symbol (Figs. 98, 99). The great importance of the art of woodcarving in the Woodlands would have remained unsuspected had it not been for the fact that in 1895 the archæologist Cushing discovered in the muck of Key Marco, in the swamps of the Florida Keys, hundreds of remarkable wooden objects: masks, statuettes, painted boards, carved tablets, boxes, stools, spear-throwers, hafted adzes, saber clubs set with shark's teeth, canoe models, etc. Many of these shrank beyond recognition in drying, but enough were saved to give us insight into a new aspect of Indian art: sculptures of animals—

FACING: *Ancient Navajo blankets. Top: a fine example of the so-called "Chief's blanket" type (Collection of Fred Harvey); bottom: an old bayeta saddle-blanket (Collection of G. Wharton James) (Wharton James, 1937).*

FIG. 95. ABOVE LEFT, *shell gorget with human figure from Spiro,
Oklahoma* (MAIHF); RIGHT, *from southeastern Missouri*
(*Holmes, 1881*); BELOW LEFT, *from New Madrid County, Mis-
souri* (AMNH); RIGHT, *sandstone disk with rattlesnakes, from
Mississippi* (OSM).

265

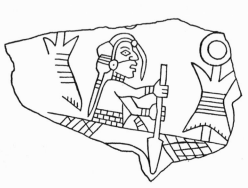

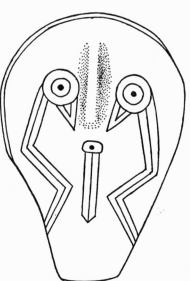

FIG. 96. *Shell art of the Temple Mound period:* ABOVE, *gorget with rattlesnake motif, Rome, Georgia (MNAM);* BELOW LEFT, *fragment of conch-shell from the Spiro Mound, Le Flore County, Oklahoma, showing Mexican influence (UO);* RIGHT, *conch-shell mask, Tennessee (AMNH).*

FIG. 97. *Gorgets of incised shell with typical "buzzard cult" motifs:* ABOVE, *Swastika, Tennessee;* BELOW LEFT, *woodpecker, Tennessee;* RIGHT, *spider, Illinois.*

pumas, deer, wolves, frigate birds, and alligators (Pl. 41, 42; Figs. 100, 101)—carved with an unprecedented delicacy and sensitive realism.

Seen as wholes, the arts and cultures of the ancient Woodlands present many tantalizing and suggestive problems. Judging by the existing evidence, there seems to be a continuity in the development of these cultures from the times of the hunters of mastodon, over ten thousand years ago, through a long period of primitive hunters and gath-

FIG. 98. Repoussé *copper plaques with hawks and birdmen:* ABOVE, *from Etowah, Georgia;* TOP AND BOTTOM, *from Malden, Dunklin County, Missouri (Fouke, 1910).*

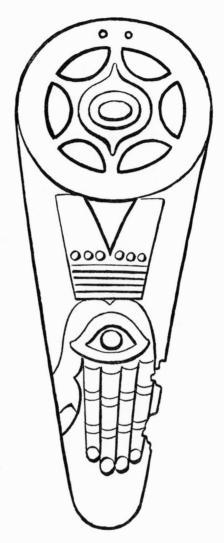

FIG. 99. *Copper plaque with* repoussé *eye-on-hand design, Moundville, Alabama (after Moore).*

erers not unlike the Cochise paleo-Indians of the Southwest, to Archaic transitional cultures marked by the appearance of a strange mixture of local, Middle American, and Asiatic traits. On the one hand are such elements, typical of early Mexico, as agriculture based upon corn, beans, tobacco, and squashes, and funerary mound-building; on the other hand are such Asiatic traits as stamped, cord-marked, and textile-impressed pottery, ground slate tools, and stemmed and socketed copper weapons of the Asiatic Bronze Age style. These mixed elements suggest two covergent currents of cultural diffusion: one from the north—

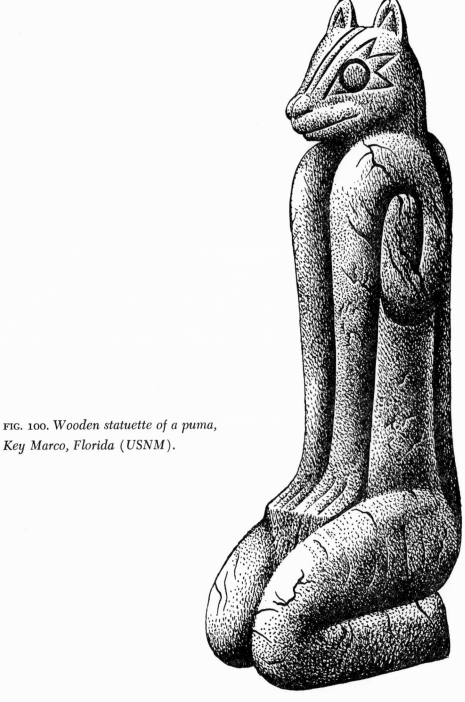

FIG. 100. *Wooden statuette of a puma,
Key Marco, Florida* (USNM).

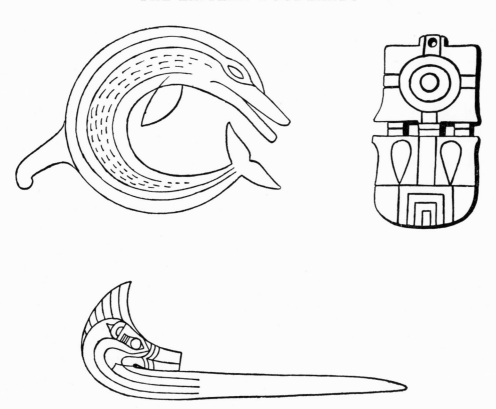

FIG. 101. ABOVE LEFT, *porpoise incised on a wooden implement, Key Marco, Florida* (USNM); RIGHT, *heavy gold ornament from the Kissine River, Fort Bassinger, Florida* (Douglas, 1890); BE-LOW, *gold ornament from Florida* (Holmes, 1881).

if not directly from Asia, through Asiatic immigrants, perhaps the Dorset Eskimo of two thousand years ago—the other from the south, from pre-Classic Mexico, probably at a time when the Mexican cultures were not yet fully differentiated.

It is a puzzling fact that copper tools and weapons appear at such an early date, over a millennium before they were known in Mexico. The "Old Copper" culture tools made by the ancient settlers of the Wisconsin-Minnesota area have unique sockets and rat-tail stems like those of Asiatic iron tools, and it is more likely that the Asiatic style of forged bronze or iron tools was translated into hammered copper, rather than that, as was formerly believed by archæologists, the native stone tools had been copied in copper. Pipe-smoking, which is one of the most characteristic Woodland concepts, also appears at an early time. It is difficult to explain why the famous Adena pipe, one of the oldest known, is carved in the Mexican tradition, for pipes came quite late to Mexico and stone pipes were unknown there.

The art of the Woodlands reached maturity in the Hopewell period, with local traits such as effigy mounds, peculiar pottery shapes and decoration, elaborate ornaments of hammered copper and silver, antlers as headdresses, stone effigy-pipes, "banner stones," silhouettes of mica, and pendants of bear-teeth set with pearls. The serene art of Hopewell faded away and a new barbaric culture rolled like a wave from the south, carrying with it many Mexican elements, probably acquired second-hand, such as pyramids to support ceremonial structures, stone statues, certain pottery styles, shell gorgets, and lurid elements from the southern cult: skulls, bones, eagle-warriors carrying severed heads, feathered rattlesnakes, and so forth. This culture also decayed, so that its grandiose traits were not evident to the early settlers from abroad. The Woodland cultures reflected the ups and downs of Mexican pre-Spanish cultures, and the character and spirit of their art is in such measure an extension of Middle American civilization that it has been called, perhaps wrongly, "peripheral Mexican."

THE ARTS OF THE HISTORICAL PEOPLES
OF THE WOODLANDS

THE North American Woodlands stretch over most of Canada, all the way from Alaska to Labrador, and from the Great Lakes area to Louisiana and Florida. Conifers predominate in the sub-arctic north and gradually give way to birches, elms, oaks, and willows. The Woodlands finally turn into the alligator-infested swamps of the lower Mississippi and the Florida Everglades. This beautiful and romantic country was once populated by Indian peoples of different languages and customs, with cultures in varying degrees of development. The northern peoples, for instance, constituted scattered, roaming tribes of hunters with only minor artistic manifestations; in the southeastern Woodlands remnants of peoples still live who in ancient times possessed now-forgotten arts and cultures of high æsthetic quality, while others, like the civilized Iroquois of New England and New York, amazed the founders of the United States by their advanced democratic political system. However varied, these people constitute a loosely bound unit because with time, the spread of certain traits, and white influence, their cultures and arts took on some uniformity.

In historical times these peoples had a homogeneous art, perhaps because of its simplicity essentially decorative, without clear connections with the known archæological cultures of these areas. Many of these peoples influenced one another, until the differences among their art styles became vague and confused. The process of acculturation after white conquest intensified this homogeneity, or in certain cases developed new areas of culture with well-defined centers, but with gradually merging frontiers. Such is the case of the Plains Indians, originally marginal Woodland peoples, who developed a new cultural outlook by the acquisition of the horse and firearms, admirably suited to their restless and warlike spirit and to the country into which they were displaced by the new pressures from the east from both Indians and whites: the vast, open Plains. Thus the sedentary agriculturists turned into wandering hunters and ferocious warriors. The introduction of glass beads, European cloth, and commerce with the whites radically modified their cultures, their dress, their arts, and their decorative styles.

The northern area was about equally divided between two great linguistic families: the Athapascans to the west, the Algonquians to the east. The Athapascans were nomadic hunters entirely dependent upon the caribou for food and using skin tents, tailored clothes, mittens, and caps. They used snowshoes and toboggans and made a meager living from the fur trade. Their art was practically nonexistent: the Kutchin of Alaska were content to decorate their skin garments with simple filleting embroidered with colored porcupine quills. Later on they learned to make European-style floral designs with glass beads. Today they have forgotten even such elementary arts, and dress in the overalls and discarded clothes of the whites. The Ingalik of the Yukon made wooden dishes and masks copied from the Eskimo, and the Sarsi imitate the beaded designs of their neighbors, the Plains Indians. The rest of the Athapascan tribes seem never to have practiced any form of art.

The Algonquians had a much greater artistic personality; the Ojibway or Chippewa, the Cree, Montaignais, Naskapi, and others made utensils and vessels of bent and sewn birchbark decorated with scraped designs representing silhouettes of animals and plantlike curvilinear, symmetric designs (Figs. 102, 103). Such vessels of scraped birchbark constitute one of the many traits these peoples have in common with Siberia. The Naskapi of Labrador decorate their white buckskin coats with fine red, blue, and yellow motifs based upon the double curve (Fig. 104). This motif, the most characteristic in the northeastern Woodlands, has its most archaic aspects in the Naskapi painted coats, becoming increasingly baroque among such eastern Algonquians as the Iroquois, Mohicans, Penobscots, and Micmacs. Were it not for the fact that the double curve appears on birchbark vessels and on wooden objects preceding European contact, the Indian origin of this motif could be doubted.

The textile arts must have been practiced intensively in prehistoric

274

FIG. 102. TOP & CENTER, *birchbark box with abstract design,*
Ojibway (AMNH); BELOW, *birchbark box with naturalistic*
animal motifs, Cree, north central Canada (DAM).

275

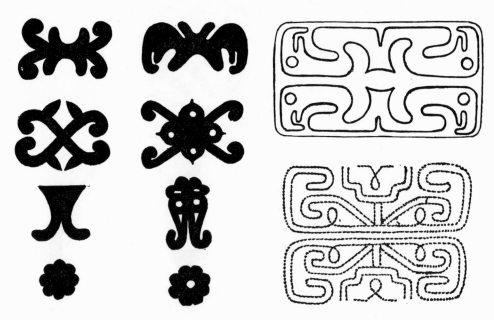

FIG. 103. LEFT, *Algonquian birchbark motifs and their probable antecedents in Hopewell cut-out metal plaques (Quimby, 1943);* RIGHT, TOP: *incised copper plaque from the Hopewell mounds;* BOTTOM: *beaded design of the New England Micmac.*

times, but they have disappeared from the Woodlands, and only a rather elementary form of weaving survives in the Great Lakes region, among the Winnebago and Menominee. It consists in the making of fiber or yarn bags woven with able stylizations of mountain lion and thunderbirds (Fig. 105), indicating the presence of an art that probably had a wider distribution in the past. Typical of the Sauk and Fox Indians of Lake Michigan are folding boxes and parfleches of rawhide painted with well-balanced geometric designs in bright colors, pointing at a link with the Plains art of skin-painting, of which they are perhaps the origin.

Perhaps the most typical of North American arts (it is unknown in the rest of the world) is porcupine-quill work. This art had its greatest development among such northern Algonquians as the Ojibway, Cree, and Winnebago, among whom it probably originated, spreading widely

FIG. 104. *Aspects of the double-curve motif of the northern Woodlands.* LEFT, TOP TO BOTTOM: *embroidered in porcupine quills, Dog-Rib Dene, Mackenzie Valley (USNM); on a Montaignais birchbark box from Labrador (ChMNH); painted on a Naskapi buckskin coat, Labrador (ChMNH); on a strip of appliqué cloth, Potawatomi, Great Lakes area (ChMNH);* RIGHT, TOP: *carved on a wooden implement, Chippewa, north-central Canada (USNM);* BOTTOM, *embroidered with porcupine quills on a Chippewa coat (DAM).*

277

FIG. 105. *Cat and thunderbird motifs from Menominee bark-fiber bags from Wisconsin (AMNH).*

278

to the north, west, and south, from the Mackenzie Valley to the Rocky Mountains and as far as New Mexico. The porcupine quills are dyed in various colors, flattened, and sewed, wrapped, plaited, or woven to form designs. Geometric styles predominate among the western tribes, while curvilinear, floral designs betraying French influence are prevalent in the east, though curvilinear motifs were used also in the west after 1860. Porcupine-quill embroidery or, rather, mosaic always has a serene, restrained character, and the soft colors and excellence of the workmanship of the older pieces give it unique distinction (Pl. 25). The complicated woven technique, of which only a few pieces have been preserved, was practiced exclusively by the Canadian Ojibway, without doubt the masters of this peculiar and highly specialized art.

The Algonquians also embroidered birchbark and buckskin with moose-, elk-, and horse-hair, an art that was soon influenced by European folk art. Quillwork and moose-hair embroidery suffered a sudden transformation of style and went into decadence during the 1890's, when manufactured cloth, silk ribbon, and glass beads were introduced. With these new materials the Indians created such new arts as beadwork and the characteristic mosaics of colored ribbons sewed on broadcloth. After reproducing the traditional quillwork designs in glass beads for a while, they adopted a heavy Victorian style of floral decoration of the bedroom slipper, watch-holder style of the 1890's. The Iroquois, Penobscot, Micmac, and others of the New York and New England area, however, adapted their old style of double curves and spirals to beadwork and created a delicate lace-like style in impeccable taste (Fig. 106) for use in their broadcloth leggings, belts, shirts, skirts, moccasins, and even papoose cradles.

The intelligent and noble Iroquois distinguished themselves for their political organization, so advanced that they had formed a great confederation of six nations with elected representatives, woman's suf-

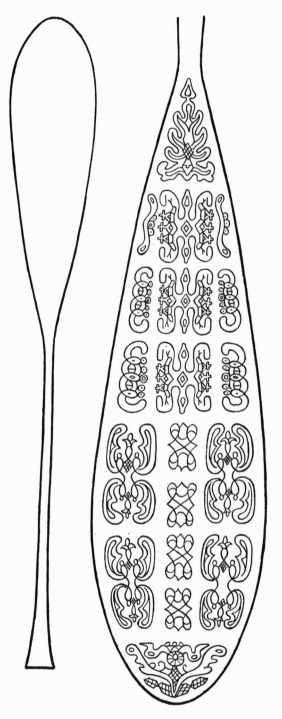

FIG. 106. *The double-curve motif among the New England Micmac:* LEFT, *on a wooden paddle (AMNH);* ABOVE, *on a beaded hood (MAIHF).*

frage, referendum, government by executives, and a council under a constitution. It is well known that among those who formulated the

FACING: *Art of the Plains Indians. (a) Crow beaded pipe-bag (DAM); (b) apron of buckskin embroidered with porcupine quills, Blackfoot (USNM); (c) Crow medicine shield of rawhide (ChMNH).*

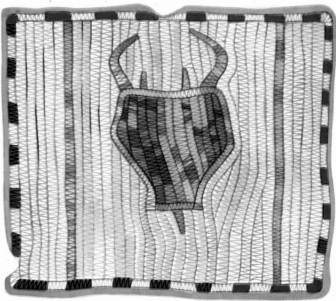

Constitution of the United States there were authorities in the study of the political systems of the Indians, and it has been said that the concept of federalism was in part derived from the Iroquois Six Nation Confederation, founded by the famous Indian leaders Dekanawida and Hiawatha.

Some Iroquois still live in the neighborhood of Buffalo, but formerly they occupied the area around Lake Erie and Lake Ontario. They lived in palisaded villages of birchbark houses; they cultivated corn, beans, and squash; hunted with bows and arrows; and fished with traps, spears, and hooks. They constructed streamlined canoes of birchbark, light as feathers, which they handled with extraordinary ability. They used to dress in buckskin garments, which were eventually replaced by those made of imported cloth and beads. In ancient times they made a peculiar type of pottery: round jars of unpainted, coarse clay with an added thick, wide rim, often squared, with simple incised geometric designs and with the suggestion of human faces and even human figures at each of the four corners (Fig. 107). This pottery was made until about 1700, when it was replaced by imported metal kitchenware. There is little evidence that the ancient Iroquois practiced sculpture except for elementary human and animal figures on clay pipes, a few bone combs topped with carved figures of animals, and a figurine or two in bone or antler. In recent times, however, they carved amusing spoons and bowls of wood with animal objects, as well as war-clubs of hardwood, designed with elegant abstract simplicity.

Perhaps the most interesting manifestation of Iroquois art is the carving of fantastic wooden masks, used by the members of the Seneca "False Face Companies" (*Hadigonsa shono*), mutual-aid societies made up of clubs of masked dancers, supposedly empowered to cure sickness. They still parade through the night wearing their gruesome masks, brandishing clubs, and shaking rattles of snapping-turtle shells

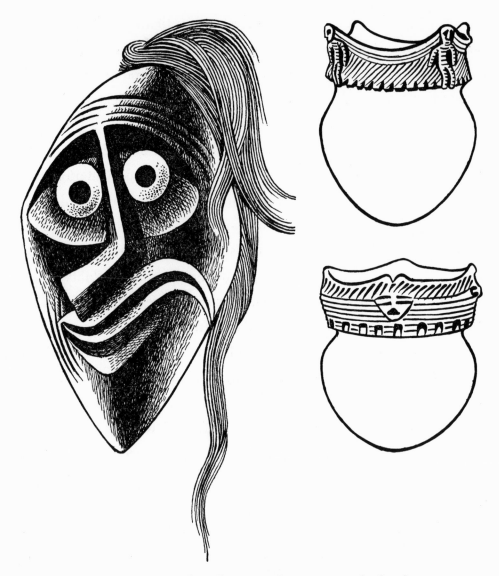

FIG. 107. *Seneca mask of the spirit whose nose was broken by a falling mountain, New York (MAIHF); two ancient pots, Iroquois, from Cayuga and Madison counties, New York (MAIHF).*

to drive out the spirits that cause disease. It is amazing that these societies still survive in western New York, even in the heart of our industrial age, though the "False Face" dancers now use automobiles to go to the aid of the sick.

Seneca masks are representations of spirits, the faces of such stone giants of Iroquois folklore as the long-nosed spirit who kidnaps children or the one whose nose was broken by a falling mountain (Fig. 107). These faces are "dreamed" by someone, who then proceeds to carve a mask out of a living tree so that it will also be endowed with the magic power of life. There is a great variety of such masks: red, black, and white ones with deformed and twisted features and violent gestures, peering out from thick locks of hair made from long horsetails—great noses, fleshy mouths, and round, startled eyes made of shining metal disks (Pl. 44). They also made masks of cornhusk, used in the ceremonies of the "Husk-face" societies (*Gaji sashono*), each of which consists of thirty members, commemorating the legend of the stranger who met in the forest thirty beings whose faces were made of cornhusks.

Other famous examples of Iroquois art, these made by the Huron and Delaware Indians, were the unique ceremonial belts with elaborate symbolic meaning, made to commemorate a treaty or negotiation. They were of wampum, small tubular beads of white and deep-purple shell, woven on a loom into a strip. Examples (Fig. 108) are the William Penn wampum belts: the first a famous historical relic preserved by the Historical Society of Pennsylvania. The other two are the proud possession of the Museum of the American Indian, Heye Foundation, of New York. The Penn belts were among the documents that sealed the land transfer of the Delaware nation to the colonial proprietors of Pennsylvania. The first belt, believed to have been given to William Penn at Shackmaxon in 1682, represents the desire for amity between the Indians and the whites, symbolized by two figures holding hands. Contrary to the generally accepted version, the large figure represents the Indian, the thin one the white man, for at the time the belt was made the Indian was in a strong position, the white man the recipient of hospitality and protection (Speck, 1925; Beaucamp, 1901). The second

283

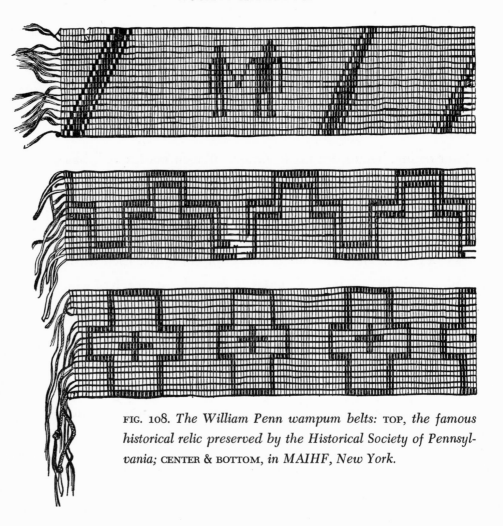

FIG. 108. *The William Penn wampum belts:* TOP, *the famous historical relic preserved by the Historical Society of Pennsylvania;* CENTER & BOTTOM, *in MAIHF, New York.*

belt, with the stepped design, was interpreted by the Onondaga chief David Sky as a "freedom belt," meaning that though the land had changed hands, the Indians reserved for themselves the right to cross it in pursuit of whatever they needed. Chief Sky, after consultation with other chiefs, refused to interpret the third belt, with the design of four crosses. This design is frequent on other wampum belts, and has been interpreted as "tribes" or "castles" in the sense of "stronghold of tribes" (Speck, 1925).

In the southern zone of the Mississippi live the broken remnants of the Muskhogean Indians, the famous "Five Civilized Tribes": the

Cherokee, Creek, Choctaw, Chickasaw, and Calusa or Seminole, peoples who had a great cultural tradition. The Cherokee, for instance, are described in the old chronicles as fabulously rich because they wore mantles embroidered with pearls. At the beginning of the nineteenth century the famous Sequoya invented a syllable system of writing in Cherokee which had such success that after three years half the tribe had learned to read and write. This alphabet was used to publish numerous books and even newspapers in Cherokee. Despite their glorious cultural background, these Indians suffered such a decadence that among them only the art of basketry survived, with an outstanding style among the Chitimacha, a small tribe of southern Louisiana, who make baskets of split cane in red and cream, with designs rather like those on the ancient pottery. The Chitimacha baskets resemble those of the Arawaks of British Guiana and, strangely enough, those of the Dyaks of Borneo. The Seminole of Florida make a fine mosaic of small geometric bits of cloth of brilliant colors sewed together. With this they decorate their garish gypsy-like costumes.

CHAPTER VI

The Plains

THE Plains Indians, regarded erroneously as the archetype of the "red-skins," the North American Indians, owe their fame to their romantic and agitated history and to their stubborn and ferocious resistance to the white invaders, whom they fought relentlessly for forty years (1850–91). The heroism of such of their chiefs as Sitting Bull, their gallant feather bonnets, and their feats with horse and rifle are the bases of the daydreams of every American boy.

It is a generally accepted fact that the peculiar character of their present culture did not materialize until after the introduction among them of horses and firearms, after 1650, when they scattered over the prairies, exchanging a semisedentary life for hectic roaming after herds of bison and constant war with their neighbors. The warlike and adventurous temperament of the Plains Indians created a psychology in which bravery and audacity, often leading to self-destruction, were more admirable than emerging victorious over an enemy. Their entire culture suffered a violent change with their new way of life. They gave up their villages of round earth lodges for temporary camps of tepees—conical, collapsible skin tents. They abandoned the ancient art of pottery-making because all of their artifacts had to be portable: skins, folding back-rests, rawhide boxes and parfleches, buckskin bags, and so forth. Because the wandering bands were constituted by peoples who spoke different languages,[1] they had to invent a common language of signs and gestures.

The Plains Indians gradually changed their semi-vegetarian diet for the abundant bison meat; the tribes shattered into small bands that met rarely, with the result that their religious and ceremonial concepts acquired strong individual characteristics. Shamanism was the general practice, however, with emphasis on the dreams and visions of the shamans. This fact probably opened the door for the introduction in 1870 of the Mexican peyote cult, which consists in ceremonial eating of a narcotic cactus that produces wonderful visions of flashes of color. The peyote cult served as an art-motivator; a whole complex of designs that decorate rattles and feather fans is related to it. The Dakotas held a famous festival, the great annual Sun Dance, as an ex-voto to propitiate the spirits and acquire magic powers. Unbelievable acts of endurance, such as hanging in mid-air from pegs driven through the performers' skins, took place in front of a tall pole surmounted by a thunderbird, symbol of the sun.

The raw materials that the hunt produced—rawhide, bison pelts, buckskin—lent themselves admirably to decoration. New wealth, acquired from the abundant game, incited the need for personal ostentation, and the Plains Indians took to decorating everything they used—their tepees, their own and their wives' clothes, moccasins, horse-trappings, and so forth—with geometric designs in which the women specialized or in a realistic, anecdotic art that was the exclusive province of the men. The realistic style of painted skins was developed into a true

[1] There are some twenty-five different languages, belonging to seven linguistic families, spoken in the Plains: Algonquin, Athapascan, Caddoan, Kiowan, Sahaptin, Siowan, and Shoshone; peoples whose original homes lay to the far north, northeast, east, and west of the Plains.

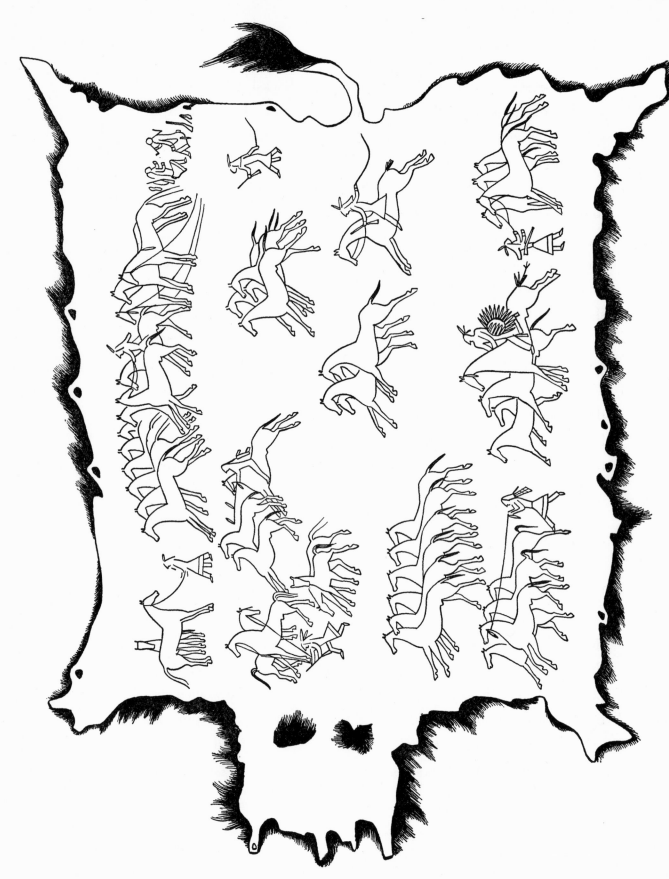

FIG. 109. *Roundup of horses on an Oglala buffalo robe* (AMNH).

form of picture-writing, and there are splendid examples of painted skins with descriptive scenes of the life and adventures of their owners, their war feats (see Pl. 47 and Figs. 109, 110), and the so-called Winter Counts, tribal annals recording events over long stretches of time. They also painted their tepee-covers, an art in which the Blackfoot Indians of the northwestern plains were outstanding, as well as their drumheads and medicine shields. These shields do not depend for their defensive powers so much on the tough bison hide of which they are made as on the magic design painted on them. The Crow are perhaps the most distinguished painters of medicine shields, and their compositions of animals, celestial bodies, or abstract forms have sometimes the vigorous spontaneity of the paleolithic rock painting of Africa or Spain, and at times are surprisingly similar in spirit to the paintings of Paul Klee or of Joan Miró. A popular motif on Crow shields is a bear or a bison facing a shower of flying bullets, represented by tadpole-like shapes (Fig. 111). The colors used are principally black and red, less frequently combined with lemon yellow, ultramarine blue, dark green, and gray.

The realistic style often bears the mark of the individual artist; the geometric style, on the other hand, is essentially traditional. It is based on triangles, diamonds, squares, circles, bands, and so forth, in combinations that show impeccable taste and a keen sense of mass-spacing. These geometric designs have names and meanings, but their arrangement has no established significance. The meanings are purely personal, changing from tribe to tribe and even from one individual to another. The artist organizes these elements to express a poetic idea, however, without overlooking the harmonious and decorative values of the whole pattern.

The geometric, abstract art is applied to various media. The most spectacular designs are painted on the inner side of bison robes, an art that seems related to the painted robes of the ancient Woodland Indians

(Ewers, 1939), and are classified into five styles: border and box, border and hourglass, feathered circle (Pl. 46), horizontal-striped, and bilaterally symmetrical (Ewers, 1939). Painted geometric designs were used also on parfleches and quivers of rawhide, clearly derived from the style of Indians of the Great Lakes area. For the decoration of lesser

FIG. 110. ABOVE & FACING: *two details of an old Sioux buffalo robe painted in the realistic style to show a dynamic battle. Collected about 1846 (MfVB).*

utensils and articles of dress they employ porcupine-quill embroidery and beadwork. The style of these probably had its origins in ancient basketry motifs, such as those of the Californians, or in the porcupine-quill embroideries from the northeast. Only porcupine-quill embroidery appears in the oldest pieces from the Plains. The introduction of commercial glass beads doomed the art of quill decoration; the women became addicted to beads, and the new art gained enormous popularity. Each tribe or group of tribes had its favorite colors and motifs. The peoples can be divided into five main groups:

FIG. 111. *Buffalo facing a semicircle of flying bullets, painted in sienna on a dirty beige background, on an old Crow medicine shield (ChMNH).*

NORTHWEST: *Assiniboin, Blackfoot, Nez Percé, Gros Ventre.*

SOUTH: *Kiowa, Comanche (and Apache, classified with the Southwest Indians).*

CENTER: *Western Sioux, Crow, Cheyenne, Arapaho.*

SOUTHEAST: *Omaha, Osage, Ponca, Pawnee, Oto.*

NORTHEAST: *Eastern Sioux, Iowa (and Winnebago, regarded as of the Woodlands).*

The Sioux were the most prolific quill- and bead-workers and made the finest examples of both bead- and quill-work. The articles were made entirely by women, from the dressing of the skins, sewing them into shirts, leggings, moccasins, and so forth, to the execution of the decoration. In former times the geometric style had a high artistic value, both because of its tasteful balance of designs and color and of dynamic or static combinations of plastic elements and because of its

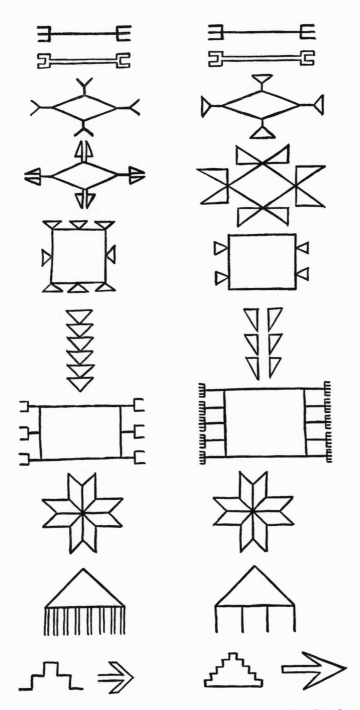

FIG. 112. *Design elements of Central Plains beadwork (right) compared with similar elements from Caucasus rugs (left) (redrawn after Lyford, 1940).*

293

technical skill, but in time it degenerated rapidly, first when it fell under the influence of the designs copied from Caucasus rugs (Fig. 112), and later when it fell under the floral French style of the end of the nineteenth century.

The men made all the ceremonial objects, the most notable of which are the calumets, the ceremonial pipes decorated with eagle feathers, beadwork, and tufts of horsehair. The pipe proper was made of catlinite, red or black "pipestone," carved in abstract or animal shapes (Pl. 46). These pipes are the only example of Plains sculpture.

Last but not least were the clothes and ornaments of the Plains Indians, particularly the great war bonnets of eagle feathers and ermine, which were made as mobiles, to be seen in motion as blown by the wind of the prairies or agitated by the gallop of the horses. The clothes and ornaments of the Plains acquire new life when seen in action, very different from the impression made by them as dead things behind the glass cases of museums. The sense of color, decoration, and drama in the art of Indians of the Plains takes on a new meaning when one sees for the first time their proud, dynamic creators in their dances or sports.

Unfortunately the natural life and vitality of the peoples of the Plains culture have ceased to exist. Their final subjection, the loss of their lands, and later the extinction of the wild herds of bison, their source of livelihood, gave the death-blow to their cultural integrity. Today the Indian population of the Plains is increasing, and there are still, on the reservations, remnants of the brave, proud redskins of forty years ago, but their function has been reduced to appearing in their war bonnets to pose for press photographs of visiting politicians and to greeting the tourists who come to the vast, wind-swept Plains.

An Album of Photographs

PHOTOGRAPHS COURTESY OF:

AMERICAN MUSEUM OF NATURAL HISTORY: *Plates: 1, 2, upper 4, 7, 8, left 9, right 10, left 14, lower 16, 17, upper 18, upper 19, 22, upper 23, upper 28, 29, 35, lower 39, 43, left 44, 47.*

BROOKLYN MUSEUM: *Plates: lower 5, upper 16, upper 31, 32, upper 36, upper 39, 48.*

CHICAGO MUSEUM OF NATURAL HISTORY: *Plates: lower 3, right 9, right 13, lower 19, upper 46.*

UNIVERSITY MUSEUM, PHILADELPHIA: *Plates: lower 3, upper 41, 42, upper 46.*

UNITED STATES NATIONAL MUSEUM: *Plate upper 3.*

METROPOLITAN MUSEUM OF ART: *Plate 6.*

RENÉ D'HARNONCOURT, MUSEUM OF MODERN ART, *and* INDIAN ARTS AND CRAFTS BOARD: *Plates: lower 15, 26, lower 27, upper 30, lower 31, left 33, lower 36, 37, 38, lower 40, lower 41, left 45.*

BUFFALO MUSEUM OF ARTS AND SCIENCES: *Plate lower 28.*

SANTA FE MUSEUM: *Plate 34.*

DENVER ART MUSEUM: *Plates: lower 18, upper right 44.*

LUIS LIMÓN: *Plates: lower 20, lower 23, lower 30, upper 40, lower 46.*

EVA SULZER: *Plates: left 10, right 11.*

WILLIAM SPRATLING: *Plates: left 11, left 13, lower 14.*

NASLI HERRAMANECK: *Plate 21.*

JUAN GUZMÁN: *Plates: lower 4, upper right 14, lower right 44, upper right 45.*

TINA MODOTTI: *Plate right 33.*

MANUEL ALVAREZ BRAVO: *Plate 12.*

MUSEUM OF THE AMERICAN INDIAN, HEYE FOUNDATION: *Plate lower 36.*

MIGUEL COVARRUBIAS: *Plates: upper 5, upper 15, upper 20, 24, 25, lower right 45.*

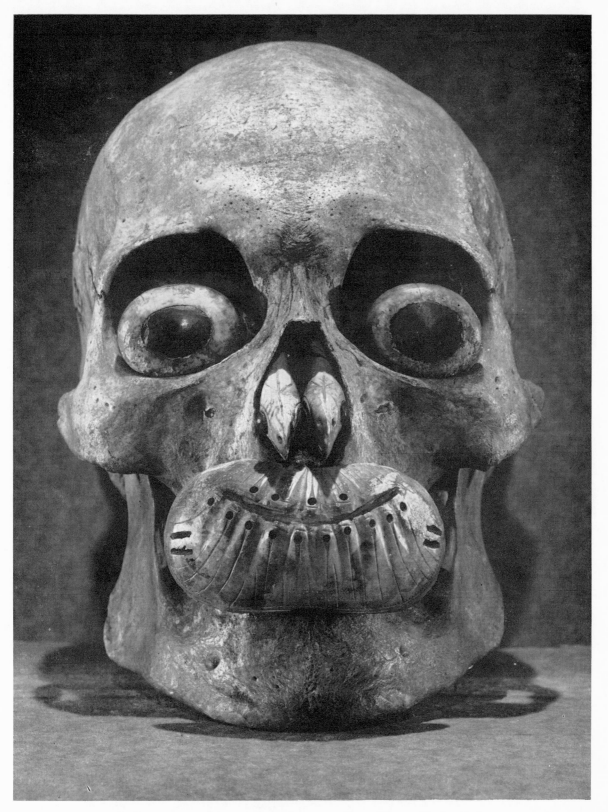

Skull from a prehistoric Ipiutak grave, Point Hope, Alaska. It has eyes of walrus ivory and jet, a carved ivory mouthpiece, and two small birds or seals to plug the nasal cavities (AMNH).

PLATE I

ABOVE: *funerary mask of carved ivory sections;* BELOW: *an
ivory seal. Both from Ipiutak graves, Point Hope, Alaska
(AMNH).*

PLATE II

ABOVE: *both sides of a winged object of fossil ivory, Old Bering Sea period, Point Hope, Alaska* (USNM); BELOW: *ancient stone lamp, probably Punuk period, Cook Inlet, Alaska* (UMP).

PLATE III

ABOVE: *Eskimo mask of driftwood and baleen representing the inua (soul) of a seal, Alaska (AMNH);* BELOW: *pair of maskettes of carved wood and fur, worn on the fingers in certain dances, Alaska (WSM).*

PLATE IV

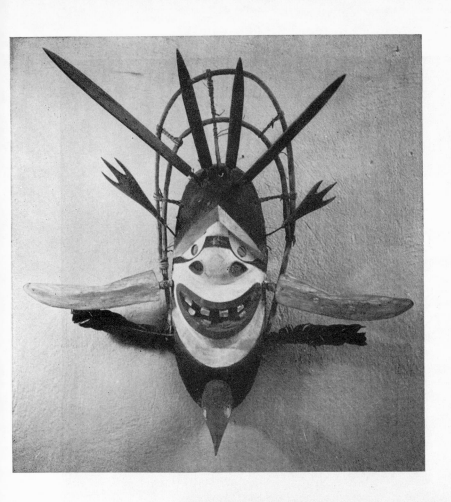

Dance masks of the Alaskan Eskimo; BELOW: *mask of driftwood from the Kuskokewin region, Alaska (AMNH);* LEFT: *the* inua *(soul) of a bird (Collection of W. Paalen).*

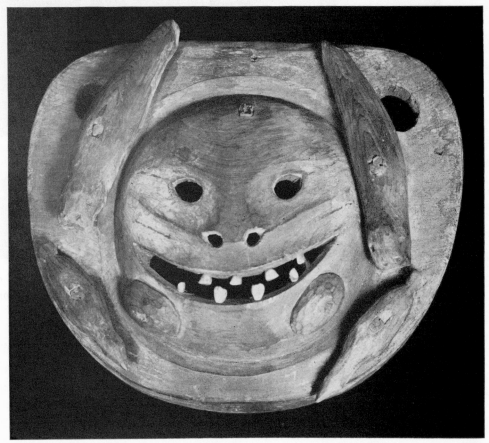

PLATE V

PLATE VI

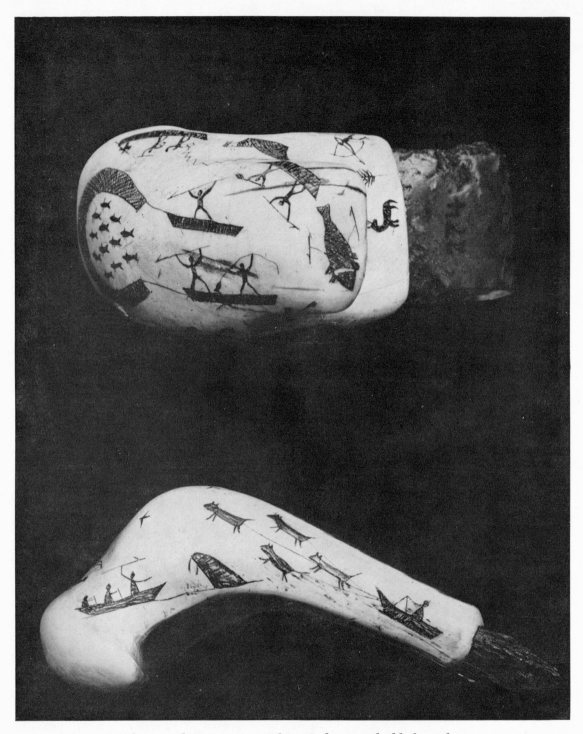

Eskimo tool for preparing skins. It has a jade blade and an incised walrus-ivory handle, and is 17.5 centimeters long (MMA).

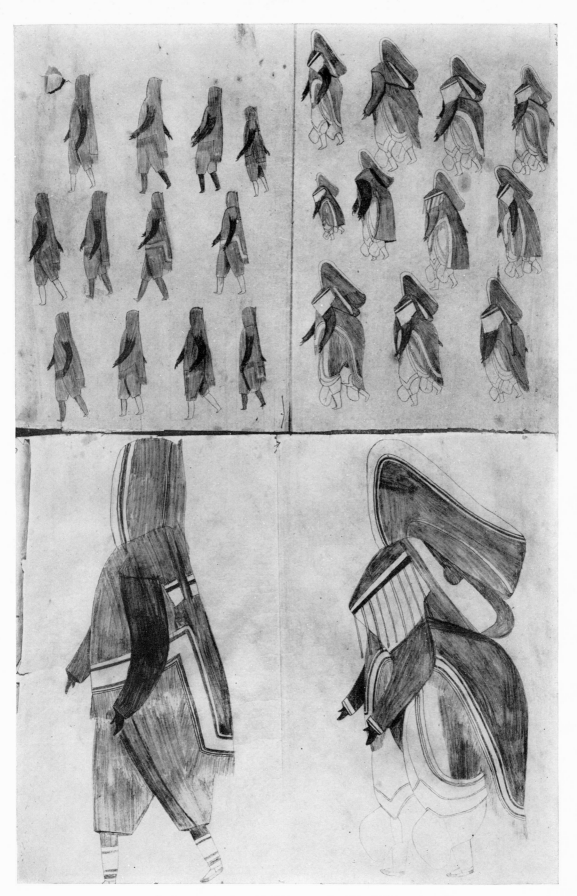

*Pencil drawings by Meliki, an Aivilik Eskimo, made
about 1890 at South Hampton Bay, Greenland (AMNH).*

PLATE VII

Old Haida totem poles from the village of Skidegate, Queen Charlotte Islands, British Columbia.

PLATE VIII

Old Haida houses, Queen Charlotte Islands, British Columbia. RIGHT: *through hole in the abdomen of the pole's lowest figure (this house was old house showing Russian influence;* LEFT: *old-style house with entrance   still standing at Massett in 1901, when Newcomb took the photograph).*

PLATE IX

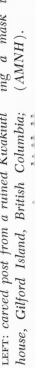

LEFT: carved post from a ruined Kwakiutl house, Gilford Island, British Columbia; (AMNH).

ing a mask to his face, Bella Coola (AMNH).

PLATE X

Monumental woodcarvings from ruined Tlingit and Haida houses. LEFT:
from Wrangel, Alaska; RIGHT: *from Gilford Island, British Columbia.*

PLATE XI

A Kwakiutl potlatch memorial statue of a chief holding a
copper. It is 1.28 meters high (Collection of W. Paalen).

PLATE XII

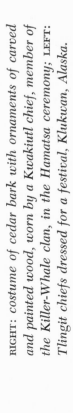

RIGHT: *costume of cedar bark with ornaments of carved and painted wood, worn by a Kwakiutl chief, member of the Killer-Whale clan, in the Hamatsa ceremony;* LEFT: *Tlingit chiefs dressed for a festival, Klukwan, Alaska.*

PLATE XIII

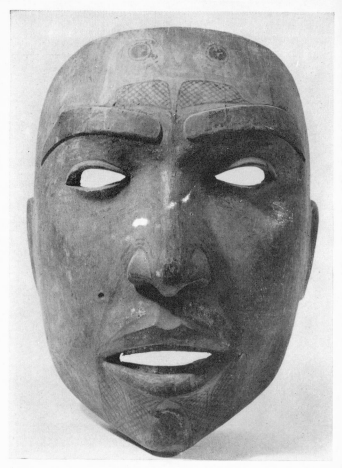

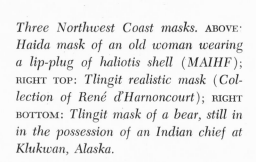

Three Northwest Coast masks. ABOVE·
*Haida mask of an old woman wearing
a lip-plug of haliotis shell (MAIHF);*
RIGHT TOP: *Tlingit realistic mask (Col-
lection of René d'Harnoncourt);* RIGHT
BOTTOM: *Tlingit mask of a bear, still in
in the possession of an Indian chief at
Klukwan, Alaska.*

PLATE XIV

LEFT: *Tsimshian mask used at potlatch dances, Port Essington, British Columbia* (MNAM); BE-LOW: *Tsimshian mask from British Columbia* (MAIHF).

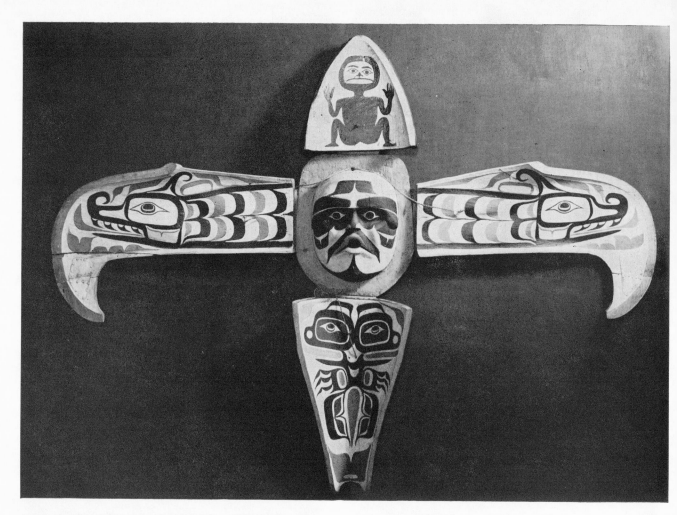

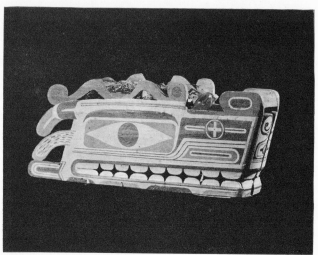

ABOVE: *mechanical Kwakiutl mask that, when closed, represents a thunderbird; when opened by a string device, it reveals the face of an angry chief, the two-headed serpent* (sisiutl), *a bear, and a crouching little man* (BM); BELOW: *two sea-wolf masks of the southerly Nootka, showing the typical concept of geometric form and design, west coast of Vancouver Island, British Columbia* (AMNH).

PLATE XVI

ABOVE: *Tlingit mask of beaten and incised copper, representing a mosquito (MAIHF);* BELOW, LEFT: *the famous "Bear Mother," a Haida slate carving 14 centimeters long, British Columbia (USNM);* BELOW, RIGHT: *a Tlingit wooden comb carved with a bear and a man, about 14 centimeters high (USNM).*

PLATE XVII

ABOVE: *Nootka partition screen of painted wood showing a thunderbird carrying a whale in its talons; on the left, a lightning serpent; on the right, a wolf (AMNH);* BELOW: *Tlingit partition screen painted with two ravens. Made about 1830–40, it measures 4.22 x 1.65 meters (DAM).*

PLATE XVIII

Two Chilkat (Tlingit) blankets or ceremonial capes of mountain-goat wool and cedarbark fiber. ABOVE: *a rare killer-whale design (AMNH);* BELOW: *a classic design (ChMNH).*

PLATE XIX

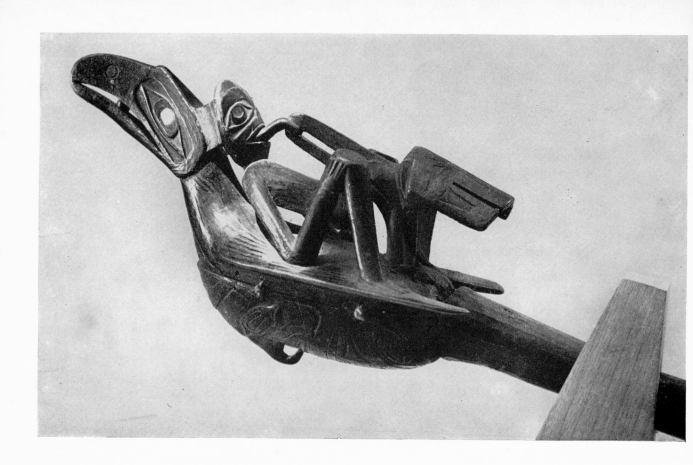

ABOVE: *Kwakiutl dance-rattle of carved wood (Collection M. C.);* LEFT: *large mask from Cowichan, Vancouver Island, British Columbia (Collection of Alice Rahon Fitzgerald).*

PLATE XX

ABOVE: *oil bowl of carved wood in the shape of a beaver;* BELOW: *Kwakiutl stone bowl in the shape of a frog* (*Collection of N. Herramaneck*).

PLATE XXI

Basketry of the Northwest Coast.
ABOVE: *two rare baskets of the Wasco, a Salish tribe (DAM);* BELOW: *an unusual Tlingit basket (MAIHF).*

PLATE XXII

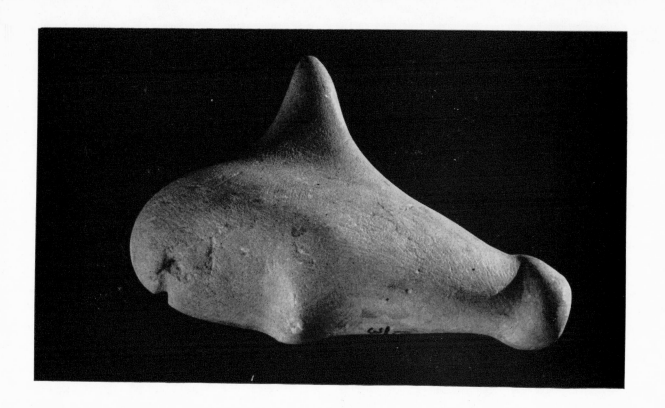

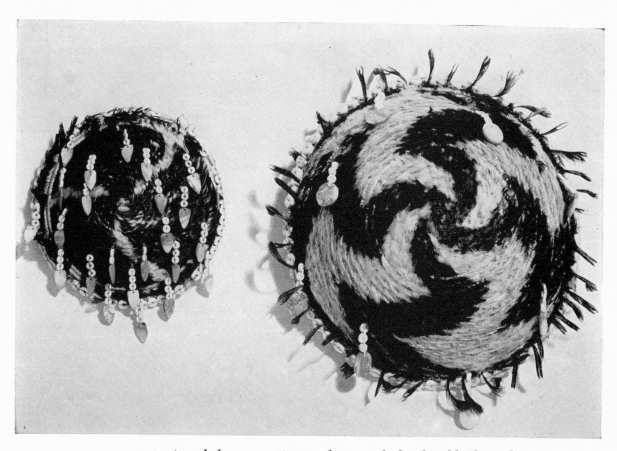

ABOVE: *steatite whale, 9.5 centimeters long, made by the old Chumash Indians of St. Nicholas Island, California (AMNH); BELOW: two "gift" or "jewel" baskets of feather mosaic, with pendants of mother-of-pearl, Pomo, northern California (right, UMP; left, Collection of W. Paalen).*

PLATE XXIII

ABOVE: *a fine Kern "gift" basket with red and black design, Tejón, Kern County, California (MNAM);* BELOW: *two Panamint "gift" baskets, Ingo County, California.*

PLATE XXIV

ABOVE: *Yakut dance-ceremonial basket, Fresno County, California;* BELOW:
LEFT, *small imbricated basket of the Lillooet Indians, Port Douglas, British
Columbia;* RIGHT, *very fine small Karok basket with design of yellow and
black porcupine quills, Humboldt County, California. (All in MNAM.)*

PLATE XXV

Rock paintings of the Basket-maker period, Barrier Canyon, Utah (photo, courtesy IACB).

PLATE XXVI

ABOVE: *Cliff Palace, Mesa Verde National Park, southwestern Colorado, known to have been abandoned about* A.D. *1300 (photo courtesy National Park Service);* RIGHT: *clay jar painted in black and gray, Anasazi culture, Pueblo III period, Kayenta style, 38 centimeters high* (LASF).

PLATE XXVII

Mimbres bowls from southern New Mexico, Pueblo III period.
ABOVE: *a warrior* (PMC); BELOW: *four grasshoppers* (BMAS).

PLATE XXVIII

Two stone palettes and a horned toad, Hohokam culture,
Santa Cruz phase, Snaketown, southern Arizona (GP).

PLATE XXIX

Basketry of the San Carlos Apache. ABOVE: *a shallow tray, 58 centimeters in diameter (Collection of Mrs. William Denman);* BELOW: *a great storage basket, 68.5 centimeters high (AMNH).*

PLATE XXX

ABOVE: *Zuñi dance mask of leather, wood, wool, and cloth, painted in turquoise blue, black, and white; it represents the Sayatasha ("Big Horn") katchina, Rain Priest of the North (BM).* BELOW: *mural painting on the adobe wall of a kiva at Awatobi, Arizona, Pueblo IV period.*

PLATE XXXI

ABOVE: *Zuñi leather mask and wooden doll representing the Anahoho katchina, Messenger of the Gods;* BELOW: *the mask of the Zuñi katchina Chichi (BM).*

PLATE XXXII

BELOW: *statuette of a Zuñi war-god, made from a pine tree that has been struck by lightning, 97 centimeters high* (BM); RIGHT: *a Hopi katchina of carved and painted cottonwood, representing Sio Humis, Messenger of the Gods* (Collection M. C.).

PLATE XXXIII

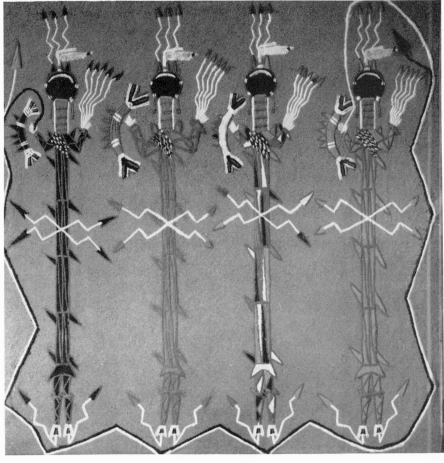

Third and fourth paintings of
the set accompanying the Female Shooting Chant. RIGHT: the
four gods; ABOVE: the buffaloes
of the four cardinal points
(SFM).

PLATE XXXIV

Modern paintings of the Southwest Indians. BELOW: *"Crowd at a Navajo n'da'a, a 'squaw dance,'" by Sybil Yassie;* ABOVE: *"Taos People at a Round Dance," by Tonita Lujan* (SFM).

PLATE XXXV

"Problematic" objects of polished stone from the early Woodland period.
ABOVE: *a "birdstone" from mounds in Kalamazoo County, Michigan (BM, Guenoll Collection loan);* BELOW: *double-crescent "banner stone," Kankakee County, Illinois, 14 centimeters wide (MAIHF).*

PLATE XXXVI

The famous Adena pipe, early Woodland period,
20.5 centimeters high, Ross County, Ohio (OSM).

PLATE XXXVII

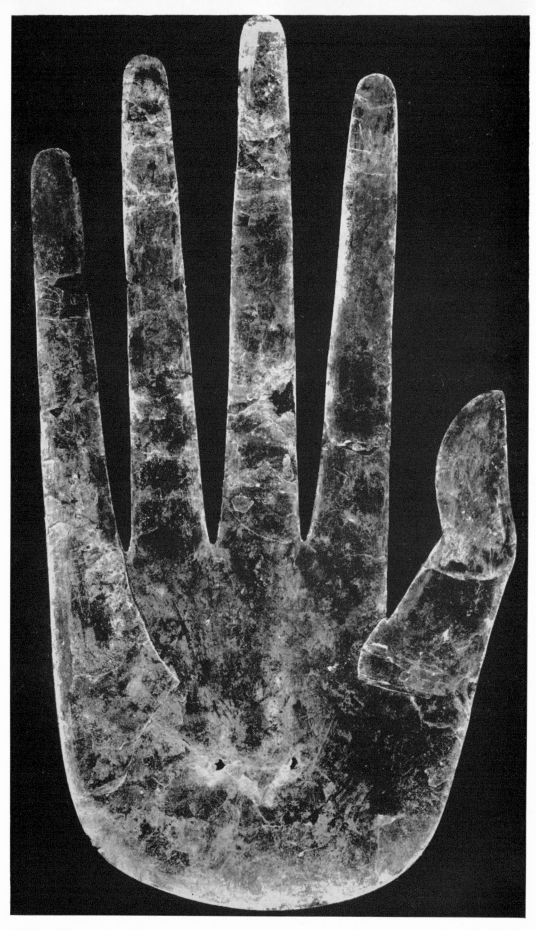

Hand-shaped ornament cut out of mica, Hopewell Mounds, Ohio, 24 centimeters high (OSM).

PLATE XXXVIII

ABOVE: *stone pipe in the shape of a puma, Hopewell style, Posey County, Indiana, about 16 centimeters long (BM, Guenoll Collection loan)*; BELOW: *platform stone pipe in the form of a hawk, Tremper Mound, Ohio, Classic Hopewell style (OSM)*.

PLATE XXXIX

PLATE XL

ABOVE: *great effigy-pipe of red bauxite from Shiloh, Tennessee, Shiloh National Military Park;* BELOW: *diorite bowl representing a male crested wood duck, Moundville, Alabama, Mississippi period (MAIHF).*

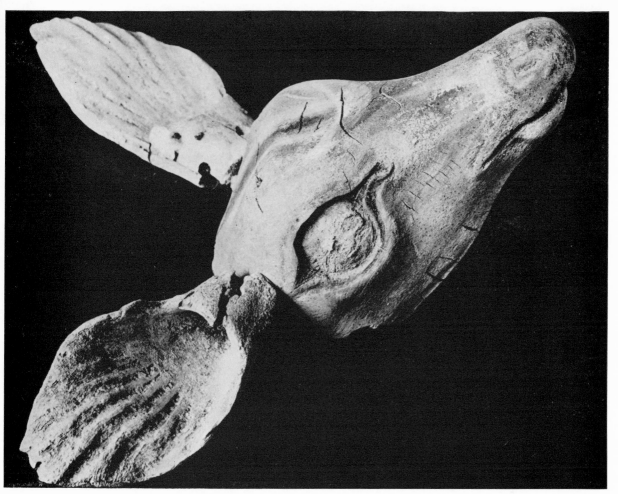

Wooden masks found miraculously preserved in the marsh mud at Key Marco, Florida. RIGHT: *head of a deer, 27 centimeters high;* LEFT: *head of a wolf (UMP).*

PLATE XLI

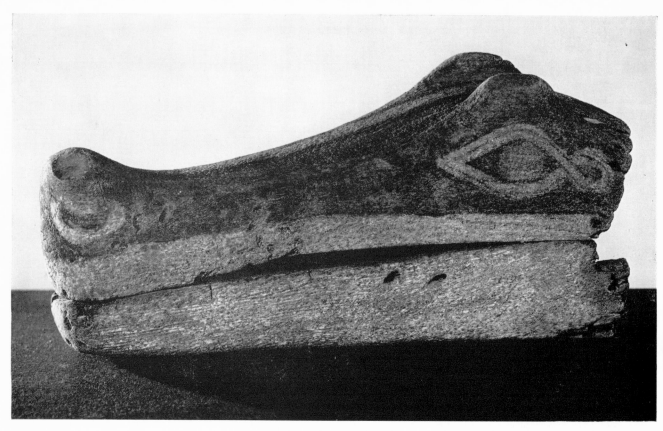

ABOVE: *head of an albatross, probably from a wooden bowl, 26 centimeters high;* BELOW: *head of an alligator, carved and painted wood, 26 centimeters long. (Both from excavations at Key Marco, Florida. UMP)*

PLATE XLII

ABOVE: *clay figurine, Turner Mound group, Hamilton County, Ohio, middle Woodland period, 9 centimeters high* (PMC); BELOW: *clay jar with openwork and two handles representing birds, Weeden Island, Florida* (MAIHF).

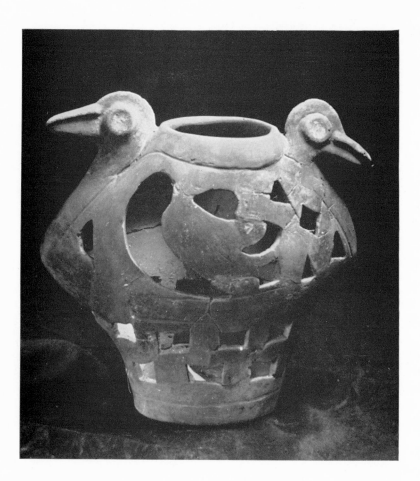

PLATE XLIII

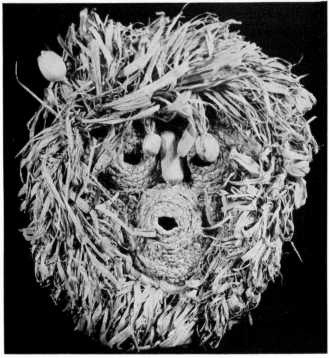

Contemporary Seneca masks, New York State, used in curative dances—two of wood, one of woven cornhusks (AMNH, DAM, and Collection of René d'Harnoncourt).

PLATE XLIV

ABOVE: *Micmac hood of broadcloth embroidered with glass beads, New England* (*MAIHF*); UPPER RIGHT: *split-cane Cherokee basket* (*IACB*); LOWER RIGHT: *Chitimacha basket, Louisiana* (*MNAM*).

PLATE XLV

ABOVE: *Sioux buffalo robe painted in the geometric style, South Dakota* (UMP); BELOW: *Sioux stone pipe representing a mountain sheep* (*United States Indian Service, Rapid City, South Dakota*).

PLATE XLVI

ABOVE: *detail of the famous painted elkhide robe, probably Sioux, Central Plains, undoubtedly by the artist-author of the skin shown in Color Plate H (Collection of Miss Amelia White, Santa Fe)*; BELOW: *ceremonial tepee of the Blackfoot Indians of Alberta, Canada, photographed in 1892 (photo, courtesy AMNH).*

PLATE XLVII

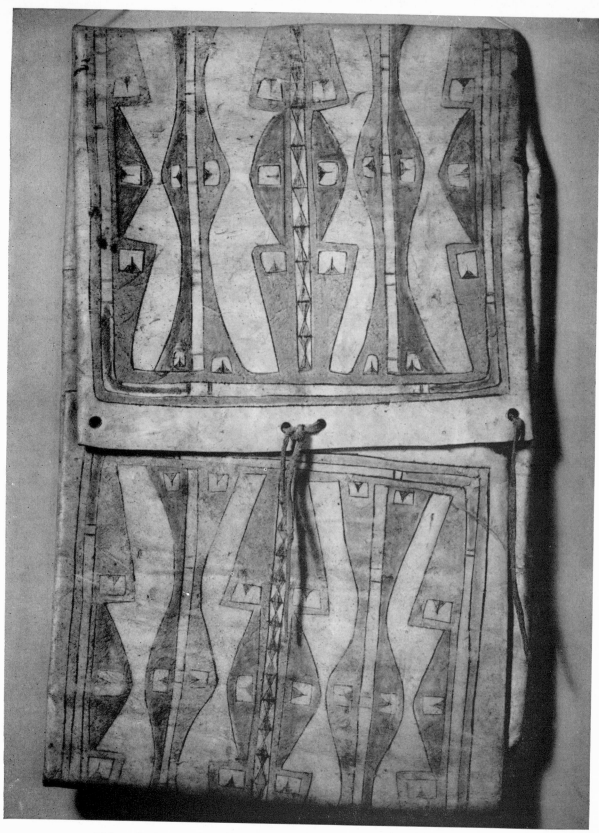

Old parfleche of rawhide painted in the geometric style, Central Plains
(Collection Herbert J. Spinden, on loan to BM).

PLATE XLVIII

Bibliography

ABBREVIATIONS USED IN THE BIBLIOGRAPHY:

AA: *American Anthropologist,* Menasha.
AJA: *American Journal of Anthropology.*
AAnt: *American Antiquity,* Andover.
AMNH: American Museum of Natural History, New York.
AMN: *Anales del Museo Nacional,* México.
AINAH: *Anales del Instituto Nacional de Antropología e Historia,* México.
APAM: *Anthropological Papers,* American Museum of Natural History, New York.
BAE: Bureau of American Ethnology, Smithsonian Institution, Washington.
CIW: Carnegie Institute of Washington.
ChMNH: Chicago Museum of Natural History.
CUCA: *Columbia University Contributions to Anthropology,* New York.
DAM: Denver Art Museum.
EFWSI: Exploration and Field Work, Smithsonian Institution, Washington.
FMNH: Field Museum of Natural History, Chicago.
GR: *Geographical Review,* New York.
IACB: Indian Arts and Crafts Board, Department of the Interior, Washington.
INM: *Indian Notes and Monographs,* Museum of the American Indian, Heye Foundation, New York.
JANSP: *Journal of the Academy of Natural Sciences of Philadelphia.*
LA: Laboratory of Anthropology, Santa Fe.
MAAA: *Memoirs of the American Anthropological Association.*
MAIHF: Museum of the American Indian, Heye Foundation, New York.
MAMNH: *Memoirs, American Museum of Natural History,* New York.
MFEA: Museum of Far-Eastern Antiquities, Stockholm.
MP: *Medallion Papers,* Gila Pueblo, Globe.
NGM: *National Geographic Magazine,* Washington.

NH *Natural History Magazine,* American Museum of Natural History, New York.

NMCA: *National Museum of Canada Annals,* Ottawa.

NMCAR: *National Museum of Canada Annual Report,* Ottawa.

OAHQ: *Ohio Archeological and Historical Quarterly,* Columbus.

PAPS: *Proceedings of the American Philosophical Society,* Philadelphia.

PNAS: *Proceedings of the National Academy of Sciences,* Washington.

PPM: *Papers, Peabody Museum of American Archæology and Ethnology,* Harvard University, Cambridge.

RMEA: *Revista Mexicana de Estudios Antropológicos,* México.

SI: Smithsonian Institution, Washington.

SM: *Scientific Monthly,* Washington.

SMC: *Smithsonian Miscellaneous Collections,* Washington.

UAB: *University of Arizona Bulletin,* Tucson.

UCPAAE: *University of California Publications in American Archeology and Ethnology,* Berkeley.

UMP: University Museum of Pennsylvania, Philadelphia.

UPMJ: *University of Pennsylvania Museum Journal.*

USNM: U.S. National Museum, Smithsonian Institution, Washington.

USNMP: U.S. National Museum, *Proceedings.*

UWPA: *University of Washington Publications in Anthropology,* Seattle.

YUPA: *Yale University Publications in Anthropology,* New Haven.

ACOSTA, José de,

1590 Historia natural y moral de las Indias, Sevilla (English translation for the Hakluyt Society by E. Grimstone, 1880).

ADAMS, Leonhard,

n.d. Nordwest-Amerikanische Indianerkunst, Orbis Pictus, 17, Berlin.

1936 North-West American Indian art and its early Chinese parallels, *Man,* January, vol. XXXVI, no. 3.

AMSDEN, Charles A.,

1934 Navajo weaving; its technique and history, Santa Ana, Calif.

1936 An analysis of Hohokam pottery designs, The Medallion, Gila Pueblo, Globe, Ariz.

ANDERSSON, J. Gunnar,

1945 Researches into the prehistory of the Chinese, Bull. 15, MFEA.

ANTEVS, Ernst,

1940 The Cochise culture, Priv. printed for Gila Pueblo, June, Globe, Ariz.

ARNOLD, J. R., and LIBBY, Willard F.,

1950 Radiocarbon dates (September 1, 1950), University of Chicago, Institute of Nuclear Studies, Chicago.

BAER, J. L.,

1921 A preliminary report of the so-called "Bannerstones," AA, vol. XXIII. pp. 445–59.

BARBEAU, Marius,

1929 Totem poles of the Gitksan, Upper Skeena, British Columbia, Ottawa.

1930 Totem poles: a recent native art of the Northwest Coast of America, GR, vol. xx, no. 2.

1939 The modern growth of the totem pole of the Northwest Coast, Smithsonian Report.

1942 Totem poles: a by-product of the fur trade, SM, December.

BARRETS, S. A.,

1921 The painted lodge or ceremonial tipi of the Blackfoot, Milwaukee Public Museum, Yearbook 1, pp. 85–8.

BEALS, R. L.,

1934 Material culture of the Pima, Papago and Western Apache, U.S. Dept. of Int. Nat. Park Service, Berkeley.

BENNETT, John W.,

1943 Southern culture types and Middle American influence, in *El Norte de México y el Sur de los Estados Unidos,* Sociedad Mexicana de Antropología, no. 3, pp. 223–41, México.

BENNETT, Wendell C., and BIRD, Junius B.,

1949 Andean culture history, Handbook Series No. 15, AMNH.

BERGSØE, Paul,

1937, 1938 The metallurgy and technology of gold and platinum among the Precolumbian Indians; The gilding process and the metallurgy of copper and lead among the Precolumbian Indians; Ingeniörvidenskabelije Skrijter, Nr. A44, Nr. A46, Copenhagen.

BIRD, Junius B.,

1943 Excavations in northern Chile, APAM, vol. 38, part 4.

1946 The archeology of Patagonia, in *Handbook of South American Indians,* BAE, Bull. 143, pp. 17–24.

1947 A Pre-Spanish Peruvian ikat, Bull. Needle and Bobbin Club, vol. 31, nos. 1–2, New York.

BIRKET-SMITH, K.,

1936 The Eskimos, London.

BOAS, Franz,

1888 The central Eskimo, 6th Annual Report, BAE.

1897 The social organization and the secret societies of the Kwakiutl Indians, Annual Report, USNM.

1908 Decorative designs of Alaskan needle cases, USNMP, 34, pp. 331–4.

1927 Art of the North Pacific Coast of North America (in Primitive Art, Instituttet for Sammenlignende Kulturforskning), Harvard Univ. Press, Oslo.

1933 Relationship between Northwest America and Northeast Asia, in *The American Aborigines, their origin and antiquity,* pp. 357–70, Toronto.

1938 Anthropology, in *Selections from the Encyclopedia of Social Sciences,* edited by E. R. A. Seligman and Alvin Johnson, Macmillan Co., New York.

BOGORAS, Waldermar,

1902 The Folklore of northeast Asia as compared with that of northwest America, AA, n.s., vol. 4, no. 4.

BOURKE, J. G.,

1884 The Snake Dance of the Moquis of Arizona, New York.

1892 Medicine Man of the Apache, 9th Annual Report, BAE.

BRADFIELD, Wesley,
> 1931 Cameron Creek Village, Monographs of the School of American Research, no. 1, Santa Fe.

BREW, J. O.,
> 1937 The first two seasons at Awatobi, AAnt, vol. 3, pp. 122–37.
> 1939 Preliminary report of the Peabody Museum Awatobi Expedition of 1937, AA, vol. 5, no. 2.
> 1941 Preliminary report of the Peabody Museum Awatobi Expedition of 1939, Plateau, vol. 13, no. 3.
> 1946 Archeology of Alkali Ridge, southeastern Utah, PPM.

BRYAN, Kirk, and RAY, Louis L.,
> 1940 Geologic antiquity of the Lindermeier Site in Colorado, SMC, vol. 99, no. 2.

BRYAN, Nonabah G., and YOUNG, Stella,
> 1940 Navajo native dyes: their preparation and use, Education Division, U.S. Office of Indian Affairs, Hasket Inst., Lawrence, Kansas.

BUNZEL, Ruth,
> 1929 The Pueblo potter, a study of creative imagination in primitive art, CUCA, 8.

CARRION CACHOT, Rebeca,
> 1931 La Indumentaria en la antigua cultura de Paracas, *Wiracocha*, no. 1, Lima.

CARTER, George F.,
> 1953 Plants across the Pacific, in *Asia and North America, Transpacific Contacts,* Mem. Soc. for Amer. Archeology, AAnt, vol. 18, no. 3, part 2.

CASO, Alfonso,
> 1946 Contribución de las culturas indígenas de México a la cultura mundial, in *México y la Cultura,* México.
> 1949 El Mapa de Teozacoalco, Cuadernos Americanos, año 8, no. 5, México.

CATLIN, George,
> 1841 Illustrations of the manners, customs and condition of the North American Indians, London.

CHAPMAN, Kenneth M.,
> 1939 The pottery of Sto. Domingo Pueblo, LA, Memoir 1.

CLARKE, Eleanor,
> 1935 Designs on the prehistoric pottery of Arizona, UAB, vol. VI, no. 4.

CODEX VATICANUS 3738,
> 1900 Edit, Duc de Loubat, Paris.

COLBERT, E. H.,
> 1942 Association of man with extinct mammals in the Western Hemisphere, *Proc. 8th Amer. Sc. Cong.,* vol. 2, Anthrop. Sciences, Dept. of State, Washington.

COLLINS, Henry B., JR.,
> 1926 Prehistoric art of the Alaskan Eskimo, SMC, vol. 81, no. 14.
> 1935 Archeology of the Bering Sea region, Smithsonian Annual Report for 1933, pp. 453–68.
> 1937 Archeology of St. Lawrence Island, Alaska, SMC, vol. 96, no. 1.
> 1939 Exploring frozen fragments of American history, NGM, vol. 75, no. 1.
> 1940 Outline of Eskimo prehistory, SMC, vol. 100, pp. 533–92.
> 1943 Eskimo archeology and its bearing on the problem of man's antiquity in America, PAPS, vol. 86, no. 2.

1945 The Aleutian Islands, their people and natural history, SI, War Background Series, no. 21.

COOK, Captain James A.,

1784 A voyage to the Pacific Ocean undertaken by the command of His Majesty for making discoveries in the Northern Hemisphere, 1776–1780, London.

COOLIDGE, Dane, and ROBERTS, Mary,

1930 The Navajo Indians, Boston and New York.

COSGROVE, H. S. and C. B.,

1932 The Swarts Ruin, PPM, vol. xv, no. 1.

CUSHING, F. H.,

1888–9 Sand-painting of the Navajos, 10th Annual Report, BAE.

1889 Zuñi Fetiches, 2nd. Annual Report, BAE.

1896 Exploration of ancient Key Dwellers' remains on the Gulf coast of Florida, PAPS, vol. 35, no. 150, pp. 329–432.

DALL, W. Healey,

1884 On masks and labrets and certain aboriginal customs, 3rd Annual Report, BAE.

DAVIDSON, D. S.,

1928 Decorative art of the Têtes de Boule of Quebec, INM, vol. x, no. 9.

DAVIS, Robert Tyler,

1949 Native Arts of the Pacific Northwest, from the Rasmunssen Collection of The Portland Art Museum, Stanford University, Los Angeles.

DE LAGUNA, Frederica,

1932–3 A comparison of Eskimo and paleolithic art, Am. Jour. Arch., vol. 36, no. 4; vol. 37, no. 4.

1934 The archeology of Cook Inlet, Alaska, Univ. of Penna. Press, Philadelphia.

1936 Indian masks from the lower Yukon, AA, vol. 38, no. 4.

DENSMORE, Frances,

1918 A study of Chippewa material culture, SMC, 68, no. 12.

DE TERRA, Helmut, ROMERO, J., and STEWART, T. D.,

1949 Tepexpan Man, Viking Fund Pub. in Anthrop., no. 11, New York.

DIXON, Captain George,

1789 A voyage round the world but more particularly to the Northwest Coast of America . . . , London

DIXON, Roland B.,

1900 Basketry designs of the Maidu Indians of California, AA, vol. 2, pp. 266–76.

DOUGLAS, Frederic H.,

1934 Apache basketry, DAM, Leaflet 64.

1936a Parfleches and other rawhide articles, DAM, Leaflets 77–8.

1936b Plain beads and beadwork designs, DAM, Leaflets 73–4.

1940a Main types of Pueblo wool textiles, DAM, Leaflets 94–5.

1940b Southwestern twined, wicker and plaited basketry, DAM, Leaflets 99–100.

DOUGLAS, Frederic, and D'HARNONCOURT, René,

1941 Indian art of the United States, Museum of Modern Art, New York.

EKHOLM, G. F.,

1940 Prehistoric lacquer from Sinaloa, RMEA, vol. 4, nos. 1–2.

1943 Relations between Middle America and the Southeast, en *El Norte de*

México y el Sur de los Estados Unidos, Sociedad Mexicana de Antropología, no. 3, pp. 276–83, México.

1950   Is American culture Asiatic? NH, vol. 59, no. 8, October.

1953   A possible focus of Asiatic influence in the late classic cultures of Meso-america, in *Asia and North America, Transpacific Contacts,* Mem. of the Soc. for Amer. Arch., AAnt, vol. 18, no. 3, part 2, January.

EMMONS, George T.,

1903   The basketry of the Tlingit, MAMNH, vol. 3, part 2.

1907   The Chilkat blanket, MAMNH, vol. 3, part 4.

1923   Jade in British Columbia and Alaska and its use by the natives, INM, no. 35.

ENCISO, Jorge,

1947   Sellos Antiguos de México, México.

ERNST, Alice Henson,

1933   Masks of the Northwest Coast, *Theatre Arts Monthly,* vol. XVII, no. 8, August.

EWERS, John C.,

1939   Plains Indians painting, Stanford Univ. Press, Palo Alto.

1944   The story of the Blackfeet, Indian life and customs, Pamphlet 6, U.S. Indian Service.

1945   Blackfeet crafts, Education Division, U.S. Office of Indian Affairs, Hasket Inst., Lawrence, Kansas.

FEWKES, J. W.,

1898   Archeological expedition to Arizona in 1895, 17th Annual Report, BAE.

1903   Hopi katchinas, 21st Annual Report, BAE.

1904   Two summers' work in Pueblo ruins, 22nd Annual Report, BAE.

1909   Antiquities of Mesa Verde National Park, Spruce Tree House, 41st Annual Report, BAE.

1911   Antiquities of Mesa Verde National Park, Cliff Palace, 51st Annual Report, BAE.

1912   Casa Grande, Arizona, 28th Annual Report, BAE.

1914   Archeology of the lower Mimbres Valley, New Mexico, SMC, vol. 68, no. 10.

1916   Animal figures of prehistoric pottery from Mimbres Valley, New Mexico, AA, n.s., vol. 18, pp. 535–45.

1919   Designs on prehistoric Hopi pottery, 33rd Annual Report, BAE.

1923   Designs on prehistoric pottery from Mimbres Valley, New Mexico, SMC, vol. 74, no. 6.

1924a   Additional designs on prehistoric Mimbres pottery, SMC, vol. 76, no. 8.

1924b   Preliminary archeological explorations at Weeden Island, Florida, SMC, vol. 76, no. 13, pp. 1–26.

1928   Aboriginal wooden objects from southern Florida, SMC, vol. 80, no. 9.

FORD, J. A., and QUIMBY, G. I.,

1945   The Tchefuncte culture, an early occupation of the lower Mississippi Valley, *Memoirs of the Society for Amer. Archeology,* supplement to AAnt, vol. x, no. 3.

FORD, J. A., and WILEY, Gordon R.,

1940   Crooks Site, a Marksville period burial mound in La Salle Parish, Louisiana, Louisiana Dept. of Conservation, Anthropological Study no. 3, New Orleans.

1941   An interpretation of the prehistory of the eastern United States, AA, vol. 43, no. 3, pp. 325–63.

FOWKE, Gerard,
1896   Stone art, 13th Annual Report, BAE, pp. 47–178.
1910   Antiquities of central and southeast Missouri, BAE, Bull. 37.

FUHRMANN, Ernst,
1922   Tlinkit und Haida, *Kulturen der Erde*, 22, Hagen und Darmstadt.

FULTON, William S.,
1934   Archeological notes on Texas Canyon, Arizona, contributions from the MAIHF, vol. XII, no. 2.

GEIST, Otto W., and RAINEY, Froelich G.,
1936   Archeological excavations at Kukulik, St. Lawrence Island, Alaska, NMCA, Report for 1931, Bull. 50.

GIFFORD, E. W.,
1931   Indian basketry, Exposition of Indian Tribal Arts, New York.

GLADWIN, Harold S.,
1947   Men out of Asia, New York.

GLADWIN, Harold S., and Associates,
1937   Excavations at Snaketown, MP, nos. 25–6.

GLADWIN, Winifred and Harold S.,
1931   Some Southwestern pottery types, Series II, MP, no. 10.

GODDARD, Pliny E.,
1931   Indians of the Southwest, AMNH, Handbook 2.
1934   The Indians of the Northwest Coast, AMNH, Handbook 10.

GREENMAN, E. F.,
1932   Excavation of the Coon Mound and the analysis of the Adena culture, OAHQ, vol. 41, no. 3.

GRIFFIN, James B.,
1942   Adena pottery, AA, vol. VII, no. 4, pp. 244–58.
1943a   Archeological Horizons in the Southeast and their connections with the Mexican area, en *El Norte de México y el Sur de los Estados Unidos*, Sociedad Mexicana de Antropología, no. 3, pp. 283–6, México.
1943b   The Fort Ancient aspect, Ann Arbor, Mich.

GRIFFIN, James B. (editor),
1952   Archeology of eastern United States, Univ. of Chicago Press.

GUERNESEY, S. J., and KIDDER, A. V.,
1921   Basket-Maker caves of Northeastern Arizona, PPM, vol. 8, no. 2.

GUNTHER, Erna, and HAEBERLIN, Herman,
1930   The Indians of the Puget Sound, UWPA.

GUTHE, Carl E.,
1925   Pueblo pottery making, Papers Phillips Academy, New Haven.

HAEBERLIN, Herman K.,
1918   Principles of esthetic form in the art of the North Pacific coast, AA, vol. 20, pp. 258–64.

HALL, H. U.,
1926   A buffalo robe biography, UPMJ, vol. 17, no. 1.

HALLIDAY, W. M.,
    1935   Potlatch and totem and the recollections of an Indian agent, London.
HAMY, E. T.,
    1899   Note sur d'anciennes peintures sur peaux des Indiens Illinois, Journal de la Société des Américanistes de Paris, vol. 2.
HARRINGTON, Lyn,
    1949   Last of the Haida carvers, NH, vol. LVIII, no. 5, May.
HARRINGTON, M. R.,
    1920   Certain Caddo sites in Arkansas, INM.
HAURY, Emil W.,
    1936a   Some Southwestern pottery types, MP, no. 19.
    1936b   The Mogollon culture of southwestern New Mexico, MP, no. 20.
HAURY, E. W., and HARGRAVE, L. L.,
    1931   Recently dated Pueblo ruins in Arizona, SMC, vol. 82, no. 11.
HAWKES, E. W.,
    1913   The Inviting-in feast of the Alaskan Eskimo, Mem. 45, no. 3, Anthrop. Series, Canadian Dept. of Mines, Geology Study, Ottawa.
HEINE-GELDERN, Robert von,
    1937   L'Art préboudique de la Chine et de l'Asie du Sud-Est et son influence en Océanie, Revue des Arts Asiatiques, t. 11, fasc. 4, Paris.
    1947   Asiatic influences in Pre-Columbian America (Lecture at the Asia Institute, March 19, 1947, New York).
    1949   Chinese influence in the Pacific and in America (Lecture at the Viking Fund, February 25, 1949, New York).
HEINE-GELDERN, R. v., and EKHOLM, G. F.,
    1951   Significant parallels in the symbolic arts of southern Asia and Middle America, in *The Civilizations of Ancient America*, Sel. Papers 29th Cong. of Amer., editor Sol Tax, Chicago.
HEWETT, E. L.,
    1905   A general view of the archeology of the Pueblo region, Ann. Rep. SI, for 1904, pp. 583–605.
HEYE, George G.,
    1921   Certain artifacts from San Miguel Island, California, vol. VII, no. 4, MAIHF.
HEYERDAHL, Thor,
    1950   The voyage of the raft *Kon-Tiki*, GR, vol. 115, January–March.
    1952   American Indians in the Pacific, the theory behind the Kon-Tiki expedition, London, Stockholm, Oslo.
HIBBEN, F. C.,
    1942   Pleistocene stratification in the Sandia Cave, New Mexico, Proc. 8th. Amer. Scientific Congress, vol. 2, Anthrop. Sc., Washington.
HIMMELHEBER, Hans,
    1938   Eskimokünstler, Stuttgart.
HODGE, F. W.,
    1924   Pottery of Hawikuh, INM, vol. I, no. 1, pp. 8–15.
HOFFMAN, W. J.,
    1897   The graphic art of the Eskimos, Annual Report for 1895, BAE.

BIBLIOGRAPHY

HOLMES, W. H.,

1883   Art in shell of the ancient Americans, BAE, 2nd Annual Report, pp. 179–305.

1886   Pottery of the ancient Pueblos, 4th Annual Report, BAE.

1903   Shell ornaments from Kentucky to Mexico, SMC, vol. 45, pp. 97–9.

1919   Handbook of aboriginal American antiquities, BAE, Bull. 60.

HOTVELD, Eric,

1944   Archeological investigations in the Thule district, Mo. G., vol. 141, nos. 1 and 2.

1947   Eskimokunst, København (with English summary).

HOUGH, Walter,

1901   Archeological field work in northeastern Arizona, Museum-Gates Expedition of 1901, report of the USNM (1903).

HRDLIČKA, Aleš,

1917   The genesis of the American Indian, Proc. of the 19th Int. Cong. of Amer., pp. 559–68, Washington.

1935   Archeological excavations on Kodiak Island, Alaska, EFWSI for 1934, pp. 42–57.

1936   Archeological expedition on Kodiak Island, Alaska, EFWSI for 1935, pp. 47–52.

1937   Archeological exploration on Kodiak and the Aleutian Islands, EFWSI for 1936, pp. 57–62.

1938   Archeological explorations on the Aleutian Islands, EFWSI for 1937, pp. 79–86.

1939   Exploration in the Aleutian and Commander Islands, EFWSI for 1938, pp. 79–86.

1940   Exploration of the Aleutian and Commander Islands, EFWSI for 1939, pp. 78–86.

1941   Exploration of Mummy Caves in the Aleutian Islands, SM, vol. 52, pp. 5–23, 113–30.

HUTCHINSON, J. B., and others,

1947   The evolution of gossypium, Oxford Univ. Press.

INVERARITY, Robert Bruce,

1941   Movable masks and figures in the art of the North Pacific coast, Cranbrook Inst. of Science, Bloomfield, Mass.

1950   Art of the Northwest Coast Indians, Univ. of California Press, Berkeley.

IVANOV, S. V.,

1928   Aleut hunting headgear and its ornamentation, Int. Cong. Amer., vol. 23, pp. 477–504.

JACOBSON, Oscar B.,

1929   Kiowa Indian art, Nice.

JAMES, George W.,

1902   Indian basketry, New York.

1937   Indian blankets and their makers, New York.

JENKS, A. E.,

1937   Minnesota's Brown Valley man and associated burial artifacts, AA, Memoirs, no. 49.

JENNES, Diamond,
   1922   Eskimo art, GR, vol. 12, no. 2.
   1928   Archeological investigation in Bering Strait, NMCA, Bull. 50.
   1932   The Indians of Canada, Bull. 65, National Museum of Canada, Dept. of Mines, Ottawa.
   1933   The problems of the Eskimo, in *The American Aborigines, their origin and antiquity,* pp. 373–96, Toronto.
JOCHELSON, Waldemar,
   1925   Archeological investigations in the Aleutian Islands, CIW.
   1928   Archeological investigations in Kamchatka, CIW.
   1933   History, ethnology and anthropology of the Aleut, CIW.
JOHNSON, Frederick, and others,
   1951   Radiocarbon dating, *Mem. Soc. for Amer. Arch.,* AAnt, vol. 17, no. 1, part 2, July.
KELEMEN, Pál,
   1943   Medieval American art, New York.
KELLY, Isabel T.,
   1930   The carver's art of the Indians of northwestern California, UCPAAE, vol. 24, no. 7, pp. 343–60.
KIDDER, A. V.,
   1916   The pottery of the Casas Grandes district, Chihuahua, *Holmes Anniversary Volume,* Anthropological Essays, pp. 253–68, Washington.
   1924   An introduction to the study of Southwestern archeology, with a preliminary account of the excavations at Pecos, Papers of the Phillips Academy Southwestern Expedition, no. 1, New Haven.
   1931   The pottery of Pecos, Phillips Academy, vol. I, New Haven.
   1932   The artifacts of Pecos, Phillips Academy, New Haven.
   1936   The pottery of Pecos, Phillips Academy, vol. II, New Haven.
KIDDER, A. V., and others,
   1946   Excavations at Kaminaljuyú, Guatemala, CIW, Pub. 561.
KINGSBOROUGH, Edward King, Viscount,
   1831–48   Antiquities of Mexico, 9 vols., London.
KISSEL, Mary Lois,
   1916   Basketry of the Papago and Pima, APAM, vol. 17, no. 4.
KNOBLOCK, B. W.,
   1939   Bannerstones of the North American Indian, La Grange, Ill.
KRIEGER, A. D.,
   n.d.   Caddo archeology, Department of Anthropology, Univ. of Texas (MS).
   1945   An inquiry into supposed Mexican influence on a prehistoric "cult" in the southern United States, AA, vol. 47, no. 4, pp. 483–515.
KRIEGER, H. W.,
   1931   Aspects of aboriginal decorative art in America based on specimens in the U.S. National Museum. SI, Publication 3102, Washington.
KROEBER, Alfred L.,
   1901   Decorative symbolism of the Arapaho, AA, vol. 3.
   1902   Preliminary sketch of the Mohave Indians, AA, n.s., vol. 4, pp. 276–85.
   1907   The Arapaho, AMNH Bull., vol. 18, Parts 1, 2, 4.

1925 Handbook of the Indians of California, BAE, Bull. 78.

1926 Basketry designs of the Mission Indians, AMNH, Guide Leaflet 55.

1946 The Chibcha, in Handbook of South American Indians, vol. 2, p. 888, BAE, Bull. 143.

KEITHAHNN, Edward L.,

1945 Monuments in cedar, Ketchikan.

LA PÉROUSE, J. F. G. de,

1798 A voyage round the world 1785–88, London.

LAVACHERIE, H. A.,

1929 Les Arts anciennes d'Amérique au Musée Archéologique de Madrid, Anvers.

LEE TANHER, Clara, and FORBES, Anne,

1948 Indian Art Fund Collection of Painting, El Palacio, vol. 55, no. 12, December, Santa Fe.

LEWIS, Gilbert N.,

1947 The beginning of civilization in America, AA, n.s., vol. 49, no. 1.

LILLY, Eli,

1937 Prehistoric antiquities of Indiana, Indianapolis.

LINTON, Ralph,

1940 Crops, soils, and culture in America, in *The Maya and Their Neighbors,* pp. 23–40, New York.

1941 Primitive art, Kenyon Review, vol. 3, no. 1, Ohio.

LOCHER, C. W.,

1932 The serpent in Kwakiutl religion, Leiden.

LOWIE, Robert H.,

1922 Crow Indian art, APAM, vol. 21, part 4.

LYFORD, Carrie A.,

1940 Quill and beadwork of the western Sioux, U.S. Office of Indian Affairs, Washington.

1945a The crafts of the Ojibwa (Chippewa), Education Division, U.S. Office of Indian Affairs, Hasket Inst., Lawrence, Kan.

1945b Iroquois crafts, Education Division, U.S. Office of Indian Affairs, Hasket Inst., Lawrence, Kan.

LUMHOLTZ, Carl,

1902 Unknown Mexico, New York.

MacCURDY, G. G.,

1913 Shell gorgets from Missouri, AA, n.s., vol. 15, pp. 395–414.

MALASPINA, Capitán Alejandro,

1885 La Vuelta al Mundo por las Corbetas "Descubierta" y "Atrevida," Madrid.

MALLERY, Garrick,

1893 Picture writing of American Indians, 10th Annual Report, BAE.

MANGELSDORF, P. C., and REEVES, R. G.,

1939 The origin of Indian corn and its relatives, Bull. of the Experimental Agricultural Station in Texas, no. 547, May.

MANGELSDORF, P. C., and SMITH, C. E.,

1949 New archeological evidence on the evolution of maize, Botanical Museum Leaf, Harvard Univ., vol. 13, no. 8, Cambridge.

MARTIN, P. S., QUIMBY, G. I., and COLLIER, D.,
1947   Indians before Columbus, Univ. of Chicago Press, Chicago.

MARTIN, Paul S., and RINALDO, John,
1939   Modified Basket Maker sites, Ackmen-Lowry region, southwestern Colorado, FMNH, Anthrop. Series, vol. 23, no. 3.

MARTIN, Paul S., and WILLIS, Elizabeth,
1940   Anasazi painted pottery in Field Museum of Natural History, Anthrop. Memoirs, FMNH, vol. 5.

MARTÍNEZ DEL RÍO, Pablo,
1943   Los Origenes Americanos, 2a. Edición, México.
1952   El Mamut de Santa Isabel Iztapan, *Cuadernos Americanos,* Año II, Julio-Agosto, México.

MASON, J. Alden,
1929   Turquoise mosaic from northern Mexico, Museum Journal, UMP, vol. 20, pp. 157–75.
1930   Excavations of Eskimo Thule culture sites at Point Barrow, Alaska, Proc. 23rd Int. Cong. Amer. 1928, pp. 383–94, New York.
1935   The place of Texas in pre-Columbian relationship between the United States and Mexico, Bull. of the Texas Archeological and Paleontological Society, vol. 7, pp. 29–46, Abilene.
1937   Further remarks on the pre-Columbian relationship between the United States and Mexico, Bull. of the Texas Archeological and Paleontological Society, vol. 9, pp. 120–9, Abilene.

MASON, Otis T.,
1904   Aboriginal American basketry; studies in a textile art without machinery, Report of the USNM.

MATHIASSEN, Therkel,
1930   Inugsuk, a medieval Eskimo settlement in the Uppernivik district, West Greenland, Medel Gronland, no. 77, pp. 147–339, Copenhagen.
1937   The Eskimo archeology of Greenland, Ann. Rep. for 1936, BAE, pp. 397–404.

MAXIMILIAN, Prince of Wied,
1906   Travels in the interior of North America, Cleveland.

MERA, H. P.,
n.d.   Navajo textile art, LA.
1937   The "Rain Bird," a study in Pueblo design, Mem. LA, vol. II.
1938–9   Navajo blankets, LA, General Series, Bulls. 2, 3, 5, 6, 7.
1939   Style trends of Pueblo pottery, LA.
1943   Pueblo Indian embroidery, Mem., LA, vol. IV.

MERRILL, E. D.,
1937   Plants and civilization, Harvard Univ. Press, Cambridge.

MILLS, William C.,
1902   Excavations of the Adena Mound, OAHQ, vol. X, no. 4.
1907–17–26   Certain mounds and village sites in Ohio, Columbus.
1916   Exploration of the Tremper Mound, OAHQ, vol. xxv, no. 5, pp. 262–398.

MOORE, Clarence B.,

1894–6 Certain sand mounds of the St. John River, Florida, JANSP, vol. x, pp. 5–103, 129–246.

1899 Certain aboriginal remains of the Alabama River, JANSP, vol. xi, no. 3, pp. 289–348.

1901 Certain aboriginal remains of the Tombigbee River, JANSP, vol. xi, no. 4, pp. 497–514.

1905 Certain aboriginal remains of the Black Warrior River, lower Tombigbee River, Mobile Bay, etc., JANSP, vols. xii and xiv.

1907 Moundville revisited, JANSP, vol. xiii, pp. 337–405.

1908 Certain mounds of Arkansas River. Part II, lower Yazoo and lower Sunflower rivers, Mississippi. Part III, The Blum Mounds, Mississippi, JANSP, vol. 13, pp. 481–600.

1909 Antiquities of the Ouachita Valley, JANSP, vol. 14, pp. 7–249.

1910 Antiquities of St. Francis, White and Black rivers, Arkansas, JANSP, vol. 14, pp. 255–362.

1911 Some aboriginal sites on Mississippi River, JANSP, vol. 14, pp. 367–476.

1912 Some aboriginal sites on the Red River, JANSP, vol. 14, pp. 483–640.

1913 Some aboriginal sites in Louisiana and Arkansas (Atchafalaya River, Lake Larto, Tensas River, Bayou Macon, Bayou d'Arbonne in Louisiana; Saline River in Askansas), JANSP, vol. 16, pp. 7–99.

1915 Aboriginal sites on Tennessee River, JANSP, vol. 16, pp. 169–422.

1916 Some aboriginal sites on Green River, Kentucky, JANSP, vol. 16, pp. 440–87.

MOOREHEAD, Warren K.,

1908 Fort Ancient—the great prehistoric earthwork of Warren County, Ohio, Phillips Acad., Bull. 4, pp. 31–163, New Haven.

1922 The Hopewell mound group of Ohio, FMNH, Anthropological Series, vol. 6, no. 79.

1928 The Cahioka Mounds, Univ. of Illinois, Bull., vol. 26, no. 4 (includes observations printed in vols. 29, no. 35, and 21, no. 6), pp. 1–176, Urbana.

1932 Explorations of the Etowah Site in Georgia, Phillips Acad., Dept of Archeology, Andover, New Haven.

MORGAN, Lewis H.,

1922 The league of the Iroquois, New York.

MORRIS, Earl H.,

1928 The Aztec ruin, APAM, vol. 26.

1939 Archeological studies in the La Plata district, CIW.

1941 Anasazi basketry, Basket Maker II through Pueblo III, CIW, Pub. 533.

MOZIÑO SUÁREZ, Joseph Mariano,

1913 Noticias de Nutka, Soc. de Geografía y Estadística, México.

McGUIRE, J. D.,

1899 Pipes and smoking customs of the American aborigines, based on material in the United States National Museum, Annual Report of the USNM for 1897, pp. 351–645.

BIBLIOGRAPHY

NAVAJO BLANKETS,

1942 From the collection of the Laboratory of Anthropology, Santa Fe (15 color paintings by Louie H. Ewing, Art Program of the Work Projects Administration).

NELSON, E. W.,

1900 The Eskimo about Bering Strait, 18th Annual Report, BAE.

NEVERMANN, Hans,

1933 Masken und Geheimbünde in Melanesien, Berlin.

NEWCOMB, Mrs. F. J., and REICHARDS, Gladys A.,

1937 Sand painting of the Navajo Shooting Chant, New York.

NEWCOMBE, C. F.,

1906 The Haida Indians, Congrès International des Américanistes, Quebec.

NOGUERA, Eduardo,

1930 Ruinas arqueológicas del Norte de México, Casas Grandes (Chihuahua), La Quemada, Chalchihuites (Zacatecas), Publicaciones de la Secretaría de Educación Pública, México.

NORDENSKIØLD, Erland,

1930 L'Archéologie de bassin de l'Amazone, Ars. Americana I, Paris.

1931 The origin of the Indian civilizations of South America, Comparative Ethnographical Studies, no. 9, Göteborg.

NORDENSKIØLD, G.,

1893 The Cliff Dwellers of the Mesa Verde, southwest Colorado, Transl. by D. L. Morgan, Stockholm.

NORMAN, D., and JOHNSON, W. W. A.,

1941 Note on a spectroscopic study of Central American and Asiatic jades, Jour. of the Optical Society of America.

OAKES, Maud,

1943 Where the two came to their father, a Navajo war ceremonial, Bollingen Series 1, New York.

OKLADNIKOV, A. P.,

1938 Archeological data on the ancient history of Lake Baikal region, Rev. Ancient History, vol. I, pp. 244–60, Moscow (in Russian).

ORCHARD, W. C.,

1916 The technique of porcupine quill decoration among the North American Indians, INM, vol. 4, no. 1.

1925 Fine line decoration of ancient Southwestern pottery, INM.

OSGOOD, C.,

1936 Contributions to the ethnology of the Kutchin, YUPA, no. 14.

1940 Ingalik material culture, YUPA, no. 22.

PAALEN, Wolfgang,

1944 Totem art, *Dyn,* no. 4–5, Mexico.

PEPPER, G. H.,

1906 Human effigy vases from Chaco Canyon, *Boas Anniversary Volume,* pp. 320–34, New York.

1920 Pueblo Bonito, APAM, no. 27.

1921 A wooden image from Kentucky, INM, vol. 10, no. 7.

BIBLIOGRAPHY

PETRULLO, Vincent M.,

    1929 Decorative art on birch-bark containers from the Algonquin River du Lièvre Band, INM, vol. 6, no. 3.

PINARD, Alfred M.,

    1872 Les Aléutes et leur origine, *Mémoires de la Société d'Ethnographie*, vol. 2, pp. 155–65.

    1875 La Caverne d'Aknañh, Ile d'Ounga, Archipel Shumagin, Alaska, Paris.

PROSKURIAKOV, T.,

    1950 A study of classic Maya sculpture, CIW, Pub. 593.

QUIMBY, George I.,

    1940 The Manitunik Eskimo culture of the East Hudson Bay, AA, vol. 6, no. 2.

    1941 The Goodall focus, an analysis of ten Hopewellian components in Michigan and Indiana, Indiana Historical Society, Prehistoric Research Series, vol. IX, no. 1, Indiana.

    1942 The Natchezan culture type, AAnt, vol. VII, no. 3, pp. 255–75.

    1943 A subjective interpretation of some design similarities between Hopewell and northern Algonkian, AA, vol. 45, no. 4.

    1944 Aleutian Islanders, Chicago Nat. Mus. Anthrop., Leaflet no. 35, Chicago.

    1945a Pottery from the Aleutian Islands, Fieldiana, Anthropology, ChMNH, vol. 36, no. 1.

    1945b Periods of prehistoric art in the Aleutian Islands, AAnt, vol. 2, no. 2.

RAINEY, Froelich G.,

    1936 Eskimo chronology, PNAS, vol. 22, no. 6, pp. 357–62.

    1937 Old Eskimo art, NH, vol. 40, no. 3, October.

    1940 Archeological investigation in central Alaska, AAnt, vol. 5, no. 4.

    1941 The Ipiutak culture of Point Hope, Alaska, AA, vol. 43, no. 3, part 1, pp. 364–75.

    1942 Discovering Alaska's oldest Arctic town, NGM, vol. 82, no. 3, September.

    1953 The significance of recent archeological discoveries in inland Alaska, in *Asia and North America, Transpacific Contacts*, AAnt, vol. 18, no. 3, part 2.

RAVENHILL, Alice,

    1938 The native tribes of British Columbia, Victoria.

    1946 A cornerstone of Canadian culture, Occasional Papers, British Columbia Provincial Museum, no. 5, Victoria.

REICHARD, Gladys A.,

    1936 Navajo shepherd and weaver, New York.

RELACIONES del viaje hecho por las goletas "Sutil" y "Mexicana" al reconocimiento

    1802 del estrecho de Juan de Fuca en 1792, Madrid.

RITCHIE, W. A.,

    1944 The pre-Iroquoian occupation of New York State, Rochester Mus. Memoir, no. 1, Rochester, N.Y.

RIVET, Paul,

    1926 Le Travail de l'or en Colombia, *Ipek*, vol. 2, pp. 128–41.

    1943 Los Orígenes del hombre americano, México.

ROBERTS, Frank H., JR.,

    1940 Archeological remains in the Whitewater district, eastern Arizona, part II, BAE, Bull. 126.

1942   Recent evidence relating to an early Indian occupation of North America, *Proc. of 8th Am. Sc. Cong.*, vol. 2, Washington.

ROBERTS, Helen H.,
1929   The basketry of the San Carlos Apache, AMNH, Ethnology Papers, no. 31, pp. 121–218.

ROWLEY, Graham,
1940   The Dorset culture of the eastern Arctic, AA, vol. 42, no. 3, pp. 490–9.

SAHAGÚN, Fray Bernardino de,
1938   Historia general de las cosas de Nueva España, Edic. Robledo, México.

SAPIR, E.,
1935   A Navajo sand painting blanket, AA, no. 37, pp. 609–16.

SAVILLE, Marshal H.,
1907   The antiquities of Manabi, Ecuador, Contr. to South Amer. Arch. Heye Expedition, New York.

SCHUSTER, Carl,
1951   Joint-marks, a possible index of cultural contact between America, Oceania and the Far East, Med. XCLV, Afdeling Culturele en Physische Antropologie, no. 39, Koninklijl Instituut voor de Trpen, Amsterdam.
1952   A survival of the Eurasiatic animal style in modern Alaska Eskimo art, Indian tribes of aboriginal America, vol. III, *Proc. of the 29th Cong. of Amer.*, Chicago.

SERRANO, Antonio,
1943   El Arte decorativo de los Diaguitas, Univ. Nac. de Córdoba, Córdoba, R.A.

SHETRONE, Henry C.,
1930   The Mound-Builders, New York.

SKINNER, Alanson,
1920   An Iroquois antler figurine, INM, vol. 2, no. 5.
1921   Notes on Iroquois archeology, INM.
1947   The Indians of Manhattan Island and vicinity, AMNH, Science Guide no. 41.

SMITH, Harlan J.,
1923   An album of prehistoric Canadian art, National Museum of Canada, Bull. 37, Ottawa.

SPAULDING, Albert,
1952   The current status of Aleutian archeology, in *Asia and North America, Transpacific Contacts*, AAnt, vol. 43, no. 3, part 2, January.

SPECK, Frank G.,
1914   The double-curve motive in north-eastern Algonkian art, Memoirs 42, no. 1, Anthropological Series, Canadian Dept. of Mines, Geology Survey, Ottawa.
1915   Decorative art of the Indian tribes of Connecticut, Memoirs 75, no. 10, Anthrop. Series, Canadian Dept. of Mines, Ottawa.
1920   Decorative art and basketry of the Cherokees, Milwaukee Public Museum, Bull. 2, pp. 53–86.
1921   Material culture of the Menomini, INM.
1927   Eskimo carved ivories from northern Labrador, INM, vol. 4, no. 4.
1935   Naskapi, the savage hunters of the Labrador peninsula, Univ. of Oklahoma Press, Norman.

1937   Montagnais art in birchbark; a circumpolar trait, INM, vol. 7, no. 2.

1940   Penobscot man; the life history of a forest tribe in Maine, Univ. of Penna. Press, Philadelphia.

SPIER, Leslie,

1925   An analysis of Plains Indian parfleche decoration, UWPA, vol. 1, no. 3.

SPINDEN, H. J.,

1922   Ancient civilizations of Mexico and Central America, Handbook Series no. 3, AMNH.

1944   Top of the world, Arctic lands in human history, Brooklyn Museum.

SQUIER, E. G., and DAVIS, F. H.,

1848   Ancient monuments of the Mississippi Valley, Smithsonian Contributions to Knowledge, no. 1, art. 1, pp. 1–306.

STEVENSON, James,

1880–1   Illustrated catalogue of the collection obtained from the Indians of New Mexico, 2nd Annual Report, BAE.

1891   Ceremonial of the Hasjelti Dailjis and mythical sand paintings of the Navajo Indians, 8th Annual Report, BAE.

STEVENSON, M. C.,

1894   The Sia, 11th Annual Report, BAE.

1904   The Zuñi Indians, 23rd Annual Report, BAE.

STIRLING, Matthew W.,

1939   Three pictographic autobiographies of Sitting Bull, SMC, vol. 97, no. 5.

STONER, C. R., and ANDERSON, E.,

1949   Maize among the hill peoples of Assam, Ann. of the Miss. Botanical Garden, vol. 36, pp. 355–404, September.

SULLIVAN, L. R., and HELLMAN, M.,

1925   The Punin Calvarium, APAM, vol. 23, part. 7.

SWANTON, John R.,

1911   Indian tribes of the lower Mississippi Valley and adjacent coast of the Gulf of Mexico, BAE, Bull. 43.

1943   Relations between northern Mexico and the Southwest of the United States from the view of ethnology and history, in *El Norte de México y el Sur de los Estados Unidos,* Sociedad Mexicana de Antropología, no. 3, pp. 259–76, México.

1946   The Indians of the southeastern United States, BAE, Bull. 137.

THALBITZER, W.,

1914   The Ammassalik Eskimo, Medel on Grønland, vol. 39, part 1, Copenhagen.

THOMAS, Cyrus,

1890–1   Report on the mound exploration of the Bureau of Ethnology, BAE, 12th Annual Report.

UNDERHILL, Ruth,

n.d.   Indians of southern California, Sherman pamphlets, no. 2, Education Division, U.S. Office of Indian Affairs, Hasket Inst., Lawrence, Kan.

1940   The Papago Indians of Arizona and their relatives the Pima, Education Division, U.S. Office of Indian Affairs, Hasket Inst., Lawrence, Kan.

1945   Pueblo crafts, Education Division, U.S. Office of Indian Affairs, Hasket Inst., Lawrence, Kan.

VAILLANT, George C.,

1939 Indian arts of North America, New York.

VANCOUVER, Captain George,

1798 A voyage of discovery to the North Pacific Ocean and round the world; in which the coast of north-west America has been carefully examined and accurately surveyed . . . , London.

VATTER, Ernst,

1927 Historienmalerie und heraldische bilderschift der nor-americanische Prairiestamme, Ipek.

WHEELRIGHT, Mary C.,

1942 Navajo creation myth; the story of the emergence, by Hasteen Klah, Mus. of Navajo Ceremonial Art, Navajo Religion Series, 1, Santa Fe.

WILLEY, G. R.,

1945 The Weeden Island Culture: a preliminary definition, AAnt, vol. x, no. 3, pp. 225–54.

1949 Archeology of the Florida Gulf coast, SMC, vol. 113.

WILLOUGHBY, C. C.,

1935 Antiquities of the New England Indians, Cambridge.

WINGERT, Paul S.,

1949 American Indian Sculpture, a study of the Northwest Coast, New York.

WINTEMBERG, W. J.,

1939–40 Eskimo sites of the Dorset culture in Newfoundland, AAnt, vol. 5, nos. 2 and 4, October and April.

WISSLER, Clark,

1904 Decorative art of the Sioux Indians, AMNH Bulletin, vol. 18.

1907 Some protective designs of the Dakota, APAM, vol. 1, part 2.

1910 Material culture of the Blackfeet Indians, APAM, vol. 5, part 1.

1916 Structural basis to the decoration of costumes among the Plains Indians, APAM, vol. 17, part 3.

1927 Distribution of moccasin decoration among the Plains tribes, APAM, vol. 29, part 1.

1930 Indian beadwork, AMNH, Leaflet Series 50.

1934 North American Indians of the Plains, AMNH, Handbook 1.

1938 The American Indian, New York.

ZOLOTAREV, A.,

1938 The ancient culture of north Asia, AA, vol. 40, no. 1, pp. 13–25, January-March.

Index

i

INDEX

A NOTE ON THE

Type

The text of this book is set in CALEDONIA, *a Linotype face designed by W. A. Dwiggins. It belongs to the family of printing types called "modern face" by printers— a term used to mark the change in style of type-letters that occurred about 1800. Caledonia borders on the general design of Scotch Modern, but is more freely drawn than that letter.*

The book was composed, printed, and bound by Kingsport Press, Inc., Kingsport, Tennessee. Color lithography by Philip Klein, New York. Line and halftone engravings by Capper Engraving Company, Inc., Knoxville, Tennessee. Typography by Harry Ford and S. R. Jacobs.